TOTAL QUALITY MANAGEMENT FOR SCHOOLS

Total Quality Management for Schools

Malcolm S. Greenwood and
Helen J. Gaunt

CASSELL

Cassell
Villiers House
41/47 Strand
London WC2N 5JE

387 Park Avenue South
New York
NY 10016-8810

First published 1994

British Library Cataloguing-in-Publication Data
A catalogue record for this book is available from the British Library.

ISBN 0-304-32996-7 (hardback)
    0-304-32992-4 (paperback)

Typeset and illustrated by PanTek Arts, Maidstone, Kent
Printed and bound in Great Britain by Redwood Books, Trowbridge, Wiltshire

Contents

Foreword

During the last few years the interest in Total Quality Management (TQM) and process improvement has exploded. There are now many texts on the subject and its various aspects, but the application of TQM in schools has not been dealt with seriously – until now that is.

This book is a welcome addition to the literature in that it really does address the practical issues of applying TQM within a school environment. The authors are very well qualified to write this book, being teachers and practitioners of TQM at the school level.

The text is well founded in the established concepts of quality management and continuous improvement, particularly those expounded by the most famous quality guru, W. Edwards Deming. However, the authors have provided many practical illustrations and examples of their applicability in the school setting.

As the authors point out, many teachers may be reluctant to accept that TQM, an industrially based management philosophy, can apply in schools and colleges. Through accounts of their own and others' experiences in applying the paradigm in a school setting, they offer a convincing argument that educational processes are like all others and can be improved on a continuous basis. Indeed pupils will respond extremely well to the ideas of TQM, which they often regard as common sense.

The book's structure covers the main features of TQM, including customer needs/wants, understanding processes, culture and people changes, the costs of quality, planning systems, and even statistical process control (SPC) in the classroom. Deming's recent thinking – his theory of 'profound knowledge' – is used to fire home one of the concluding messages, that learning should be a joy for the young.

This is an excellent contribution that should help heads and teachers everywhere to understand the WHAT WHY and HOW of TQM in schools.

John S. Oakland
Exxon Chemical Professor of Total Quality Management
European Centre for TQM
University of Bradford

Acknowledgements

Of all the many people who have contributed, formally or informally to the production of this book, we owe most to the original Father of the Quality revolution, Professor W. Edwards Deming. When I first read his work, for the first time I was able to formalize the things which I had done instinctively in the classroom for many years. The works of Professor J.S. Oakland of Bradford Management Centre provided the basis for my first halting attempts to teach the Quality paradigm to students. My co-author Helen Gaunt enabled my non-mathematical mind to grasp the significance of variance, and has made major contributions to this book.

Katherine West of Computerwork converted my scribbles into artwork, for which I am grateful. My employers, Bradford Grammar School, had sufficient faith in me to allow me to develop an innovative and untried Business Studies course without question. Above all I owe a debt of gratitude to my 'champions', the group of ten brave students who took the major risk of signing up for the course on its first run: Alex Dunn, Chris Heald, Ollie Lightowler, Darren Shields, Marcus Wright, Mark Hannan, Danny Harrison, Anne Stone, Ric Tillotson and Caroline Ryan.

I was able to give the book a wider dimension thanks to Larrae Rocheleau, Theresa Hicks, John Marsh and Roger Alston, pioneers of much greater importance than us.

Last but not least, thanks and gratitude are due to my wife Annie, for her tolerance, patience and encouragement.

Malcolm S. Greenwood

Introduction

Best efforts, people charging this way and that without guidance of principle, can do a lot of damage.

W.E. Deming[1]

For many years teachers have recoiled at any suggestion that similarities might exist between education and the commercial world. This is a pity, since great similarities do exist between organizations of all kinds, whether in the public, private or voluntary sector. I think perhaps the problem lies in apparently incompatible language. Recently I attended a conference led by the Chief of Quality at IBM (UK), together with the headmaster of an English school, Roger Alston. They were describing their joint venture designed to bring to his school the quality management techniques which were being used by IBM to restore its flagging fortunes. The heads and deputy heads who had attended the conference balked at some of the language of commerce which was being used. Sadly, much of the essential truth of the message was lost. Our aim in writing this book is to bridge this cultural and linguistic gap.

Any organization must have a 'mission' or objective, to the pursuit of which it is totally dedicated. The mission of Ford might be for example to be the leading manufacturer of quality cars in volume in the world. That of a National Health Service hospital might be to provide state-of-the-art medical care for all comers free at the point of use. Oxfam might set out to provide aid to as many Third World countries as possible. A school might set out with a mission to educate the whole person, in the context of the needs of its local community. Having such a 'mission' is, however, not sufficient to guarantee the achievement of the objective. This is because all organizations are under the same basic constraints. They must all operate within financial and resource constraints which are imposed on them by their past history, by their shareholders, by government, or by their success (or lack of it) in the market-place. The organization's ability to finance essential or desirable new developments will be constrained by its ability to generate new funds by organic growth, or to persuade outsiders to become 'stakeholders' by contributing investment funds by way of share purchase, loans, or charitable gifts. The traditional role of managers in the commercial environment has been seen as planning, organizing, controlling and directing the day-to-day activities of the organization in order to ensure its survival and growth.

I think few headteachers would deny that this is how they see their job in the current climate, even though they might regret this recent development. I suspect that, like us, they would like to think that there must be a better way, which involves greater emphasis on leadership and facilitation rather than control and direction. World-class companies have found a better way, which is called, perhaps slightly misleadingly, Total Quality Management. We would like to demonstrate the relevance of this modern management technique to the world of the school.

You will notice that we have not mentioned the word 'profit'. This was the major sticking point for the teachers at the conference I mentioned earlier. For IBM the price of survival is 'profit', a residual surplus of income over expenditure, which allows the stakeholders in the business (shareholders, directors, and perhaps workforce), to be recompensed for risk taking. It is even more important in providing the flow of investment funds which are vital for development of the company and its products. It is a misconception to see 'profit' as being an inappropriate term for the activities of a public service sector organization. There may be no stakeholders to be recompensed for risk taking, but such organizations certainly need a flow of residual funds from which to make investment in improvements to product, or process or plant. This is so even if we are thinking only of a state school with a fixed budget, set by an outside authority. In this case such 'surplus' funds will only be available if resources can be used more effectively.

If Oxfam fails to generate enough funds to cover the costs of running the organization, it will be unable to provide aid for deserving causes; moreover it will cease to exist and its mission will fail. If Guy's Hospital cannot retain a surplus out of its budget, it will not be able to buy a new body scanner. If Ford consistently loses money each year, it will become insolvent and cease to exist, its market share going to some other company and its employees losing their jobs. My point is that a headteacher is in effect a chief executive operating under the same constraints. This has always been so in independent schools, if less obviously so in the state sector. Recent changes in school management rules in the UK have created a situation where the same is true for the state school. It follows that good management practice in the commercial world must be adapted and used by organizations in other sectors, including schools.

Since the advent in the UK of local management of schools, and the rapid growth of the number of grant-maintained schools, every headteacher must now manage her school within her allocated budget. This process involves the allocation of resources, buildings, equipment and staff in such a way as to most effectively achieve the objective or mission which she has set out for her school. To do this she must have some knowledge of basic accounting procedures, or hire a bursar to provide these skills. It is not our intention to provide this information since it is readily available elsewhere. What we want to do is to demonstrate that there exist important and measurable variables which can contribute to more effective management which are not taken into account in normal accounting procedures. This discovery is something of a shock to conventional management in the commercial world as well as the public sector organization.

Any organization must have a system through which to produce its product or service for its customers. To teachers, the term 'customer' may seem irrelevant in their world. We would argue that 'customer' refers to any person or group of persons which comes to an organization for satisfaction of a need. As we will see later, a school has several layers of customers, whose needs must be attended to in an increasingly competitive world. In a firm or a school there is a tendency to take for granted a system which has been in place for many years. 'If it ain't broke, don't fix it.' Any improvement programme tends to take the form of tinkering with existing structures. The fundamentals are rarely addressed in terms of the stated mission of the school. The existing system is likely to be based on some theory of behaviour or management techniques which evolved many years ago. Thus manufacturing and even service sector activities tend to be based on the concept of 'the economic order quantity', which underpins mass production. Schools tend to be organized around the concepts of the 'class', of up to thirty children, and the structured timetable of 'lessons'. In both cases the system tends to be 'producer led'. That is, the organization produces that which it thinks is appropriate, at the lowest cost possible, and then seeks to persuade customers to 'buy' that product.

Marketing strategy is essential for any organization. It must make decisions on the product to be offered, its price, where it is to be offered, and to which group of potential customers. It must let them know it is around by promoting itself and its product. In the old producer-led paradigm, the customer was the last person to be considered in this exercise. Marketing was seen as selling. This is no longer acceptable to the sophisticated and well-informed customer of today. Until recently the school had no need to even think about marketing, since its intake of customers (pupils) was directed to it by an outside authority, which made decisions against which the customer (parent) had little hope of successful appeal. This has now changed, and parents in the UK have been given a right of choice which they are determined to exercise. The school must therefore market its services to survive. It must, like Ford, become customer led. World-class organizations have adopted the Quality paradigm. We would like to demonstrate that schools both need to do so and can do so, not just in the management of the whole organization, but also at the micro-level of the classroom.

Key functions such as production, financial control and marketing all take place within an organizational structure, whether in a firm or a school. This too is likely to have ossified in a format which was appropriate to the producer-led organization. This means that all management is the management of people within structures. It is based again on old assumptions about motivation at work which may no longer be appropriate. It is assumed that people work only reluctantly, and under constant supervision and direction. It is believed that money is the only real motivator. The result in organizational terms is likely to be steeply hierarchical structures, with top-down communication, defence of departmental boundaries, staff appraisal systems of a judgemental type, and a general climate of fear. This is certainly true in school systems. The average class teacher must be three or four layers down the hierarchy of his school, and perhaps ten layers down from his ultimate boss, the chairman of the local education authority (LEA). He feels that he has little input into decision-making processes, and so will exercise little initiative to improve what he does. These ideological chains which link us to the past must be broken.

Our aim in writing this book is to encourage you to throw away the lumber of industrial and educational history, and to look afresh at what you do and how you do it, whether in the classroom or in school management. The evident success of Japanese companies in world markets since the 1970s has not been due to some inscrutable oriental philosophy, or culture. It was firmly based on the teachings of an American professor of statistics, W.E. Deming, the father of the quality revolution, which is now being used to transform companies here in the West which intend to survive in a global market-place. This new management paradigm is not just a new 'fad' which will go away. The quality revolution is here to stay, since our customers insist that it should. Those of us who work in the world of education are not immune from these changes. It is essential that we find ways of translating the Total Quality paradigm into terms which both work and are acceptable, in schools and colleges.

We have set out on this task on the basis of our own experience, and on that of a handful of schools in the USA and the UK who have gone down this route. None has regretted doing so. We hope that you will embark on an enjoyable journey towards world-class status.

Chapter 1

The Origins of Total Quality Management

We are in a stable system of wrong management, some of which may have been all right at some time. But times have changed.[1]

W.E. Deming

We will see from the examples in Chapter 2 that TQM is a system of management which can be applied successfully in a school environment. It is in fact more than just a management system. It is a philosophy, a cultural paradigm, which owes as much to the work of social psychologists as to that of statisticians or production managers. Its central propositions are that variance of performance in any system (factory, school, army, etc.) can be measured, studied and reduced. The removal of special causes of variance (e.g. illness, variability of materials used, etc.), leaves some degree of variance around the desired standard which cannot be attributed to the worker, but only to the system, and the system is the responsibility of management. However, if that variance is to be removed then well-trained and well-motivated workers are the most powerful tool for achieving improvement in the direction of 'zero defects'. Thus the central themes of TQM are that all employees must be trained in statistical techniques and problem-solving techniques, and that all employees must be seen as an asset which appreciates in value through training – unlike a machine, which depreciates over time. These themes will be developed in some detail in this book and applied to school-based examples. In this chapter we wish to trace briefly the origins of this revolution in management systems.

THE FIRST INDUSTRIAL REVOLUTION

The First Industrial Revolution was brought to its ultimate flowering in the period from 1920 to 1970, on the basis of mass production of standardized products, produced in mechanized plant on automatic machinery, in very large volumes. Henry Ford's 'T' model car epitomizes this approach: 'you can have any colour you like so long as it's black'. In such factories the worker became an adjunct of the machine. He was alienated from product, colleague and employer. Charlie Chaplin starkly but humorously illustrated this outcome in his silent film, *Modern Times*. Management was required to plan, control and direct, with specific targets of production to be met, irrespective of quality. The worker was required to work at the speed dictated by the machine. He was regarded as a commodity, to be bought in the quantities dictated by market forces, and to be discarded when no longer required, or unable to perform. The result was confrontational management, and the organization of labour in unions which sought to defend the collective rights of workers in an adversarial relationship with the employer.

The most influential figure in the development of this universally adopted management style was F.W. Taylor, whose methods (set out in his main work *The Principles of Scientific Management* (1911)) underpinned most of these developments.

Taylor was a highly successful self-taught engineer in the US steel industry, spending much of his career at Bethlehem Steel. He was obsessed by efficiency, starting from the premise that there is a best way of doing any specific job, and that this is achieved by breaking it down into its specialist component parts. Any employee could be trained to be super-efficient at any job, so long as that job is reduced to its simplest elements. He saw only 'maximum profit for employer, and maximum prosperity for employee' as motivators. He saw management and workers as being interdependent, with a common goal of prosperity. His early experiments actually used workers in a form of self-improvement 'quality circle' to seek greater efficiency. Unfortunately this aspect of his work did not take hold. His work on the measurement of and timing of tasks (Work and Method Study) did, however, capture the imagination of management in large-scale industries, and the resulting prevalence of a highly disciplined factory, with pay linked to target production figures, became the dominant theme. The assumptions which developed about the attitudes and abilities of workers were to prove counter-productive. They were that the worker only responds to direction and control, and will only be motivated to work hard and efficiently by financial greed combined with the threat of punishment. Far from producing a recognition of interdependence between management and worker, the opposite was the case.

Industry became result driven, in the sense both of profit results and of production outputs. Quality became secondary to quantity. Anyone who owned a British Leyland car in the 1970s will testify to that.

These principles have their echo in the education system which developed, especially at secondary level, during that period:

- education is done to pupils, not by them;
- they will not work without being made to do so;
- some proportion of educational 'output' is bound to be 'scrap' and 'waste', i.e. 'failures', just as high levels of waste scrap and rework are taken for granted in mass manufacture on Taylorian principles;
- all pupils' work is likely to be 'wrong', and must have quality 'inspected in'.

THE SECOND INDUSTRIAL REVOLUTION

Economic growth has since the Second World War produced increasing sophistication in the tastes of the public, and a revulsion against cheap and shoddy goods. This was particularly marked in the 1970s and 1980s. The manufacturing industries of the Western economies found themselves increasingly undermined by competition from Japan. Whole industries were destroyed, for example the UK motor-cycle industry.

A question for the reader

How many UK industrial sectors (e.g. heavy chemicals, textiles) can still command 15 per cent or more of the world market?

Answer: Only ONE (aerospace)

How many Japanese industrial sectors can control 15 per cent of the world market?

Answer: SEVENTY-TWO

Source: Dr Corcoran, Toyota Industrial Equipment (UK) Ltd

The Japanese have realized that the Second Industrial Revolution is well under way and that it is based on information, flexibility, quality, response to customer requirements, and above all investment: not just in best-practice technology but even more in people. That is why they are wiping us out. Too much of our industry, both manufacturing and service sector, is still operated on Taylorian principles. Why then have the Japanese been able to steal a march on the advanced Western economies in this way?

The answer to this question is to be found in the work of two men: W. Edwards Deming and Joseph M. Juran. Some of their disciples have developed their ideas further, or popularized them, for example Philip B. Crosby and Tom Peters in the USA and John S. Oakland of Bradford Management Centre, UK. The paradigm which they have developed, 'Total Quality Management', is now becoming recognized in all advanced economies as the only way forward for business and public service organizations. The purpose of this book is to apply this paradigm to education.

First, however, it may be helpful to see how the ideas developed historically. Because we are convinced that W.E. Deming is the single most important of these figures, we have restricted ourselves largely to demonstrating the development of TQM through the life and influence of Deming.

THE WORK OF W.E. DEMING

Deming was born in 1902, and until recently was still actively working, following a punishing six-day week of consultancy work, and conducting seminars all over the world. The first part of Deming's career, which could be said to cover his first fifty years, was centred around his work as an academic physicist and statistician. He taught briefly at Colorado, before studying for a Master's degree and then a PhD in Mathematical Physics at Colorado State University and then Yale.

In 1928 he joined the US Department of Agriculture as a mathematical physicist, and remained there until 1939. This period of the 1930s saw many of the major developments in the field of statistics and probability, including the work of Walter Shewart on statistical process control (SPC). Deming's interest in this area developed, and he studied in the UK under R.A. Fisher at University College, London.

He was particularly interested in Shewart's work, especially the identification of and discrimination between two types of variation in the industrial process: 'assignable' and 'unassignable' causes of variation (around a specification). It is important at this stage to understand this idea in essence, since it is developed further as a central feature of the application of TQM in an educational context.

An assignable cause is one which prevents the behaviour of a process from remaining constant in statistical terms. These Deming calls 'special' causes of variation, which come from outside the system itself, and which may be identified and eliminated. Before they are identified and eliminated, it is impossible to examine the true performance of the system, and the improvements which might be made to the system by changes in design, purchasing policies, training, etc. Once the special causes have been eliminated, only what he calls 'common' causes of variation remain. These are caused by faults within the system, *not* mistakes by careless workers, and may only be changed by management action to identify the causes of these variations, and eliminate them. As Myron Trybus has said, 'Workers work *in* the system, management works *on* the system.' If management fails to identify these causes accurately, attempts to improve the system will not only fail to improve it, they may actually make it worse. These thoughts had a powerful impact on Deming, and much of his reasoning about management follows from them, both his stress on the importance of SPC, and the humanitarian aspects of his thinking.

His controversial emphasis on the undesirability of performance targets and worker appraisal, which is highly relevant to our educational context, stems from here. If a target is set which is beyond the capability of the system to produce, it can only be achieved by distorting the system in such a way as to produce worse performance elsewhere. I am sure that we have all seen this happen in schools. Secondly, and a little less obvious at this stage, the amount of 'common cause' variation in the worker's appraised performance is such that it will effectively obscure the appraised person's real contribution. Juran originally estimated that the proportion of special to common causes was 15 per cent to 85 per cent. Deming later revised this figure to between 6 and 94 per cent. Improvement may only therefore be achieved where management seeks to improve the system, once the workers themselves (who are best placed to do so) have identified and rectified the special causes. Once the worker has got his part of the system into 'statistical control', he can do no more. Shewart concentrated on the impact of SPC on manufacturing processes, and it is in this area that until recently most progress has been made. Deming was the first to recognize that SPC may also be applied to non-production systems (such as schools). He demonstrated this fact in his work for a US Government department, the National Bureau of the Census, in 1939.

During the Second World War, Deming was invited to teach his SPC methods to industrialists and engineers, with very beneficial effects on the war effort. These advances were unfortunately not maintained in a sellers' market after the war when the emphasis was once again on shipping out production without attention to quality or efficiency. Deming's view is that whilst he got his ideas through to engineers during the war, management failed to take them in.

In Japan in 1946 as the country set out to rebuild its shattered economy, word of Deming's SPC methods reached the ears of the Union of Japanese Scientists and

Engineers, and this led to an invitation to Deming to lecture to the Union in 1950. At the first meeting, Deming addressed 21 of the presidents of top Japanese companies and during the following year he reached a further 500 or so. They were astonished when he told them that if they adopted his methods they would capture many world markets in a few years. He was not, however, just stressing the importance of SPC for production control, but a whole philosophy of company-wide (or total) quality management. At this time the reputation of the Japanese was for the clever pirating of Western ideas and the production of cheap and shoddy goods for export. He convinced them that they could capture world markets by the pursuit of quality in the sense of recognition and fulfilment of customer requirements. They felt that they had nothing to lose and the key Japanese companies embraced Deming's philosophy. It fitted with their Confucian philosophy, which stresses cooperation and consensus rather than conflict, in a context of team-work. The rest is history. The success of the Japanese economy in maintaining high levels of economic growth through exports and outward investment has been the envy of the less successful Western economies.

By 1978 the Japanese economy was dominant amongst the OECD countries, and a number of formerly powerful industries in the West had been wiped out, or were about to be so, including motor-cycle manufacture, cars, electronics and steel. The economies of the USA and UK were particularly hard hit, especially in the serious recession which followed the second oil price hike in 1978/9. It was only at this point that anybody in these countries began to hear the Deming message, despite the fact that for many years the most prestigious award in the Japanese economy had been the Deming Prize for Quality.

The first leading US industrialist to hear of Deming was W.E. Conway, of Nashua Corporation, a Fortune 500 company manufacturing computers and machinery. By the late 1970s the company was struggling to cope with increasing competition from Japan, not only on price, which was not new, but also on vastly better quality. Conway had heard of the Deming Prize in 1974, but did not really make the connection until 1979, when a colleague mentioned that Deming had been employed by a previous employer years before as a statistical consultant. Conway invited Deming to visit the company in March 1979, the first time Deming had been approached by a US company. Deming was by this time 78 years old. He was invited to consult for Nashua, and he refused, unless Conway himself as Chief Executive was prepared to act as chief agent of change. Conway agreed, and despite the difficulties of achieving the necessary culture change in the company, he began to see vast improvements. He than started to spread the word about Deming for he had recognized the importance of statistics, despite his own prior lack of knowledge of this subject. He himself said, 'The Japanese success is based on the statistical control of quality, introduced to them by an American.'

Whilst preparing a programme for NBC ('If Japan can why can't we'), Clare Crawford-Mason was pointed to Deming in the course of her preliminary research. She found her extensive interviews with Deming difficult but exciting. How could it be that a man who was five miles from the White House had the answer to Japanese competition, but no one would listen to him? The fact was that no one in the Administration had heard of him. She visited Nashua, where she filmed her documentary with both Deming and Conway. This was in June 1980 and from that moment Deming's phone was red hot.

Deming responded to this massive surge of interest in his work by commencing his now famous series of four-day seminars. The result of this programme has been the conversion of many major US companies to the Deming philosophy, including Ford, Honeywell, ATT, Campbell Soups, Kimberley Clark and Velcro. Public utilities are also becoming involved, e.g. city and state governments in Madison, Wisconsin and the Florida Light and Power Company. The word has more recently spread to Europe, in both private and public sectors. Recent success stories in the UK have included British Steel and Rover Cars, whilst British Gas and British Rail have just begun programmes to introduce TQM, as have some government agencies, for example the Legal Aid Department. Of course it takes time to see an improvement, two years perhaps for a small company (or a school) but as long as twenty years for an organization as large as British Rail.

In Europe as well as the USA, large numbers of academics and consultants have been influenced by Deming and his disciples include men such as Crosby and Trybus in the USA and Oakland and Atkinson in the UK. The result is that more and more consultancies are seeking to introduce TQM in a wide variety of business environments as companies and organizations realize that the old ways will no longer work. It is only in the last four years that the Deming philosophy has begun to percolate through into the educational system, first in the USA, and more recently in the UK. Where experimental programmes have been undertaken by individual teachers who have come under Deming's influence with their own classes, and by headteachers who have begun to apply TQM to the whole school organization, it has been evident that it is possible to seek and achieve 'continuous improvement', both in the way the school operates and in the performance of groups of individual students. We hope that this book will do something to introduce teachers and school managers and governors to Deming and his work, and spark off a transformation such as that which has brought so much success to Japan.

NOTE

1. This and the epigraphs to other chapters are all from Deming's book *Out of the Crisis* (see bibliography).

Chapter 2

The Pioneers

Adopt the new philosophy. We are in a new economic age. Western management must awaken to the challenge, must learn their responsibilities and take on leadership for change.

W.E. Deming

The purpose of this book is to invite the reader to consider the possibility that there is a better way to run schools than any with which most of us are familiar. Our proposition is that it is not only possible, but essential, to apply the management paradigm developed by a number of theorists, in particular W.E. Deming, and applied with enormous success by the Japanese to manufacturing industry in the first instance, but more recently to every type of business organization, and the public services. Our aim is to set out the key features of this paradigm and to demonstrate how it might be applied to an educational context.

Many, perhaps most, teachers and educationalists are reluctant to accept the possibility that any management theory stemming from a capitalist industrial background can possibly apply in schools and colleges. This being so, first we must convince you that it is possible. To do this we intend to introduce you to some of the pioneers of Total Quality Management principles in schools. Some of the few known pioneers are breaking the first rule of TQM by being very reluctant to make public their experiences of the 'continuous improvement' journey which they have undertaken. For this reason our account cannot be complete.

An account of our own experiences in applying the paradigm within the context of a Business Studies A-level course, is available elsewhere.[1] Here we would like to tell you the story of two outstanding teachers in the USA who have in quite different and contrasting contexts applied the TQM paradigm to their work with great success, and considerable acclaim across the USA. We would also like to introduce you to the work of a well-known American management consultant who has thought through the application of TQM to schools and education, and presented them in 1992 in an address to the British Deming Association. A full account of this paper is available elsewhere.[2]

THERESA HICKS

Theresa Hicks is an elementary school teacher in the Wilmington City schools, Wilmington, Ohio. She set out an account of her own personal journey towards the application of Deming's principles in a paper delivered to the British Deming Association's National Forum 1992.[3]

President Bush, like recent British Conservative governments, launched a campaign to 'reinvent education'. There, as here, the programme is grounded in principles which are in many ways the antithesis of the TQM paradigm. However, the search for increased voluntary involvement in education of parents and community, including business, and the desire to encourage students to become life-long learners, which are at the root of both US and UK planning, are entirely in line with TQM principles. Hicks, like us here at Bradford Grammar School, took the view that the search for a proposed partnership between education and industry was the most valuable starting point of government educational initiatives. She, like us, was influenced by the ideas of W.E. Deming, and felt that his so-called 'System of Profound Knowledge' was applicable to our own daily routine in the classroom. Our experience was with able pupils in an independent school Sixth Form, commencing an A-level course in Business Studies prior to going up to university. Her experience was at the opposite end of the educational spectrum, with 8 to 10-year-old mainstream and special needs pupils in elementary schools. She, like us, soon realized that it is possible to conduct a controlled experiment within one classroom, but that the wider application of the paradigm cannot be accomplished by the teacher in isolation.

Our starting point was to find a way a of developing in A-level students a greater degree of independence, self-esteem and self-motivation, in order that they be more effective independent learners at the university. Hicks began from the premise that special needs pupils needed to have individual learning programmes tailored to their specific needs. Together with her principal she had been involved in research in this area, and also studied the literature related to this research. She discovered that more student- or pupil-centred programmes produced significant attainment gains. As she points out, 'Cooperative learning encourages students to interact and investigate reading in a non-threatening manner.' Other research from the 1980s indicated that 'students learn best when they work with other students in teams'. The vital process of creating a 'need to know' can be accomplished 'by asking the students to help the teacher with the teaching process'. The recognition of this truth led her to wonder whether the same 'need to know' may be created by asking what business had found to be productive in this process and whether team-work and shared management responsibility was important in 'best practice' in industry. In this way Hicks came into contact with the ideas of Deming. She was fortunate in being able to attend various seminars on his work, and eventually to work with Deming himself. Within a year of this contact (1991) she had transformed her classroom management techniques on the Deming model. At this time she met another of our 'pioneers', David Longford, and shared her experience with him.

Basically as a result of these experiences, Hicks set out to attempt four things:

Hicks' objectives

- Actively use business management training and contacts as a way of encouraging students to become life-long learners.
- Adopt management principles (TQM) in teaching methods and lesson plans.
- Train 'customers' – identified as parents and students – in tools of statistical analysis applicable to their personal life experiences.
- Research the needs of the third 'customer', future potential employers.

I am struck by the similarity of these objectives to ours working with students ten years older, in a different school and national environment.

Hicks' methodology

The first step was the recognition of the customer–supplier relationship, and its application in the classroom within Deming's interaction triangle (Figure 2.1). The class was taught to see itself as a business, and then teams within the class as divisions of that business. The teacher at some times played the role of Chief Executive, and at other times the customer of the business.

The teaching process itself served a dual purpose. The principles of the Deming approach to problem solving (set out later in this book) were themselves taught, and were the foundation paradigm of classroom management. The course material proper was delivered within this context. The application of the Deming approach in the classroom was found to facilitate the learning process. As Myron Trybus was later to comment, 'it works as a lubricant for learning'.[4] We also found this to be true with our sixth-form students at Bradford. It was relatively easy for us with older students to go further than this and involve the students in the process of planning the organization and delivery of the course. It is much more remarkable that Hicks was able to do so with students as young as nine or ten years. She, like us, felt that this was an important step

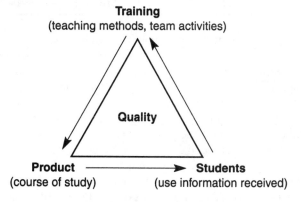

Training
(teaching methods, team activities)

Quality

Product ⟶ **Students**
(course of study)   (use information received)

Figure 2.1 *Deming's interaction triangle*
Source: W.E. Deming and Theresa Hicks

towards enabling the students to establish 'ownership' of (and so responsibility for) the learning process. By this approach students become 'co-managers' of their education. 'Knowledge becomes something sought after, instead of something done to them.' Competition between students is downplayed, since judgements of relative merit are inevitably subjective. Instead the self-esteem of the class is raised simply by telling them when they have done a good job. Hicks creates in their minds 'a school without grades', although they have to be told that the system requires that she impose grades on their work. This is similar to our experience. Hicks feels strongly that teachers should stop ranking students and dishing out rewards and punishments. She believes that 'ranking results in the suboptimisation of the system'. Students must be encouraged to have good feelings about their work. We have had similar thoughts about the effects on students of the imperative of ranking in the public exam system in the UK. The most positive outcome which she found, and one that was replicated in our experience, is that students have a feeling of self-control which is not present in other classes. In our case the contrast between their experience with us as against more orthodox A-level courses which they are also following causes a certain amount of anxiety.

Central to the learning experience provided by Hicks is an understanding that new knowledge is what we add to that which we have already learned in the past, and on the basis of which we can manage or predict the future. From this basis Hicks demonstrates in simple terms with everyday examples the importance of Deming's principle that the management of any system is based on prediction along with revision and extension of what we have observed. This leads to the development of the simple problem-solving devices such as the fishbone diagram, and the various ways in which information can be collected, displayed and analysed. Examples are used which are part of the child's everyday experience. Deming does not deny the existence of competition, but Hicks seeks to diffuse its worst effect of creating fear of learning, through the teaching of simple statistics, which cause even young children to see that ranking (of results) will happen, as a result of different ability or characteristics, but that this is not necessarily a permanent judgement. She believes that the system must offer not the certainty of failure, but the chance to fail and then to learn from failure, in order to continuously improve.

In pursuit of continuous improvement, she has amended the Deming cycle to:

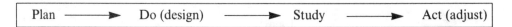

Plan ⟶ Do (design) ⟶ Study ⟶ Act (adjust)

She seeks to teach her pupils that if improvement of their work is to take place, the first step is to develop a plan, then put it into a form which may be implemented. Then the outcome must be carefully examined (by gathering and examining data), recognizing the existence both of special and of common causes of variation in outcomes (see Chapter 8). The fourth step follows from this analysis, and involves doing something to correct the causes of variation, by planning the process or system in a new way in order to improve the outcome further. The cycle is never-ending, since we must always seek continuous improvement of 'product' and 'process'. We must not create a climate of fear of reprisal for failure. Teachers want to do a good job; so do students.

Like us, Hicks believes that we must 'drive out fear' by using grades and ranking only as a means of, in a neutral way, describing what skills and knowledge have been mastered, and as a guide to the next step in the cycle of continuous improvement. Rewards, such as gold stars, prizes, etc., in Hicks' view place undue emphasis on extrinsic motivation (just as payment by results does in business), and the giving of rewards will extinguish intrinsic motivation for learning if we do not take care.

Hicks concludes by reminding us that we must do something to end the cycle of underachievement. As she says, 'We must look at the mistakes made by business and learn from them.' We need also to look at the alternative, which is the successes of business. 'Ask any company and they will tell you there is more to it than gathering and analysing data. Most of them keep quality records just as we keep results of standardized tests! It is what you *do* about the results you collect that matters.'

LARRAE ROCHELEAU AND DAVID LONGFORD

Rocheleau became superintendent (headteacher) of Mt Edgecumbe High School, Sitka, Alaska, USA, some seven years ago. For many years this residential school had been run by the Federal authorities, under the Bureau of Indian Affairs. In 1985 it became a State school, run by the Alaskan authorities. It is situated in the south-eastern panhandle of Alaska, and has always catered for students from scattered rural communities, most of whom (80 per cent plus) are of either American Indian or Inuit (Eskimo) origin. These communities are amongst the most disadvantaged in the USA, and in this case 40 per cent of the students are considered on entry to be 'at risk'. There are some 215 students and 16 teachers in the school. Under his leadership, Rocheleau states, 'the school has developed a culture that is different from any I have seen or heard about'. Assisted by David Longford, computer coordinator, Rocheleau set out five years ago to implement in the organization and operation of the school the ideas of W.E. Deming. The essence of this approach is that there must be total commitment from the top of the organization to a programme of continuous improvement of every aspect of the organization, and that this can only be achieved if the people in the organization are 'empowered' to make change and improvement happen.

After four years of the Continuous Improvement Programme, some remarkable results have emerged. In the most recent survey of graduates for the school, some 45 to 50 per cent were at college or university, in most cases studying business courses. The latest unemployment data for the various districts of Alaska shows rates of between 15 and 30 per cent, whilst the 1991 crop of leavers from Mt Edgecumbe shows only 2 per cent unemployment. A comparison with data from a school in the UK with similar problems amongst its students on entry would be revealing. Moreover, this obscure outback high school has emerged as a 'world-class school'. Its reputation is now well known throughout the USA and is even becoming known in Europe. Its students have offered presentations of the methods which have brought this success at major business and educational forums and conferences throughout the USA and most recently at the British Deming Association National Forum in 1992. The students operate a business enterprise as part of their normal curriculum, processing and exporting salmon, which has brought fame to the school in Japan and other parts of Asia. Accounts of its work have appeared in journals and newspapers and on TV across the USA. Remember, this is a school catering for ethnic minority youngsters in the remotest part of the USA. It is analogous to an inner-city comprehensive in Leeds becoming more famous across the world than Eton College. How do Rocheleau and Longford see the secrets of their success?

The change started at the top. For most of his working life, Rocheleau sees himself as having been a 'benevolent dictator'. Now he sees himself as 'coach' and 'facilitator'. He believes that the successes which they have achieved have stemmed from a determination to break the cycle of deprivation, low expectation and dependency amongst students, and old-fashioned ideas amongst the staff, through which grading and ranking systems simply created self-fulfilling prophecies of failure. The attempt to apply Deming's methods has worked in his view because the staff's beliefs are reinforced by action and regular schoolwide training. He has sought to create a climate in which there is no fear, and where motivation is intrinsic not extrinsic. As a visiting reporter put it, 'To those who labour in traditional school settings, it would seem that Mt Edgecumbe is founded on an outlandish affirmation of joyful learning.'

This may to the reader sound incredible and unattainable. It was not easy. The programme of continuous improvement which Rocheleau set up is founded on very hard work by students and staff, cooperating to produce a more exciting curriculum, and a method for engaging 'buy in' by as many pupils and staff as possible. The teaching is cross-curricular and is also very demanding, since it includes, in addition to the normal basic curriculum required in all US schools, the study of Japanese, Russian or Chinese as part of the attempt to base the curriculum around a study of the place which Alaska and its people has in the Pacific Rim and Asian economy and culture. The teaching of Business Studies and the operation on the mini-enterprise are part of this attempt to engage the interest of the pupils. It has worked. In addition to having this demanding academic diet, the students are also deeply involved in a dialogue with staff in the search for improvement of the system within which they operate. The starting point of this remarkable turnaround was a 'quality audit' of what was happening in the school in order to identify possibilities for improvement. Rocheleau provided the leadership and the mission. This 'corporate mission' was based firmly on a version of Deming's original 'Fourteen Points', (see Table 12.1, p. 146), amended to fit a school rather than a business.

Mt Edgecumbe High School, Sitka, Alaska:

Mission Statement

Mt Edgecumbe High School is a paradigm shift in philosophy to the usual high school program. Each curricular area offers innovative teaching methods that not only enhance opportunities for Mt Edgecumbe High School students, but serve as models for other high schools.

Mt Edgecumbe High School provides new and important education opportunities for Alaskan students. The school places high expectations upon students, administrators, and staff. Program and curriculum are based upon a conviction that students have a great and often unrealized potential. The school prepares students to make the transition to adulthood helping them to determine what they want to do and develop the skills and the self confidence to accomplish their goals.

Mt Edgecumbe High School students are required to pursue rigorous academic programs that encourage students to work at their highest levels. Administrators, teachers, and other staff are required to keep current on educational advances and to initiate innovative, challenging, and stimulating classroom programs and activities.

Teachers and staff analyze issues to anticipate future social and economic needs of Alaska, such as Alaska's economic position among the Pacific Rim nations, and to integrate an educational approach to these issues into the curriculum. A strong curriculum in English, social studies, mathematics, science/marine science, computers/ business, career exploration, Asian languages, and physical education is provided.

Special emphasis is placed on the study of both historical and contemporary topics specific to Alaska. Study of the history, culture, and languages of the Pacific Rim are a major curricular area and to the extent possible Pacific Rim studies are applied across the curriculum.

Vocational eduction is stressed through entrepreneurship and work study. Cottage industries are run by students. Traditional vocational education is offered on a limited basis.

Opportunities for leadership, public service and entrepreneurship are integrated into the program, both during and after regular school hours. The school prepares students for the academic demands of being away from home and managing time effectively. Some students are selected for admission who are having a difficult time with their local environment. Staff work within available resources to help these students become productive citizens

Mt Edgecumbe High School as a boarding school offers students a wide range of support activities in both academic and residential programs, to assure the success of all students. To facilitate personal growth and decision making skills, each student is assisted, guided, and challenged to make choices about future academic or technical schooling and alternative methods of making a living. Students are respected for their cultural background and diversity. Students and teachers are encouraged and expected to offer insights to increase the effectiveness of the school.

Purpose: Why do we exist? What is the basic need we fulfill?

The purpose of Mt Edgecumbe High School is to provide quality education for youth, in its day, for its future, in order to add value to society.

Vision: What are we striving for? What do we want to become?

The aim or vision of Mt Edgecumbe High School is to:

- enable *quality* individuals.
- create a learning and working environment for all students and employees which is stimulating, provides a sense of belonging, and nurtures long term growth and development both personally and professionally.
- provide for parents the assurance that their children will live and work in a safe environ- ment, learn to freely cooperate with others to cause positive improvements, adjust and participate in a changing global society, and gain enthusiasm for life-long learning.
- provide the State of Alaska a continuous model for educational advancement and a cadre of productive citizens who will shape the future of the State.
- pass the torch for continuous quality improvement to the next generation.

Quality: A definition

Quality education is the continuous improvement of systems to enable the optimum state of personal, social, physical, and intellectual development of each individual which will result in society and colleague loyalty now and in the future.

Rocheleau's version of Deming's 'Fourteen Points'

Our actions, at Mt Edgecumbe High School, are based on the following beliefs:

1. Human relations are the foundation for all quality improvement.

2. All components in our organization can be improved.

3. Removing the causes of problems in the system inevitably leads to improvement.

4. The person doing the job is most knowledgeable about that job.

5. People want to be involved and do their jobs well.

6. Every person wants to feel like a valued contributor.

7. More can be accomplished by working together to improve the system than by working individually around the system.

8. A structured problem solving process using statistical graphic problem-solving techniques lets you know where you are, where the variations lie, the relative importance of problems to be solved and whether the changes made have had the desired impact.

9. Adversarial relationships are counterproductive and outmoded.

10. Every organization has undiscovered gems waiting to be developed.

11. Removing the barriers to pride of workmanship and joy of learning unlocks the true untapped potential of the organization.

12. Ongoing training, learning and experimentation is a priority for continuous improvement.

Educational operational definitions

School Boards, Superintendents, Principals and central office support personnel are:

Management – These individuals have the responsibility to lead by enabling, to foster project teams and to constantly seek opportunity for improvement in every process and service of the school organization. They have systems level responsibility.

Teachers are:

Leader/managers – Teachers continually work on improving their classroom systems and they work with students to improve the instructional process. Teachers are expected to continually look for improvement opportunity in both special and common causes in organizational processes. Teachers are the experts in their work area and are considered first level managers.

Students are:

Co-managers – They are responsible to manage and improve their own personal processes and participate with the teacher in the management of the classroom.
Customers – Each student involved in the education process is receiving a service and deserves to be happy, satisfied and to have their needs anticipated.

Product – Students are the product produced by the education process.
Managers – They are capable of improving their own quality of life by monitoring their own actions and managing themselves, their work processes and peer groups.

Parents, businesses and community are:

Customers – Parents, businesses and community are paying for education service and are customers who deserve to have their requirements met or exceeded.
Co-managers – We also want parents to be part of the decision making process and actively involved in improvement processes.

Support Services are: (i.e. Contracted services such as food service, security etc.)

Suppliers of product and service, are expected to learn quality methodology, implement continuous improvement within their organization and work to establish long term relationships.

Students Sources

Any school, organization, or parental structure which educates incoming students is a student source or supplier. MEHS works with these sources to improve incoming students and to establish long term, cooperative relationships.

A summary of the quality audit results, including the actions taken to cure identified problems, is set out in Table 2.1. This may be helpful for the reader when attempting (as we hope you will) to apply the TQM paradigm in your school. We in Bradford Grammar School invited a group of 18 Business Studies students to undertake a similar exercise some months ago, before we had heard of Mt Edgecumbe High School. The amazing similarities of both diagnosis and recommendations cause us to believe that the similarities between schools, viewed as organizations, are greater than the differences. Why not try it in your school? The rest of this book seeks to set out the techniques which underpinned Rocheleau's successful experiment.

Table 2.1 *Continuous improvement at Mt Edgecumbe High School*

Problem	Recommendation	Gains
Pinball curriculum/class structure Seven periods per day, of 50 mins – causes 'waste' through excessive pupil movement	Four 90 min classes per day	Large time saving – permits 90 mins per week for training for *all* staff
		Permits varied teaching styles, in-depth study, projects, fieldwork etc.
		Reduces didactic teaching
		Increases student involvement and motivation
Student apathy	Students invited to help plan class activities	Focus on quality not quantity
		Increased pride in workmanship
	Change education from what is done *to* students, to working *with* students as 'coaches'	Peer tutoring

Table 2.1 *Continued*

Problem	Recommendation	Gains
		Cooperative learning
		Increased student self-esteem
Students generate poor quality work	Improve communication	Better equipment provided (40 computers in place of 10)
	Increase trust	Teachers stress quality and improvement, not grade and ranking
	Stress quality not quantity	
	View students as customers	Teachers focus on student needs – even if it needs more work
		Library and IT better used – evenings as well as day
		Improved curriculum at student request – e.g. US History, Russian, Physics
		Average homework commitment up to 15 hrs per week
		Achievement becomes a habit
Truancy/lateness/discipline	Cooperation between staff and students to bring improvement	Lateness down from $^{34}/213$ to $^{10}/213$ per week
	Identify reasons and causes of variance	Reduced waste of office time and classroom time
	Improve system, educational and organizational	Students arrive early
	Teach time management skills	Students help identify and control discipline problems
		Improved classroom productivity
		Teacher time on discipline problems reduced to zero
		Teachers cooperate instead of acting defensively
		Learning becomes skill development, not rote learning
		Withdrawals from school reach new low of 1 per cent 1990
Organizational problems	Develop mission statement	1990/91 teacher turnover zero
Lack of staff focus	Use Deming's Fourteen Points	Vastly improved atmosphere
Low teacher morale	Improve the system to help the teacher	Students see lessons as a challenge, not a chore
Poor internal 'climate'		
Lack of cooperation between teachers and administrators	Involve everyone in decision making	Moved from the 'they' syndrome to 'we'
Low morale of admin staff	Develop induction programme	Consensus decision making established as 'norm'
Lack of participation in decision making	Involve administrators as part of educational process	Team teaching and flexible approach to all activities
	Motivate students	

Table 2.1 *Continued*

Problem	Recommendation	Gains
Inefficient use of technology	Use 90 mins per week for training and meetings involving all staff	'Glasnost' established as school philosophy
Hierarchical structure and poor communications		
Lack of training	Train all to use technology	
Lack of long-term planning	De-emphasize job titles and descriptions – be flexible	
	Teach all project management techniques	
Teaching methods	Change timetable to 90 min classes to save time for staff training and student self-directed activity	Increased extra-curricular developments
Lack of planning and preparation time		Students seek to reduce variance in own performance
Lack of student self-responsibility	Students track own progress against quality goals	Internal drive for achievement
Boring lessons	Constantly review curriculum contents	Students involved in classroom management
Lack of pride in work		
Static methods	Reduce emphasis on grades and emphasize quality and intellectual curiosity	Sharing of information and skills
Lack of 'relevance' in courses		Greatly improved IT provision
Inadequate use of technology	Involve students in current issues within curriculum	
	Give all teachers a computer	
	Teach all students TQM techniques	

A cynical reader may perhaps think that the school has invented these supposed improvements, but I have to say that the outcomes described at the beginning of the chapter suggest that there is more to it than that. Why not try your own experiment with a small group of older pupils? You might be surprised at their perception and enthusiasm.

I have included as Figure 2.2 a piece of work submitted by a 13-year-old boy in an English class. This was written in response to being asked to redesign the school in the event of its having been burnt down. It illustrates the ability of even quite young pupils to think creatively about the process of education in which they are involved.

We will end this chapter with a summary (Table 2.2) of the key points of the three experimental TQM programmes which we have mentioned at Mt Edgecumbe, Wilmington elementary schools and Bradford Grammar School, together with some first-hand comments on the experiments from pupils at the two secondary-level schools. I hope that you will have found in this chapter enough food for thought to prompt you to read the rest of the book and then seek to apply the Deming approach in your school. There is no reason why your school should not achieve world-class status.

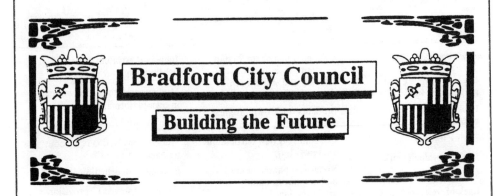

Here at Bradford City Council we have a commitment to all citizens of the Bradford area. This commitment extends itself to you, as a parent of a B.G.S. pupil. After the arson attack of May 1993, we set about designing the world's most efficient school building, incorporating design features from architectural studios worldwide. We are sure that you will find it most agreeable. This is also the first building project to use information supplied by its future users: we received more than five-hundred returns of our survey to find the views of pupils from the school. The building, which will be completed in early 1996, is detailed in the following pages; we hope that you will like it!

Figure 2.2 *A 13-year-old boy's redesign of his school following an imaginary arson attack. (Continued on pp.19–22).*

The School as a Whole

The Overall Design

The most obvious aspect of the overall design is the circular shape both of the inner and outer 'districts'. This cornerless structure allows rapid access to every part of the school. Nowhere in the building can be more than the diameter of the outermost circle away. The gap between the inner and outer precincts allows sufficient space for the main building not to cause a shadow to fall onto any of the outer 'form' blocks during school hours. (From 7:30am to 2:45pm).

Classrooms

The classrooms within the main building have been a great source of debate among the architects assigned to their design. The most obvious problem, of the rooms having to fit within a circular layout, (See Fig ii) proved to be immaterial: the shape of the classrooms (See Fig i) tends to focus the pupils' attention on the teacher, especially as the rooms are banked towards the centre of the building.

Central rooms have a large VDU (Visual Display Unit) at their fronts, with control from Television, Video, Satellite, and Computer sources. All rooms are decorated and equipped in a similar way:

1) All rooms are painted in a tranquil shade of blue-green.
2) All rooms are carpeted.
3) All rooms have white-boards and marker pens, rather than blackboards and chalk.
4) Hard plastic chairs are replaced by soft cushioned chairs, for pupil comfort.

(Fig i)

Pupils use the main building only when they have a lesson with a need for special equipment. (e.g. Physics, Chemistry, Biology, lectures. library periods, etc.) In all other circumstances pupils use their own form room in one of the separate blocks.

After the success which was obvious with the introduction of girls into the lower and upper sixth year groups, it has been decided by the school governors that all years should become coeducational.

This means the selling of the Girls' Grammar School, which will assist finances for the new Bradford Grammar School, and allow us to offer boarding facilities for the first time in the school's history. This advance should allow a wider spread of cultural identities in the school, as pupils will now be able to attend the school from much further afield.

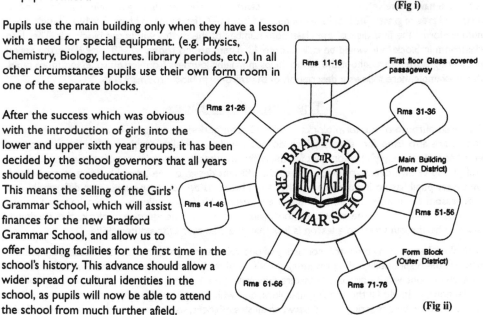

Rms 11-16

First floor Glass covered passageway

Rms 21-26

Rms 31-36

BRADFORD GRAMMAR SCHOOL · CuR HOC AGE 1001

Main Building (Inner District)

Rms 41-46

Rms 51-56

Form Block (Outer District)

Rms 61-66

Rms 71-76

(Fig ii)

Facilities within the Main Building

A fully catlogued library is located on the second of the three stories, with computer search capabilities which extend to all the networked computers, in the main building as well as in the form blocks.

In the field of Information Technology, fifty IBM compatible PCs are available for all to use. All computers in the school are networked (electronically linked) in order to be more efficient. For example, the Headmaster, in his third floor office, is able to send letters to the printer of a form block, so that pupils there receive them as quickly as possible without having to rely on an individual to carry them over. Computers form an important part of the design of the school as a whole. All form blocks are supplied with six computer terminals, one for each classroom, which only members of staff are permitted to use. A pilot scheme, involving the use of laptop computers by pupils, will be put into operation for the third-year shortly after the opening of the school in 1996. A similar study proved to be successful in Northern Ireland in the late 1980s, and it is hoped that the same will be true here. For, if the scheme is successful, all pupils will be issued with a laptop computer to note-down and produce work. Close association with computer technology will also benefit pupils wishing to use such facilities in later life.

School Power Sources

For environmentalists, a high degree of insulation is implemented, and solar panels are fitted to the roof of the main building. All other electricity is produced by the latest in environmentally friendly (and cheap) technology: an algae-powered generator. Algae are grown under controlled conditions using the sun's energy, then dried and compressed to form a diesel-like substance. This is then burned in a combustion chamber, with little in the way of pollutants given-off, to produce electricity. After the initial cost, no further expenses need to be considered, and the school will pay nothing for its power, except minimal maintenance costs, thus reducing the fees for parents such as yourself.

The Form Blocks

All the outer blocks are virtually identical in structure, most consisting of six equally-sized classrooms (L6 and 6 having twelve), a common area with central fountain and vending machines, and a rear ballustraded area of grass. The blocks are numbered from 1–7, (First year to Upper sixth) and their block number forms the first digit of the classroom number of the rooms within the block. e.g. The third classroom in block four would be called room 43. There are no rooms 47, 48, or 49, but the logical numbering system throughout the school helps in making journeys from lesson to lesson more rapid. As an example, here follows a description of the third-form block, rooms 31-36.

The Third Form Block

The main purpose of the form blocks is to hold form periods and registration; however, the classrooms are also used for lessons which do not envolve specialist equipment (such as laboratory benches and gas supply). Lessons last for thirty-five minutes, to maximize concentration of students, and period change-overs are quick due to the efficient design of the school building as a whole. A third-year pupil has no lessons in any other form block, as do no other pupils from different blocks have lessons in his/hers, and so he/she alone is responsible for its upkeep, as no other year groups will ever use it. As he/she only uses the main building and the third-year block, the maximum distance he/she can travel to a lesson is less than the diameter of the outer circle.

Each block has its own commitee, consisting of one volunteer from each of the six forms. This voulounteer has the responsibility of representing the views of his fellow classmates in the monthly meetings. At such meeting will be discussed matters concerning the running of the block. For instance, which confectionary should fill the vending machines, and which activities should be carried-out on which day. Every quarter, a meeting is held between all seven blocks, to air views on the school as a whole. A member of staff is present at all these meetings to act as a chairperson.

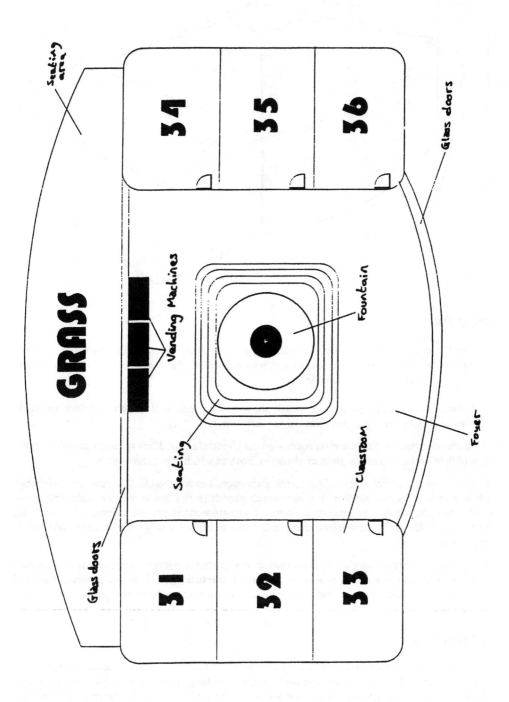

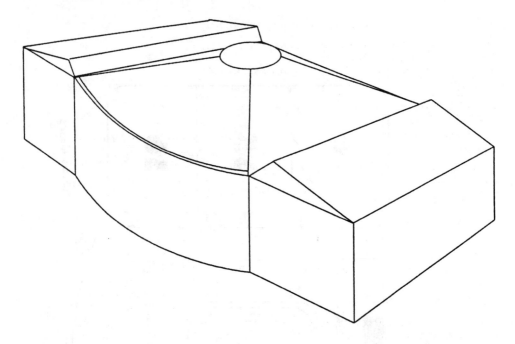

Other Details

One of the most important areas of school design is to create the correct atmosphere and environment in which to work. To this extent we have included some features which have never before been used in a school building:

1) Tinted, double-glazed glass roofs, which allow an excellent level of light in which to work. Filtered neon striplights are also installed for duller days.

2) To counter glare due to the glass roofs, vertical blinds of about 30cm in depth, allow in a great deal of light without creating glare or shadows, both of which can disturb work.

3) A full climate control system. Due to the glass roofs, heating the block in summer is far more efficient than in the old building. The temperature tends to rise above an acceptable limit, however, when the sun is very intense; therefore a climate control system is installed to cool the whole block down. We have found that pupils work much more diligently in cooler, less humid conditions.

4) Vending machines. There is no tuck-shop in the school any longer. Instead, various vending machines will sell everything that was on offer in the old tuck-shop. This also removes the need for prefects to spend time working in the shop, as the vending machines are fully automated, and cut down on queues.

In Conclusion

The building of the new Bradford Grammar school will take in the region of three years; after which time you will be able to see and evaluate the new design for yourself. This building is a first in the education industry worldwide, and we hope that you and your son/daughter will appreciate it to the full of its potential.

Table 2.2 *Similarities between three experimental CIP programmes*

LR	=	L. Rocheleau, Mount Edgecumbe High School, Alaska
TH	=	Theresa Hicks, Wilmington, Ohio
MSG	=	M. S. Greenwood, Bradford, Grammar School, UK

Objectives	Methods
Establish leadership, not control	*Examine the system and seek continuous improvement*
Go from you to 'I' to 'we'; establish interdependence. LR	Students and teachers are expected to offer insights to increase the effectiveness of the school. LR
Create a need to know in students. TH	Involve students in how the lessons develop beyond the planning stage. TH
Aim for student-centred (as against teacher-centred) learning. MSG	Seek the student's view of the development of the course. MSG
Develop skills as well as knowledge	*Stop blaming people*
Give students skill and experience. LR	If a school system has been dysfunctional for years, then all the people, including the students, will be dysfunctional. Quit blaming people for the problem and start fixing the system. LR
Students successful in developing skills help others. TH	
Stress decision-making and problem-solving skills. MSG	Teachers cannot achieve a transformation alone, we work within a system. An entirely different approach to that system is needed. TH
Empower students to feel ownership of their studies	Norm referencing limits the possibility of continuous improvement, and creating expectations based on past experience. MSG
Students become actively involved in the learning process through intrinsic motivation and trust. LR	*Develop problem-solving techniques*
What better way to establish a need to learn than through actually feeling you own the lesson? TH	Train everyone in quality techniques. LR
Learning should be owned by the student, not imposed on him. MSG	Students must be challenged to analyse what factors contribute to variance in an experiment. TH
Develop team-work and flatten the hierarchy	Provide a set of benchmarks for process of analysis of any presented problem. MSG
I now would consider myself as a team facilitator rather than a benevolent dictator. LR	*Use intrinsic, not extrinsic, motivation*
Students must be equipped with the ability to work together to a common end. TH	De-emphasize standardized (tested) achievement, and emphasize intellectual curiosity and the individual's learning needs. LR
Stress a range of communication, leadership and team-work skills. MSG	The effect of competition is suboptimization and driving fear into a system. I create for them in their minds a school without grades. TH
Delight customers	
The school prepares students to make the transition to adulthood, and develop the self-confidence to accomplish their goals. LR	A heavy work rate based on regular testing will cause students to sacrifice quality for quantity. MSG
Train my customers (students and parents) in the specific tools of analysis applicable to their life experience and what is required by future employers. TH	
Develop a high level of self-confidence, initiative, self-discipline and personal organization. MSG	

The quality revolution is beginning to gather pace in schools, but there is a long way to go yet. An anti-quality culture is actually being reinforced in schools by government diktat in both the UK and USA, in the name of reform. In this climate, any head or serving teacher who happens to read this book will probably feel that it is idealistic, and impossible. Perhaps, but the experience of Mt Edgecumbe High School suggests otherwise:

- 50 per cent of the last four graduating classes are at university or college, mostly studying business.
- 36 per cent of last year's leavers found work.
- The drop-out rate is only 1 per cent.
- The unemployment rate of recent former students is only 2 per cent as against 15 – 30 per cent in other Alaskan school districts.
- The school runs a successful salmon-processing business, exporting its product to Japan.
- Three major corporations are now engaged in supporting the school.
- Pupils and staff have done major presentations on their CIP programme at major conferences in Texas, California, and for the British Deming Association in the UK.

This is truly a world-class school.

Let the students of Mt Edgecumbe High School and Bradford Grammar School speak for themselves.

Jason Edwards MEHS 'People are needed to take part in the process of improvement. It is unbelievable what happens when you lose your fear.'

Greg Lundhal MEHS 'MEHS students are not just going to get soft when they go to college, and slide back into the old paradigm, we are going to fight.'

Lis Pohl MEHS 'I used to be ashamed to be an Indian, but now I am proud to be an Indian. We will initiate a CIP programme into every college when we get there.'

Chris Nutter BGS 'The circle [of expectations] must be broken and a climate of cooperation and team-work introduced to the students and then extended between all levels in the hierarchy.'

Nick Woolley BGS 'The main advantage of the TQM paradigm is that the onus is placed on the student, which is good preparation for university, and later life. However, it is difficult immediately to adjust to the fact that teachers are no longer spoonfeeding the information to you.'

Let Myron Trybus have the last word. In his 1992 address to the BDA conference in the UK he said:

I can think of no other activity which promises more leverage in the improvement of society than the development of a generation which understands quality and is equipped to improve it.' [5]

NOTES

1. *Managing Service Quality*, published by IFS/MCB, January and May 1992.
2. British Deming Association, conference papers, 1992 National Forum, British Deming Association, 2 Castle St, Salisbury.
3. Theresa Hicks, 'Applying Deming's Profound Knowledge in the Classroom', British Deming Association, 1992 National Forum. 'A system of Profound Knowledge', BDA pamphlet.
4. British Deming Association, as note 2.
5. As note 2.

Chapter 3

What is Quality Anyway?

Create constancy of purpose for improvement of product and service.

W.E. Deming

We all think we know what we mean by quality in any context. But do we? Make a mental checklist of the instant responses you would give to the following questions.

Give a named product which typifies for you high quality in each of the following categories of goods and services.

1. Motor cars
2. Watches
3. Shoes
4. China
5. Banking
6. World cruises

It is very likely that you composed a list which would look something like this.

1. Rolls-Royce (or BMW or Mercedes)
2. Rolex
3. Gucci
4. Aynsley
5. Coutts & Co.
6. Cunard

If we had asked you to provide a name for the highest-quality university it is likely that you would have instantly responded with Oxford, Cambridge or Harvard. Or if we had asked you for a high-quality school, you would probably have instantly responded with Eton, Manchester Grammar School or Holland Park Comprehensive.

We are not for a minute suggesting that any of the above, or any which you named are bad providers of goods and services, but I am suggesting that if this was your instant response (not your considered response when you were looking for the catch), it suggests that you should definitely read on.

If you responded as we suggested you might, then your definition of quality would be something like this: 'A product or service delivered to a very high specification at a very high price, only accessible to customers or clients who have high incomes and wealth.' The implication of this attitude is that products and services delivered for consumption by the majority of less well-off customers must necessarily be of lower specification, and lower price. In other words, you get what you pay for.

It is not surprising that for many years suppliers of volume-produced cars, washing machines, rail services, banking services, and, dare we say it, education, have been able to get away with products and services which are both cheap and nasty.

In 1951 the leaders of Japanese industry learned a completely new approach from an American, W. Edwards Deming, who had been ignored at home. Since then they have systematically eroded the market share worldwide of major US and European industries. It is simply not true that their methods will only work in Japan's apparently regimented and conformist society, nor is it only possible within a Confucian culture. It can and is being done in any society, including our own, Our objective is to show how to apply the secrets of Japanese success to your school, Do not feel that somehow your pure vision of education as an end in itself, to which only educationalists have access, will be prejudiced.

Now let us take a fresh look at the concept of 'quality'. In recent years customers for all kinds of products and services have become much more sophisticated in their tastes. They are also more demanding. They are no longer willing to accept substandard products in any market-place, including education. Even British Rail commuters have rebelled against being treated like cattle, and have gone so far as to occupy a train until BR were willing to send it where the passengers wished to go. This new attitude has enormous implications for our definition of quality.

Our new definition of quality should then read:

> 'Meeting customer requirements', 'fitness for purpose' and perhaps even 'delighting our customers'.

This need amplifying somewhat. What are customer requirements?
1. *Availability*
   The product or service must be there when the customer requires it, not just when the producer is willing to put it on offer.
2. *Delivery*
   The product or service must be delivered to the customer at a time and place which is convenient to him.
3. *Reliability*
   The product or service must live up to customer requirements at all times. It must never let him down.
4. *Cost effectiveness*
   The product or service must satisfy the customer's needs at the lowest possible cost.
5. *Performance*
   Above all else, it must do what the customer wants it to do. For example, in the classroom you need a watch. It must tell the time accurately, and be virtually unbreakable. It matters much less what it looks like. However if you were the wife of

the US Ambassador to the Palace of St James, it would be important that your watch demonstrated and confirmed your power and influence, your grace and good taste. In this case it would be much more important for the watch to look good than for it to tell the time accurately, or be unbreakable.

Perhaps we should develop the idea of quality a stage further. From the point of view of the supplier of the service or product, two matters are crucial:

1. *Quality of design*
   By this we mean the product or service must be designed in such a way as to do the job required of it in the best way possible.
2. *Quality of conformance to design*
   This sounds difficult, but in essence all it means is that the system used to produce the product or service must be capable of producing it to the design specifications set out. Or, to put it the other way round, the design of the product must be capable of being produced with the system which is available. If this is not so, then either the design or the system must be changed.

What we are saying is that the producer (in your case the school), must establish a system (curriculum, timetable, organizational structure, culture) which is capable of fulfilling the requirements of the customer, and, better still, 'delight' him.

I can imagine that at this point in the argument you are saying to yourself, 'This is all very well, and may be appropriate to a car manufacturer, a plumber, or even a bank or British Rail, but I do not have a customer, so how can it apply to me as a headteacher, or a classroom teacher? Our view is that it does apply to you. So who is this 'customer' whose every requirement we must satisfy?

THE CUSTOMER CHAIN

Every organization has two kinds of customers: external and internal. It also has suppliers, who provide inputs of materials and services. This is just as true for a school as for a factory, except that in the case of the school, the picture is more complex.

External customers are those outside the organization to whom the product is 'sold'. The transaction is more indirect in the case of a maintained school, because the service is supplied free at the point of use, and the payment is indirect, via taxes and Council Tax or charge.

Who then are the customers of a school?
1. *The pupils*, to whom we supply 'education'.
2. *The parents*, who directly or indirectly pay for their children to be educated.
3. *Institutions of higher education and further education*, for whom the pupil will be an input into their educational process.
4. *Employers*, who need to recruit suitably educated and skilled staff.
5. *The nation*, which requires a better-educated and trained workforce if the economic system is to remain capable of generating better standards of living and quality of life.

Our problem as teachers is that the needs of these different 'customers' may be to a degree incompatible. Later in this chapter we will consider ways in which we might go about finding out exactly what these requirements are. Until we do so we cannot design either our 'product' or 'system' to meet their requirements, and we will be tempted to make the mistake of offering what we think is appropriate, rather than what our customers require.

First we must consider the less commonly recognised phenomenon of the internal customer. Inside any organization are many employees who may seem to be very remote from the external customer, for example, caretakers, secretaries and technicians. They will often see their function as being 'to do a job'. They will rarely want to do anything which is not in their job description and perhaps within parameters set for them by a trade union. Much of their energy may be expended in avoiding going beyond these limits and in defending the boundaries of their department. We will consider this phenomenon in more detail later. The point to be made here is that each of these operatives does have a 'customer' and each of them has a responsibility to meet their customer's requirements. Each of them also has a responsibility, however remote, to the external customer. Any organization also has supplier organizations, from which are obtained inputs of materials, machines and services of all kinds. This is obvious, but what is less obvious is that each of us acts inside our organization as a 'supplier' to the next person in the chain of production. This customer–supplier relationship, both external and internal, is best described in diagrammatic form as in Figure 3.1. Before turning to Figure 3.2 (p.30) in which we have represented in simplified form the customer/supplier chain in the case of a school, you might find it useful to reflect on the chain within your own school. Does it resemble Figure 3.2? You may have produced a list something like this:

Customer/supplier relationships within a school
1. Transfer from primary to secondary school
2. A parents' evening
3. A staff meeting
4. Teacher appraisal
5. Appointment procedures
6. Contracting a supply teacher
7. Preparing the school handbook

How well does your school manage these relationships? Are any attempts being made to measure customer satisfaction in these cases? If not why not? Could such measures be obtained? How might they help to improve our relationships with customers and suppliers? In Figure 3.2 these relationships are represented in a simplified form, but even at that level it must strike you that this is a very complex network of relationships, with lots of potential for disaster if it is not properly managed. It has lots of potential for improvement provided we are prepared to make the effort to seek to establish exactly what each customer requires from his supplier at every point in the chain, both internal and external.

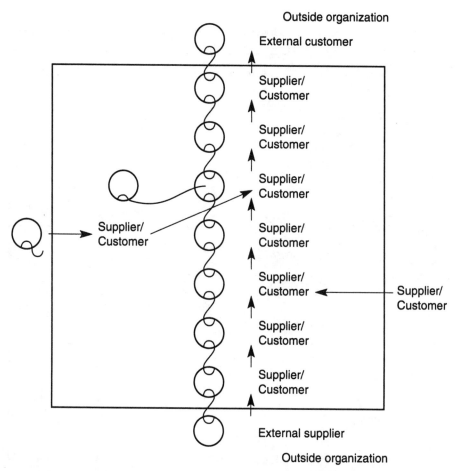

Figure 3.1 *The quality chains.*
Source: Oakland (1989)

HOW DO WE KNOW WHAT OUR CUSTOMERS REQUIRE?

We pointed out earlier in the chapter that it is important to supply our customers with what they require. It is not much use merely knowing who our customers are if we have no idea at all about what they actually do require.

The particular problem of a school is that we have a number of ultimate customers whose requirements may not appear to be compatible. But it is certainly true that we will not fulfil the requirements of any of them, except by accident, unless we take steps to find out what *they* see as their requirements. With this information we may have a chance of reconciling the conflicting requirements of parents, who may want an academic education for their child, with those of the employer, who is looking for skills,

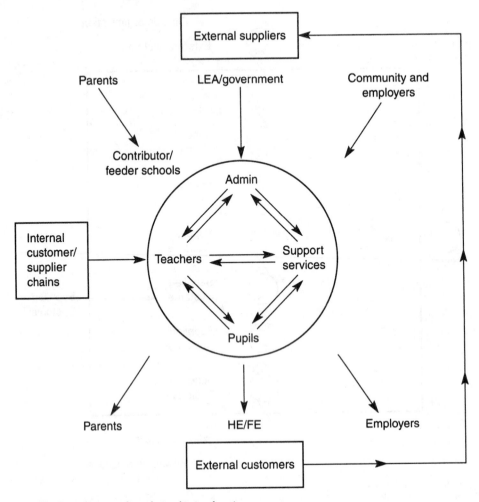

Figure 3.2 *Customer – supplier relationship in education.*

and the pupil himself, who wants something which he sees as relevant to his life now, not in ten years time. If we cannot reconcile these conflicting requirements, then at least we must establish what is desired by the people who choose to send children to us. At least then our chances of survival in a more competitive market-place are improved. The ways in which we might obtain this information are developed in Chapter 4. Meanwhile a brief story may make my point.

A parable

A major local authority with a large immigrant population composed mainly of Asian families has quite a number of inner-city comprehensives, which have had their short-comings publicly exposed by the introduction of league tables. Asian families, especially the poorest ones, are very anxious that their children receive a good academic education. Under the new rules which allow parents to choose schools from anywhere within or even outside the authority, a large subgroup of the immigrant population put their children down to attend much more successful schools on the fringe of the city. The LEA still allocated them to the weak inner-city schools. The parents took legal action, or at least threatened to do so. The LEA offered places in a school 12 miles away. The parents refused to be fobbed off and are still asserting their right to choice. The point of the story is that there has been no suggestion that the wishes of the parents are being seriously heard, or that there is any plan to insist on major improvements in the weaker schools. The 'customers' are not being heard by the 'suppliers', who insist that they know best what is good for the customer. You could not run a fish and chip shop on that basis, could you?

Teachers often recoil at the suggestion that 'marketing' has any part to play in school management. We make no apology for suggesting that it is the starting point of the educational process. Every school has a 'mission', or set of objectives which it pursues. These are often not articulated in print but are taken as read. They may bear no relationship to what the customers would say they wanted if they got a chance to do so. They may not even have been communicated clearly to the employees of the school. Marketing is not about selling the mission like soap. It is about listening to the customer's view of what he wants, and formulating the mission to match the need. The new mission must then be communicated to every member of the organization. We will then be in a better position to identify and reach potential new customers.

Let us take two examples: a neighbourhood school, with a mixed socio-economic catchment area, and a similar school serving the same area. The first school may have as its 'mission' 'the provision of a suitable education for all ability levels, with special emphasis on skills development'. The second school, originally a highly selective grammar school, sets out its mission as being 'to provide a traditional academic education for all who wish to proceed to higher education'. In both cases the function of marketing activity is to establish more exactly what potential 'customers' (parents) require, and what is appropriate for customers (children). In order to get the internal system for the provision of 'education' right, we also need to find out what other external customers require (higher education institutions, further education institutions, employers). The market research techniques needed to acquire this information are set out in more detail in Chapter 4.

This effort to discover the true needs of our external customers is, however, not sufficient. We must also identify chains of internal customer–supplier relationships. If we do not find out in detail who our internal customers and suppliers are, and ensure that these chains are working well, we will be unable to develop our system or process in order to satisfy out external customers. We have set out a plan for conducting an internal quality audit in Chapter 10, and in the training materials in Appendix 1 and 2.

Once we have understood the significance of the customer–supplier chain, it is a small step forward to recognize that the achievement of quality is a never-ending search for CONTINUOUS IMPROVEMENT. We must seek to design and create a SYSTEM or PROCESS through which we can transform inputs into outputs in such a way as totally to satisfy all customer requirements. Better still, we must seek to delight our customers by giving them *more* than they anticipated. This may sound impossible, unless we remember that we are talking about a JOURNEY, not a destination.

Chapter 4

What Does Your Customer Want?

Improve constantly and for ever the system of production and service, to improve quality and productivity.

W.E. Deming

THE NEED FOR A POSITIVE APPROACH TO MARKETING

Marketing is often incorrectly equated to increased and/or intensive promotion and selling, which is why many educationalists disagree with it in principle. There is a lot more to marketing than promotion; indeed, promotion is a relatively small part of any marketing planning process.

Marketing focuses on the needs of the customer, and satisfaction of these needs is achieved by attention to the product/service and the whole cluster of things associated with creating, delivering and finally consuming it. It applies equally to both profit- and non-profit-making organizations.

Identification, anticipation and satisfaction of customer needs and requirements is then the primary focus of any marketing-orientated organization. Satisfaction of these needs and requirements is achieved through the provision of quality. Therefore marketing should be used as an endless cycle of quality monitoring, quality control, quality improvement and the proven display of that quality.

Schools must market themselves for the following reasons:

(a) marketing is the central feature to accountability and responsibility; and

(b) good reputations are hard to achieve and easy to lose, therefore they should be nurtured and protected.

The success of these factors affects the school's ability to attract, retain and adjust the balance of pupils and, of course, pupils generate resources.

Positive marketing will enable a school to determine:

(a) who its customers are;

(b) what their needs/requirements are;

(c) whether the school has the capabilities necessary to meet these requirements and, if not, what must change in order for it to improve its capabilities;

(d) whether requirements are continually met and, if not, what prevents this from happening when the capabilities exist; and

(e) how to monitor changes in the requirements.

DEVELOPING A POSITIVE APPROACH TO MARKETING A SCHOOL

The decision having been made to incorporate marketing into the school development planning process, it is important to get the commitment of all those associated with the school. The establishment of a marketing culture is probably the most difficult part of marketing a school.

Everyone associated with the school will act, to some extent, as an ambassador for the school. Therefore commitment towards a marketing approach must be obtained from all teaching, ancillary and administrative staff, governors, parents, pupils and regular visitors so that there are consistent messages emanating from the school.

It must be accepted that the customer is the most important person in the school. The quality of contact, in person, in writing, or by telephone is the key to a successful relationship.

Factors worthy of consideration include:

(a) the needs and wants of the customer should be provided in a professional way;

(b) customers are not additional to the school, without the customer there is no school; and

(c) whereas the customer is dependent upon the school for the provision of an education, the staff of the school are dependent on the customer for their jobs.

Senior management will have the responsibility for introducing a marketing approach into the school, but it can and should be managed by a marketing team. There will be a need for internal marketing, i.e. to market marketing itself. Marketing should be incorporated into the organization's work and culture.

The whole point is to develop an 'outward' rather than an 'inward' looking school which is responsive to the needs/requirements of its customers, and which takes a positive approach to the constant monitoring of changes in those needs/requirements.

DETERMINATION OF CUSTOMER NEEDS/REQUIREMENTS

The customers of a school will require, among other things, quality in at least some of the following: academic standards; the school climate/culture; pastoral care; extra-curricular activities; adequate preparation for the next stage of life, and so on.

Different groups of customers will have different needs/requirements. Customer groups which have similar characteristics/needs should be grouped together in order to determine their expectations/perceptions in more detail. This process of dividing customers into groups with similar needs/requirements is known as 'market segmentation,' the groups being called 'market segments'. Their is no single way to segment a market. For commercial purposes the major variables used in segmentation are demographic, geographic, psychographic and behavioural.

Once market segments have been identified, the school should choose six, at most, of these segments to target, and develop unique marketing strategies for the individual target segments in order to achieve maximum effectiveness. This process of market segmentation and target marketing is fundamental because it is more productive than treating the whole market in an undifferentiated way.

Market segmentation and target marketing is widely used in both profit- and non-profit-making organizations.

Advantages for schools

(a) It may help a school to identify marketing opportunities. For example, the division of the local community into segments such as businesses and firms would allow schools to focus their attention on developing links of mutual benefit between the schools and the companies involved.

(b) It might place schools in a better position to develop the 'right' service for each target market. For example, the timing of the school day and the provision of schools may be very important for mothers who work part-time.

(c) It might allow the school to adjust its public image in order to reach the target market more effectively. For example, in an area where the majority of parents are middle class, more importance may be placed upon a strictly defined school uniform. Thus instead of scattering its marketing effort, a school could focus it upon those potential customers who have most 'need' for it.

MARKET SEGMENTS APPLICABLE TO A SCHOOL

The following is a list of market segments which may apply to a school. There may be others and, conversely, some of them may not be considered relevant for your school. You should try to make a list of those segments which are relevant for your school.

Internal markets
Pupils
Parents
Staff (teaching and non-teaching)
Governors
Regular visitors

External markets
Prospective pupils
Prospective parents
Prospective staff
FE and HE establishments
Other schools
Commerce and industry
LEA
HMI
National bodies
The local community

The school should decide which of these (or any other) market segments it wishes to target, remembering that it should choose six at most for maximum effectiveness. The decision as to which markets to target will of course depend upon the marketing objectives of the school, which should be clear. For example, if one of the school's marketing objectives is to increase the number of first choice applications it receives by 10 per cent then possible target markets may include: prospective parents and pupils, feeder schools and the local community.

MARKET RESEARCH

Having determined its target markets, further analysis and evaluation of each of these markets should be made. Information regarding the characteristics, needs/requirements and the perceived image of the school by each of the target markets will need to be obtained.

Market research is the systematic collection and analysis of this information. It is a means of quantifying and qualifying the nature of customer needs and wants and of monitoring the school's effectiveness in satisfying those needs and wants.

Market research should be carried out in the following sequence:

(a) identification of information needs;

(b) planning the market research activity;

(c) collection and analysis of the market research information; and

(d) reporting the results of the market research.

METHODS OF CARRYING OUT MARKET RESEARCH

Market research may be carried out because it has not been done before, or it may be carried out in order to update information which has been gathered on some previous occasion. Some information will be readily available internally (for example, records of past examination results, numbers of pupils staying on past the age of 16, rates of absenteeism and staff turnover); it is important not to duplicate efforts. Therefore always check first to determine whether the required information is on record. If the information has not already been collected there are various ways of carrying out market research. Some of the most useful and effective ways for schools are:

(a) Questionnaires
(b) Interviews
(c) SWOT analyses

Questionnaires

Questionnaires are a useful way of collecting information. The most efficient way of getting responses to questionnaires is for someone to ask the questions and to record the responses. At least then you are assured of a particular response rate. Questionnaires may also be given out at, for example, open days and parents' evenings, offering an incentive to those who return their completed questionnaires before leaving. A free raffle for a bottle of whisky, or something along those lines, will usually ensure a high rate of response. Postal questionnaires are worth considering but can be costly. Also, the rate of response is usually only of the order of 20 to 30 per cent.

The design of questionnaires should be such that they can be answered and analysed as simply as possible. Where the answer to a question is one of several given alternatives it enables the respondent to focus upon the way in which the question should be answered and also makes analysis much more straightforward.

The following example shows part of a questionnaire which was designed to determine both those factors which were considered important to parents of existing pupils in School X, and how effective the same parents felt the school was in satisfying those requirements. Some questions which were more specific to the school that conducted this survey have been omitted.

In looking at both importance and effectiveness School X was able to determine which factors were most important to parents and also to determine areas in which parents perceived the school not to be fulfilling their requirements. This type of analysis measures where there is a gap between what is wanted and what is being provided. In this case there proved to be quite a large gap between the importance of pastoral care and the perception of the school's effectiveness in providing what parents felt was an adequate pastoral system. The school then had to decide how to go about improving its pastoral care system and, having done so, communicating this to parents. By using similar questionnaires for potential parents, but omitting the question about its effectiveness, the school was able to decide which factors to stress in any form of promotional material which was seen by both present and potential parents.

SCHOOL X: MARKET RESEARCH QUESTIONNAIRE

The following are a list of attributes which may or may not be important to you when choosing a school for your child. In the column headed 'I' please indicate how important they are to you, and in the column headed 'E' please indicate how effective you feel School X is in fulfilling your expectations. The following scales should be used:

Importance:

1 irrelevant
2 not important
3 important
4 very important
5 crucial

Effectiveness:

1 poor
2 inadequate
3 adequate
4 very good
5 excellent

Example: If you feel that discipline is very important and that School X achieves an adequate level of discipline indicate thus:

	I	E
Discipline	4	3

	I	E
1. Discipline		
2. Academic achievement		
3. Facilities		
4. Extra-curricular activities		
5. Geographical location		
6. Profile of headteacher (low/high)		
7. Prestige/name of school		
8. Specialist staff		
9. Good communications between school and parents		
10. Adequate preparation for next stage of life		
11. Liaison between school and industry and business		

Later questions from the same questionnaire enabled School X to determine which methods of communicating with current and prospective parents would be most effective, what the perceptions of the school prospectus were and how most people found out about the school in the first place:

SCHOOL X: MARKET RESEARCH QUESTIONNAIRE (continued)

20. Have you ever seen any of the School X advertisements attached to the back of this questionnaire?   Yes _____ No _____

21. Where did you see them? _____

22. Which newspapers do you take regularly?

    Daily (local/national) _____

    Sunday   _____

23. How did you find out about School X? (please tick those which apply)

    Newspaper   _____

    Word of mouth _____

    Previous connection with school (please specify) _____

    Radio _____

    'Good schools guide' _____

    Other (please specify) _____

24. Have you seen the School X prospectus? Yes _____ No _____

25. If you have seen the prospectus, please comment on

    a. its presentation _____

    b. Its contents (does it contain in your opinion sufficient appropriate information?) _____

Interviews

Interviews may be used in both formal and informal ways in order to gather information. On a formal level the interviewer may have a set list of questions which he or she wants to ask, which may or may not be shown to the interviewee prior to their meeting. The advantage of the interview over the questionnaire is that it gives the interviewer the opportunity to explore points in more detail. Responses may be noted or taped depending upon which the interviewee finds less distracting. Interviews may also take the form of group discussions.

On a less formal note, information may be obtained from people simply through conversations. These are basically informal interviews, where the persons being questioned may not realize that they are being interviewed. Schools can use this type of information gathering in order to determine what other, competitor schools are doing, either successfully or unsuccessfully. It is no secret, and is accepted, that in the business world people find out what other organizations are doing by visiting them, looking at their products or services and asking members of the public what their opinions of these products or services are (the extreme case of this is industrial espionage). The advantage of the informal over the formal methods of information gathering are that people may be more honest when they do not realize they are being interviewed.

SWOT analysis

Significant use is now being made of SWOT analysis in educational establishments. It focuses on key aspects of an organization and can be applied to the whole school or to sub-groups: for example, individual year groups or particular curriculum areas.

SWOT stands for Strengths, Weaknesses, Opportunities and Threats. Strengths and Weaknesses are internal to the organization and Opportunities and Threats are external factors affecting the organization from the environment within which it functions.

A SWOT analysis is based upon the perceptions of the staff and the customers of an organization. They are asked to list what, in their opinions, are the Strengths, Weaknesses, Opportunities and Threats, and their responses are collated. The four or five factors which are listed most frequently in each category are then addressed. An example of the results which may be obtained for a school is shown in Table 4.1.

Table 4.1 *SWOT analysis*

	School Y	
	Staff perceptions	Customer perceptions
Strengths	Caring, motivated staff Supportive head Smallish class sizes Extra-curricular activities	Good exam results Pleasant atmosphere Smallish class sizes Sports facilities
Weaknesses	Inconsistent discipline procedures State of fabric of building Lack of career development Links with governors	Not strict rules on uniform Making phone contact in morning Pupils not stretched enough Ageing staff
Opportunities	Adult learners Letting of premises New technology Crèche on site	Widen community links Industry links Develop more languages
Threats	Competitor schools Difficulty recruiting certain staff High cost of current staff Lack of vision of senior management	Shortage of specialist staff Effect of national politics Resource shortages

Strengths and weaknesses

Having identified certain strengths and weaknesses, the school must plan to capitalize on its strengths and to overcome, or minimize the effects of, its weaknesses. To capitalize on strengths it will be necessary to: seek ways of communicating them to the internal and external audiences; look for opportunities to apply its successes in other ways; ensure that reinforcement and praise are given; and ensure that such activities continue to receive support. When addressing the need to overcome weaknesses we are looking at quality control. However, it may be that weaknesses were only perceptions of a problem which did not really exist. For example, parents may feel that there is a need for more frequent newsletters from the school when, in fact, it is simply that pupils are not delivering them. In this case the school will have to decide how to ensure that this information actually reaches parents.

Opportunities and threats

Having identified opportunities the school can prioritize. In order to do so the school will have to decide which opportunities will be lost if they are not grasped relatively quickly and which ones it can afford to leave until later.

Potential threats must have action taken against them in order to avoid them. For example, a school which will potentially lose pupils to a neighbouring school because of the provision of better facilities could consider improving its own facilities in order to prevent this from happening. On the other hand, it may stress other advantages which it possesses which the neighbouring school does not have, for example, better qualified and more specialist staff.

In stressing different factors it is actually differentiating itself. This type of marketing can be more effective than trying to compete head on. It is important to match opportunities with the school's strengths. For example, if a school is lacking in financial resources at a particular point in time, it will be unable to exploit any opportunity which could incur high costs.

THE MARKETING PLAN

Having determined the market segments which are going to be addressed, and having analysed the needs and requirements of potential customers, the school management will be in a position to define the 'marketing mix', or 'four Ps'. These concepts were defined in Chapter 3. The marketing mix is simply a method used to formalize a marketing plan, which will be a constantly updated point of reference when strategic management decisions have to be made. For example, the only remaining Latin teacher announces her retirement. Rather than simply replace her permanently, the management team would want to consider whether Latin is to have a place in the curriculum which appears to be required by the 'customers' over the next ten years. If not a tempory replacement might be sought, and consideration given to increasing manpower in a department which clearly figures strongly in customer requirements, perhaps IT.

We have set out below ways in which the marketing mix, i.e. the four Ps of product, price, place and promotion, might be used by schools.

The product

The 'product' (in our case education) provides the means by which organizational objectives are met only if 'customers)' needs are simultaneously met. This point emphasizes the importance for any organization to know its customers, and establish their true needs and requirements. The organizational objectives which are to be met will already be set out in the school's mission statement.

A mission statement for a school

A suitable mission statement might be:

School X strives for academic excellence and personal development in a caring and challenging environment, so that each individual may achieve his or her full potential.

An actual example from Mt Edgcumbe High School, Alaska, may be found in Chapter 2. The specimen example which is given here may be interpreted in more detail as follows.

ACADEMIC EXCELLENCE traditional learning values, and high levels of achievement

CARING ENVIRONMENT encouraging and expecting individuals to strive for improvement and excellence

PERSONAL DEVELOPMENT educating the whole person

EACH INDIVIDUAL members of the school community are treated as important individuals, not items to be processed

ACHIEVE FULL POTENTIAL delivering the most important performance indicator (be it A levels, GCSE or SATS)

We should remember that the mission statement is central to the school's purpose and function as well as being central to the marketing plan.

Using the mission statement

The mission statement should be used in several ways:

- to inform the development of the school's aims
- to establish the products and services needed to achieve the mission
- to act as the touchstone against which the potential of new initiatives may first be checked
- to help focus the marketing process by giving a clear indication of what the school is trying to do
- to enable any 'ambassador' to explain clearly what the school is trying to achieve and to ensure that the various ambassadors put out the same message

Governors, staff, pupils and parents thus get a clear message as to what the school does and what it wants to do in serving customers' needs. The products and services which the school supplies consist not only of the range of subjects which are offered. The National Curriculum after all has reduced to a degree the choice of subjects which can be provided. However, the ways in which these subjects are delivered may be adapted, or varied. Also, the complete range of optional courses provided and the range of extra-curricular activities are an important ingredient. The provision of special features in the environment and facilities of the school (e.g. for disabled children or gifted musicians), and services such as special transport are important.

Price

Price may be an especially important factor to independent schools which charge at the point of use, but it is not irrelevant to state schools. In one important independent day school, a customer survey revealed the important information that in a list of characteristics of the school to be listed in order of importance to the customers, fees came 13th out of 14. This ran entirely counter to the belief held by the governors that the level of fees had to be kept lower than that of competing schools in the area if the school was to survive. In a state school the price is in fact the income per capita which the school derives either from LEA or direct from government. So far as the customer is concerned he is not really conscious that he is paying indirectly for his children's education. He is, however, very much aware of the direct costs of particular schools: travel to and from home, school meals, uniform and games equipment. There are other 'costs' more directly relevant to the educational process, such as larger or smaller classes, more or less experienced staff. The school needs to be sure that its potential customers are prepared to pay these extra 'costs', at the level it sets, or else change them if they are not willing to pay. Again, they must be asked.

Place

Place has two aspects. The location of the school in relation to it target markets geographically must be considered. An unpleasant environment may be improved by screening with trees, for example, and more care of school grounds and gardens. Special buses, or arrangements with British Rail, might widen potential catchment area.

The other aspect of 'place' is those various organizational activities which make the product available to the target market: for example, open days and school visits.

Promotion

It is common for promotion to be mistaken for marketing, ignoring the other elements of the marketing mix. Promotional activities are those which communicate both the mission of the school, and its merits, in a manner designed to both inform potential parents and persuade them that this school is the best for their child. Any promotion must follow from and not precede the attempt to establish customer requirements through a customer survey. Promotion includes the following activities: advertising, publicity, personal 'selling' by school 'ambassadors', provision resulting from dealing with potential customer enquiries and visits, open days, parents' evenings, school publications, such as magazines and newsletters, sporting activities, assistance to community organizations and so on.

Marketing must involve everyone in the organization. At the very least, every employee at all levels, and every pupil, is an 'ambassador' for the school wherever he or she goes. It is important that everyone is working towards the same objectives.

Control and feedback

Constant checks must be made to find out whether objectives in terms of those which are essential to meeting customer requirements are being achieved.

To conclude this chapter, it is worth stressing that effective marketing does *not* mean putting other factors before the welfare of children in our care. In fact, it really means being orientated towards the individual needs of pupils, those needs being defined by the pupils themselves and their parents, as well as our experience as professional educators. In short, it is about delivering *quality* in education.

Chapter 5

Understanding Processes

Some understanding of variation, including appreciation of a stable system, and some understanding of special and common causes of variation, is essential for management of a system, including leadership of people

W.E. Deming

In Chapter 2 we set out to demonstrate that it is possible to transform the process which we call 'education', provided that we are prepared to take the risk of throwing away many of our preconceptions. In Chapter 3 we sought to show how important it is to establish more clearly what is required by our various 'customers', and what might delight them. We demonstrated the importance of listening to what William Scherkenbach has called 'the voice of the customer'.

Now we must seek to understand what he calls 'the voice of the process'. This is much more difficult to grasp since it requires some understanding of simple statistics. It is very important to persevere since if we can grasp this principle in its essence, the argument set out in the rest of the book will become much clearer. The statistical logic which underpins the whole paradigm which we are examining is set out in much more detail in Chapter 8.

In Chapter 1 we stressed the critical importance of an understanding of the principle of variance in any process. To do so we must first be clear what we mean by 'process'. (Note that, like Deming, we have in this book used the words 'process' and 'system' as synonyms.) John Oakland, a leading quality consultant in the UK, tells the story of his meeting with the six operational directors for the six regional divisions of one of the largest companies in the UK. He carefully offered his presentation on the importance of controlling variance in a process if continuous improvement was to be achieved. At the end one of his clients asked him, 'What *is* a process anyway?' The answer to his rather surprising question is that everything we undertake in life involves a process. Getting up, making breakfast and driving to work is a process; planning a journey is a process; organizing a children's treat, planning a series of lectures or lessons, producing bottles of cola are all processes which involve transforming inputs into outputs. This may be illustrated with a simple diagram.

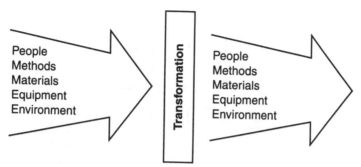

Figure 5.1 *Definition of a process.*
Source: Scherkenbach (1991)

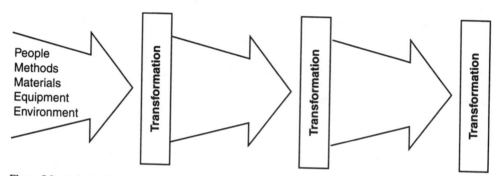

Figure 5.2 *A chain of processes linking supplier to customer, whether within the organization or between the organization and its external customer.*

Processes may be said to be linked in 'chains'. An external supplier is linked through the customer–supplier interfaces within an organization, to an external customer. However, it is more complicated than this, since the 'chain' may perhaps be seen as an independent *network* of processes. This is illustrated in Figures 5.3 and 5.4. Two points emerge, first that the network may well over time have become much more complex than it need be and secondly that some breakdown may occur at any of the connecting points.

We saw in Chapter 3 that a customer survey may reveal considerable differences in the perceptions of what the school is providing, and its value, between the parents questioned (or pupils), and the school. Scherkenbach explains this dissonance as being between the 'voice of the customer' (established by the survey), and the 'voice of the process', as indicated by the way education is delivered, its measured outcomes, and the teachers' own perceptions of delivery and outcome. The recent publication of GCSE result league tables produced some interesting examples of this dissonance. In the case of an inner-city comprehensive school with a very high population of Asian children, the scores measured in terms of the percentage of pupils achieving grades A–C were far below the national average. (This in itself is, of course, not surprising since any measure of this kind will produce 50 per cent above and 50 per cent below average.) The point I am making is that if the parents of those children had been asked on entry what they wanted from the school, they may well have placed first in importance good end-results

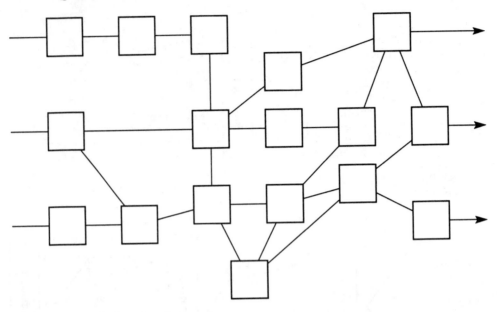

Figure 5.3 *A network of interdependent processes.*
Source: Scherkenbach (1991)

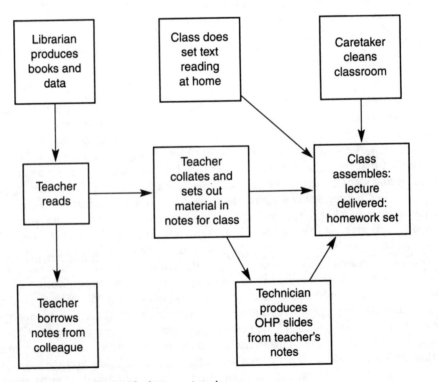

Figure 5.4 *Network of processes involved in preparing a lesson.*

and, possibly, a very disciplined environment. The school saw its task rather differently, and explained away it relative lack of success by reference to the difficulties of teaching children where English is the second language, the poverty of many of the home backgrounds of the pupils, and a lack of resources provided by the local authority. It is doubtful whether this explanation cut much ice with the parents of the unlucky children. In Scherkenbach's terms the two 'voices', of the process and of the customer, are out of line. The task of the leadership of the organization must be to realign them. The voice of the customer may be changed, perhaps by talking to customers, persuading them, etc. But for the most part it must be heard and accepted, and recognized as not necessarily being predictable. Matching the two voices therefore rests heavily on being able to understand what the voice of the process is telling you.

Naïve management thinks that if People did as they were told (Methods), used their expensive Equipment, making the most of the Materials (carefully selected by management), in the recently developed cooperative Environment, then all the 'product' would be of exactly the same standard. All our pupils would get A grades. In reality we know that this is not how processes work. If we teach the same course, from the same notes to sets of pupils of matched ability, using the same visual aids, year after year, we will despite our best efforts achieve a spread of results. Some will be above average, some below. This is in the nature of mathematical measurement. Or so it seems. It is too easy for this phenomenon to become an iron law which causes us to condemn as failures a proportion of our students. What we should be doing is recognizing that in any process variation will occur. What we need to do is develop techniques for efficiently managing this variation around whatever specification is set, and for using the data generated to discover ways of improving the capability of the process, continuously, setting as our (unattainable) goal zero defects. The mission which we have set ourselves as a company or a school will indicate the target in terms of the reduction of variance.

Before we can use the concept of variance as a means to develop a programme of continuous improvement of 'product' and 'process', we must have a much clearer understanding of the idea introduced earlier in the book of SPECIAL (assignable) causes of variance, and COMMON (non-assignable) causes. This idea is at the heart of Deming's work, and indeed of all development of the Quality paradigm. The statistical mechanics of this concept are developed for those with a mathematical turn of mind in Chapter 8, and used to illustrate ways in which the paradigm might be applied to classroom management in Chapter 9. What we want to do here is help you to understand the concept by undertaking some little experiments which Deming has developed over many years to graphically make his point in his famous seminars.

The old method of maintaining Quality in manufacturing environments was by 'inspecting quality in' at the end of the line. In other words, any product which was below specification was either scrapped or sent back for rework. If it just made the specification but might fail when the customer used it, it would be passed fit, and the consequences seen as the customer's problem. Is this not what happens to our students? We push them through a teacher-led course, cram them for an exam, constantly inspecting quality in on the way by telling them that their work is sub-standard and must be reworked. After the final exam, external examiners mark their papers, and, whatever the raw marks may be, an 'appropriate' percentage is passed, and the remainder failed, i.e. scrapped. Near misses may be encouraged to return and repeat the course (rework). In both cases it is assumed that nothing can be done to prevent things being like this.

Take the case of the comprehensive school discussed above. The outcry provoked by the advent of league tables of school results is in a sense the 'voice of the customer'. The school may be jolted into recognizing that something must be done. The question is, what? Suppose the headteacher decides that the problem is the second language. He may decide that the answer is bilingual teaching, i.e introduce teachers who are capable of delivering basic key material in the pupils' first language. Even supposing that there is only one ethnic minority language, this will not necessarily work. The side effects may in fact make things worse. This would be what Deming refers to as 'tampering', which is always likely to make things worse because a 'special' cause of variance has been treated as a 'common' cause.

What we must do now is to understand exactly what the difference is between the two. To do so we must understand how processes work. Actually, ineffective management of processes stems more from 'knowledge' than ignorance. We think we know exactly how children's learning develops, and what we may expect of any teaching system. We expect a level of performance, and a range of outcomes, which reflects our misunderstanding of the nature of the normal curve of distribution that has conditioned our perception of learning for fifty years. This 'knowledge' is very dangerous since it prevents us from seeing the road to continuous improvement, and so better outcomes for our students. We are rather like the little girl described by Deming. She explained her recipe for making toast, which she had learned by watching her mother: 'First you put the slice of bread in the toaster, then turn it on, when it is burnt you take it out and scrape it.' This is why we must start afresh if we want to understand better the processes which we manage in a school. To do so we would like you to attempt this simple experiment which Deming has used over and over again in his seminars.

EXPERIMENT 1: THE RED BEADS

The resources required are as follows:

People	Foreman
	6 willing workers
	Recorder
	Chief Inspector
	2 Inspectors
	Audience
Materials	Beads
	White (80 per cent total) Red (20 per cent total)
Equipment	Whiteboard
	Marker pen
	Paddle (wood or plastic) with 50 holes cut or bevelled
	1 plastic ice-cream box
	1 A4-sized plastic tray
	3 clipboards with paper
	3 pens
Environment	Indoors
	Dominant 'traditional' foreman
Method	Set out in the flow diagram as shown in Figure 5.5.

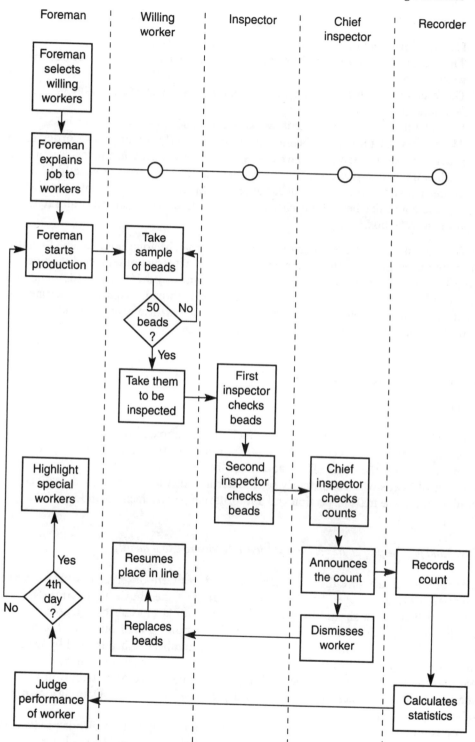

Figure 5.5 *Flow diagram of the red bead experiment.*
Source: Scherkenbach (1991)

In conducting the experiment the following points should be remembered.

1. The experiment involves four days' work for the six workers.
2. The recorder should record the statistics on a matrix previously set out on the whiteboard.
3. The foreman should be as angry and dominating as possible to drive the workers by fear of failure.
4. He is free to dismiss 'incompetent' workers at the end of each day if he wishes.
5. The process of taking the beads should be carefully monitored in order to be exactly the same each time. The beads are initially placed in the ice-cream box. Each worker then pours the beads into the tray, holding the box exactly 50 centimetres above the tray. After each worker has taken his 50 beads with the paddle, and the count has been done, checked and recorded, he should pour all the beads back into the box.

The exact manner of conducting this experiment may be adjusted of course to match the resources available to the experimenter. The above instructions are slightly different from Deming's own version (Deming uses 3,000 white and 750 red beads), and was developed for our own use in a school environment. Provided that the experiment is replicated each time exactly, the outcome in terms of statistical results should make the same points that emerge each time in Deming's seminars.

Lessons of the red bead experiment

Quality is made at the top

The leaders of an organization have a much greater impact on the outcomes from a process, and thus the success of an organization, than the efforts of willing workers trying hard to do their best. The leaders, not the workers, made the decisions to use a supplier of beads who consistently sent material that was 20 per cent defective (red beads), and to use mass inspection and authoritarian management methods.

Rigid and precise procedures are not sufficient to ensure exact quality

The foreman made sure that the precise procedures were observed – you can make them as precise and specific as you like, adding to the above instructions others such as which hand should be used, tilting the paddle a prescribed degree, and so on. However precise the foreman may be, the samples pulled out with the paddle will contain varying numbers of red beads. If the numbers of beads used by Deming are observed, you will find that the range of counts of red beads will be from 2 to 18, and the mean about 10. They will form a normal curve of distribution around the mean. This has been consistent over a period of 35 years of Deming's own use of the experiment.

We can therefore say that the number of red beads likely to be drawn is predictable within a range of values, but that the precise number drawn will not be predictable.

People are not always the dominant source of variability in a process

Variability will occur in all processes, and it may be caused by any combination of Equipment, Material, Methods, Environment or People. In this experiment the effects of the latter on variability have been deliberately eliminated. It is therefore not possible to say (as your foreman probably did) that the variability was caused by people making mistakes, not listening to instructions and so on. Yet there are still too many red beads (defective product) being produced. The major contributors to variance are the beads (red beads in incoming supplies), the paddle, and the failure to allow the workers to make any attempt to improve the process themselves on their own initiative.

Data that are rank ordered may be misleading

Whilst the customer is within his rights to say that one number is better than others, i.e that zero red beads only is acceptable, the process is telling us that there is no difference between 3 red beads and 18 red beads. All are equally likely to happen. Thus to rank order workers as 'good', 'average' or 'bad' is meaningless, since any worker is just as likely to produce 10 red beads one day, 18 the next and 2 the next. Any rank order of workers on which rewards are judged, or dismissal decided, is meaningless.

Sacking the 'bad' workers and keeping only the 'best' does no good

This statement follows logically from the previous point. All that you may predict about the future performance of a particular worker is that he is likely to produce defective products somewhere in the range of between 2 and 18 red beads. This is because the process is stable. It is in statistical control.

Numerical goals are often meaningless

Willing workers cannot influence the number of red beads produced, nor may they influence the process itself. Thus if the foreman translates the voice of the customer into a specification of say 3 red beads only in each 50, this set target will have no effect on the number of red beads produced, no matter how the foreman seeks to motivate the workers to reach the target. It was the leaders of the organization who set up the process.

Mechanical and random sampling will give different results

If each 50 beads were chosen from 3,000 white and 750 red beads, each of which was numbered by choosing a random selection of numbers, then the average number of red beads selected would be 10 . However, we are using a paddle. If several different paddles were used, each only slightly different from the others, we would derive an average number of red beads which would not necessarily be 10. Deming has used four different paddles, each of which produced a different average.

This being so, it is possible that wrong deductions might be made. If you set a break-even point for the process of 10 red beads, and then produced an average of 9.3 say, would you be making a profit? Not necessarily. The paddle is telling you that things are better than they really are. By changing the process you might do better. It is no longer good enough to say 'we are close to the target or break-even result, so why worry?' It is possible to improve the outcome, if the process is improved. People are only one part of the process.

Elimination of red beads by inspection and prior removal is an expensive way to improve

You are probably thinking to yourself that the obvious answer to the red bead problem is for the workers to be asked to inspect incoming material, and remove red beads before the process begins, or better still require the supplier to do so before delivery. This is just an expensive way of scraping the burnt toast. There is a better way.

The prevention of defects

It is far better to prevent defects by seeking a different way to manage the process, seeking constantly to improve its efficiency. This critical message is examined in more detail in Chapter 8. The use of statistical methods is the key to the prevention of defects. We need to satisfy customer requirements always, constantly, and the customer has the right to demand zero defects. It is up to management to seek means by which we may journey towards that destination. This experiment is developed further in Appendix 1.

If the world were deterministic rather than variable, it might make sense to 'tamper' with processes, by varying the combination of inputs when things go wrong. Since the world is variable, tampering may well make things worse. If variance is understood, it is possible to change the process in order to reduce and eliminate defects by prevention rather than inspection. It is a much cheaper approach – as we will show in Chapter 8. A worked example of a modified version of the red bead experiment is shown in Appendix 1. However, you may prefer to conduct your own version on a Training Day. If so you should use the calculation methods shown in Chapter 8. Doubtless your Head of Maths will enjoy the challenge of organizing the experiment.

EXPERIMENT 2: THE FUNNEL

In the red bead experiment Deming deliberately eliminated ways in which the 'willing workers' might influence the process. In the funnel experiment Deming seeks to make two very important points:

- In many processes the workers may and do affect outcomes by altering the procedures.
- If they use inappropriate methods to affect outcomes (tampering), chaos may occur.

This situation is particularly true of the process of teaching. As you read this section you will almost certainly recall examples. It may well be that you will see the point of this experiment simply by reading the account, but nevertheless it might be fun to try it on a Training Day.

The resources required are as follows:

People	Any willing volunteer
Material	A marble
	Tablecloth
Equipment	Funnel
	Table
	Water soluble pen
Environment	Indoors
Method	See Figure 5.6 (process flow diagram). You will note the influence of scientific method here. For our purposes it may prove to be a flawed paradigm.

Rule 1 The funnel should be held in a fixed position over the cloth by using a clamp, at say one foot above it. A target point is marked on the cloth. The volunteer drops the marble through the funnel and the pen is used to mark the point where it lands. A series of drops will produce a cluster of points around the target.

The volunteer should be invited to undertake a fresh sequence of drops following the rules below, which are intended to improve the result by adopting an approach based on the scientific method.

Rule 2 After each drop, move the funnel from its previous position to a point equal in distance but opposite in direction from the last error (i.e. point hit other than the target). The point is to move the funnel to compensate for previous error, and hit the target. Although this sounds a logical way to seek improved results, it will, according to Deming's results, produce a stable distribution of points with a spread which is 41 per cent *greater* than that obtained under Rule 1. Thus the process is now more unpredictable than it was before.

Rule 3 After each drop, move the funnel to a point equal in distance but opposite in direction from the previous error,

The aim is again to compensate in order to hit the target. In this case, however, the result is an unstable process, which will explode into infinity in two directions.

Rule 4 After each drop, move the funnel to a point over the last drop. In this case you have abandoned the target and are settling for getting the same result each time. Unfortunately, all you will get is another unstable system, which will get progressively worse.

If you use this experiment on a Training Day, why not ask your people to think of examples of each rule in operation in their daily working lives?

Let us at this point summarize the lessons which we should derive from these experiments:

- Quality is the responsibility of top management.
- Rigid and precise procedures will not ensure quality outcomes.
- Failure by people is not always the main source of variability in a process.
- Rank-ordered data are misleading.
- Getting rid of 'weak links' from the workforce will not work.

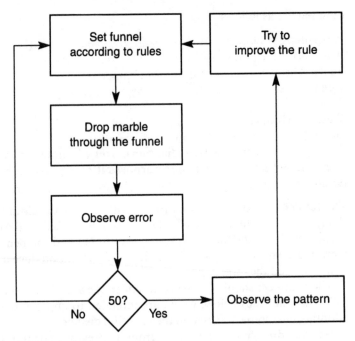

Figure 5.6 *Process flow diagram for the funnel experiment.*
Source: Scherkenbach (1991)

- Numerical targets are meaningless.
- Random and mechanical sampling procedures will give different results.
- Inspection of quality into the product is an expensive, wasteful and ineffective method of ensuring quality outcomes.

If you can see why this is so by attempting one or both of these experiments, you will find the rest of the argument which we set out in this book much easier to understand. To do so, however, you may well have to abandon perspectives which you have taken for granted for a lifetime. On the other hand, you may feel that all we are doing is putting a formal structure on to what you have instinctively felt and practised during your career.

The question then becomes, what should we do? Everything we do is a 'process', and any process you think about is likely to be relatively inefficiently carried out. What we need is a method by which the process might be improved, not just as a one off, but continuously for ever. This book sets out to make you think afresh about how you might improve the processes in that organization which we call a school, and how we might communicate this vital perspective to the next generation by involving them in the continuous improvement programme. At this point let us go back to Deming. He suggests that we should at all times adopt a 'cycle of activities'. These are a series of eight action steps.

PLAN – DO – STUDY – ACT

These four activities contain the following eight steps:

Develop a plan for improvement.

1. PLAN   Step 1. Identify the opportunity for improvement
            Step 2. Document the present process (by flow chart)
            Step 3. Create a vision of the improved process
            Step 4. Define the scope of the improvement effort

2. DO   Carry out the plan
            Step 5. Pilot the proposed changes on a small scale

3. STUDY   Study the results of the pilot
            Step 6. Observe what you have learned about the improvement of the
                    process

4. ACT   Adjust the process on the basis of your new knowledge
            Step 7. Operationalize the new mix of resources
            Step 8. Repeat the cycle on another improvement opportunity

All that follows is designed to help you to undertake this process with confidence.

Chapter 6

Changing the Culture

Institute leadership. The aim of supervision should be to help people to do a better job.

W.E. Deming

All organizations have a 'corporate culture' – the way we do things around here. This is determined by external constraints, and the management style of the leader. It is transmitted through the organization by a process which is best described in diagrammatic form (Figure 6.1).

This corporate culture will become solidly entrenched, and over time will influence other key characteristics of the organization. These will include the following:

- What the perceived 'mission' of the organization is to be.
- What its quality standards are to be.
- The type of customers it will attract.
- Its relationship with competing organizations.
- The expectations which society at large will have of the organization.

All this is as true of a school as of any other business.

At this point it would be helpful for the reader to attempt to analyse his own school under the above five points.

In fact, it is not only true of a school, but is even more important than in a business. This is because the 'product' of a school is a living human being, who has acquired as part of his permanent mental equipment some or all the key elements of the culture of the school. The set of values which he has acquired during his school life he will transmit to his own children, and also to anyone else with whom he has close contacts in social or working relationships.

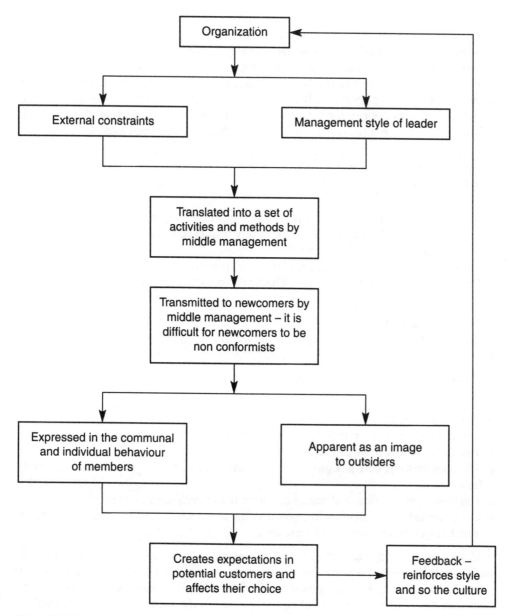

Figure 6.1 *The process by which corporate culture is determined and maintained.*

At this point the reader should think about his own school days, and list the key values which were evident in those days at his school. He might then consider (on a scale of 1–5 low to high) how important they still are in his life.

These values, be they political, moral, or intellectual, will be reflected in adult life in response to day-to-day events, and even more so in highly stressful or stimulating circumstances. Thus a school may develop a value set which tends to lead to many of its former pupils making careers in particular areas, be it as lawyers, judges, MPs, sportsmen, army officers, clergy or maybe even criminals. This is turn creates expectations in society, parents, and pupils, that it will continue to do so. And so it will. This can be seen nationally in the products of major public schools, for example, Eton (MPs), Winchester (radical politicians) and so on. But it can also be seen at local level.

> Now consider your present school. What are its key values? How are they reflected in predominant expectations?

This organizational culture may be strongly positive, or it may be negative, in terms of its value system. Either way it will strongly influence the outcome of the school's efforts on behalf of its pupils and staff.

These sets of values which comprise the culture of the school will relate to key aspects of the activities and objectives which are present in some form in all schools:

- The purpose of education.
- The nature of education.
- The type of education seen as appropriate for the pupils in this particular school.
- The methodology of the delivery of education to pupils in this school.

They will also influence the mechanics of the operation of the organization from day to day:

- The nature, shape and functions of the control hierarchy.
- The communications systems down, up and across the organization.
- The delegation of tasks and responsibility.
- The relationships between members of teaching staff, and between them and ancillary staff.
- The level of motivation and degree of commitment evidenced by the staff.
- Communications systems with parents, 'the customers', and the outside working world, which is the other set of 'customers'.

Who then sets this agenda of values? In most schools in the maintained sector the agenda will be determined by the LEA acting through its network of advisers and inspectors. They often hold the power to offer both INSET training, and of preferment. Thus they can inform the culture of all schools within the authority, limiting the ability of the individual Head to create his own agenda.

The education 'industry' was therefore producer led, in the sense that 'experts' had the power to define education, and to impose it on the customers, whatever they might think about it. The agenda set varied considerably from authority to authority, but was heavily influenced by the work of 'educationalists' in the universities and teacher training colleges. The value system created in this way was all-pervasive, and ran counter to the values which government in recent years would have liked to impose. The effect, and perhaps purpose, of recent educational reforms has been to break the agenda, and to impose a new and nationally defined set of values in the form of a National

Curriculum. Local management of schools was not intended simply to transfer responsibility for financial control to schools, but to break the power of the local authority to impose the agenda.

The new state-imposed agenda is itself derived from a number of values held by people of a right-of-centre political persuasion. These are centred around a belief in the efficacy of capitalism as a means of creating and distributing wealth, and in self-help on the part of the individual. It is believed that the state should retreat from an interventionist stance, on the grounds that the evidence here, and more so in Eastern Europe, is that interventionism and the corporate state do not work. The search for equity and equality in a classless society was abandoned in favour of a more individualist view. The contrasts may be traced back to the competing perspectives and values of nineteenth-century liberalism (stemming from J.S. Mill) and Fabian or more extreme versions of socialism (stemming from the work of Engels and Marx, Webb and Keynes). The educational value system which was prevalent in the 1960s and 1970s was attributable to the latter ideologies, or chains of ideas linking us with earlier generations. This is the value system which is second nature to many mature members of the teaching profession trained in that period, or indeed through to very recent years. There is therefore a major culture clash between the profession and its customers. This makes the creation of a new culture for schools, based on the best aspects of modern management, and the value system which stresses excellence in an individual and collective sense, very difficult. This book is intended to show that the best of *both* cultures can work in a school.

At a deeper level there exists in every school culture a hidden agenda, which stems from the work of certain psychologists. This determines the immediate expectations as to what pupils can do. These in our view are:

- The concept of measurable general intelligence. (Largely rejected in principle, but influential in practice – some pupils are always assumed to be more 'able', or 'intelligent', than others.)
- Behaviour modification, via stimulus/response, as developed by Skinner.
- Developmental stages, as set out by Piaget.
- The statistical concept of 'normal distribution'.

> This is not the place to develop this train of thought, but the reader might like to consider ways in which the organization and functioning of his school has been and is influenced by these concepts.

To these influences might be added some accretions of English social history:

- The class system.
- The belief in inevitable social progress, aided by the intervention of the state in society and its institutions.
- The Romantic literary heritage – the 'innocence of the child'.

These various cultural influences have combined in the collective consciousness of teachers into a set of propositions about how education ought to be conducted, and for what purpose. Thus Worth's 'labelling effect' comes into play to ensure that children are placed in groups, and treated in ways which are perceived to be 'suitable' for their particular needs. (The children and even their parents are rarely consulted as to the suitability of this course of action.) This labelling process inevitably reflects the class influences, aspirations and expectations of the teachers themselves.

All this suggests to me that it is possible to identify a number of propositions (values) which would be acceptable to the majority of teachers in almost any kind of school, and which would 'fit' within the official and hidden agenda of any school.

Current educational value system

- All children want to learn, and should be enabled to do so.
- If particular children object to being educated, or fail, then it is somebody's fault, either parent, society, or government. (Ironically, the parent will usually believe that it is the teachers' fault.)
- Children differ in their ability to learn – 50 per cent are 'average', 25 per cent above, and 25 per cent below 'average'. This is seen as an iron law.
- They must therefore work at their own pace, which they effectively decide, since they cannot be made to work.
- Sanctions on poor performers are unacceptable, since it is not the child's fault.
- Competition of any kind is damaging to the spirit.
- Since children work at different speeds, it is unacceptable for them to be taught didactically in large groups.
- Therefore all the paraphernalia of the formal classroom are forbidden.
- Classrooms cannot therefore be quiet places, and children must be allowed to move about, whenever they wish, and should switch from one of a 'circus' of activities to another as they wish.

This model of educational activity has been unquestioned for many years, and is the only route to promotion to posts of influence, where it can be propagated further. Most front-line classroom practitioners would privately express a weary cynicism at many of these propositions, especially the last three. They would, however, I suspect concur with the rest in principle at least. Since their experience runs counter to the practical implications of these idealistic principles, an alternative model can be constructed, from the point of view of the practising teacher.

An alternative value system

- Children are natural anarchists, who will avoid concentrated work wherever possible.
- This not the teacher's fault, but that of society, authority or government, parents, etc.
- Children do fall into average, above and below average according to the principles of the normal curve, but where 'average' falls is wherever they deem appropriate for their pupils. It follows that there is nothing they can do to change things.
- The children must work at their own pace, because it will make no difference to the outcome if they are pushed harder, except that the teacher will be more exhausted.
- Since neither sanctions nor praise are officially approved, nothing can be done about poor work or behaviour, except to pretend that it is not happening, or only to be expected.
- Teachers know that it is sensible and economical to explain new material to a larger group first, and to explain it in detail through smaller group activities.

This is not allowed, and so much time is wasted giving the same explanation several times with small groups.

- Classrooms are bound to be noisy, anarchistic places, in which the bully and attention seeker thrives, and the quiet, shy child disappears.
- Children will labelled successes or, more likely, failures by the system, whatever the teacher does. There is nothing to be done to change things.

I hope that these two stereotypical models will illustrate my point: that a value system has been put in place which inhibits good teaching and learning and guarantees failure. Is this really the best we can do? Is it not possible to change things for the better?

Robert Tressell put it far better than I can in his influential novel *The Ragged Trousered Philanthropists*, way back in 1905.

From their infancy they (the working men) had been trained to distrust their own intelligence, and to leave the management of the affairs of the world – and for that matter the next world too – to their betters, and now most of them were absolutely incapable of thinking of any abstract subject whatever. Nearly all of their betters were unanimous in agreeing that the present system was a very good one and that it is impossible to alter or improve it.

Have we moved on very far in all these years, and if not, what can we do about it?

Two biographies

Jenny X

Jenny was at a comprehensive school, and her O level preparation was ruined by the breakdown of her parents' marriage. She left school with no exam passes, and worked as a book-keeper for many years. She married, unhappily, and when her marriage broke down, she decided to make a fresh start at the age of 30. She became an Open University student, and despite her total lack of self-confidence, the high expectations which the OU has of students gradually overcame this trepidation, and her academic work blossomed. She gained Distinctions in both the foundation course and a second-level course in Economics. A supportive tutor suggested that she ought to become a full-time student, and that she was able enough to apply to Oxford. This she did and was accepted to read PPE, in which she has graduated. She plans to become a teacher.

Graham Y

Graham was a pupil at a famous boys' independent grammar school from the age of ten. He did well throughout his school career, and eventually won a place at Merton College, Oxford to read PPE. He was also a fine rugby player who narrowly missed a Blue as well as taking a good degree. It was only at the very end of his school career that his sixth-form master happened to look at his file. There he discovered his record card from his primary school, on which it was claimed that his IQ at that time had been measured as 92. Had he been in a comprehensive, he would have been placed in a class on that basis, and would probably have ended up taking a bunch of mediocre GCSE passes. His grammar school automatically had higher expectations of him.

These examples simply illustrate the enormous power which the expectations of a school or university can have on a student's self esteem, and subsequent academic performance. The aspirations and expectations of children are set by society, and school, where they are strongly reinforced. Education can enslave rather than liberate children. But it can do the opposite. Most children are denied access to 'abstract' knowledge which might teach them to think, and to control their own lives, because it is seen as unsuitable for them. In the past, thinking workers and citizens have been seen as a threat to capitalism and the established order of society. Capitalism in its old form required unthinking 'hands' such as Tressell's 'ragged trousered philanthropists'.

This view is no longer acceptable. Capitalism has proved to be less bad than the alternative, and has changed in fundamental respects. Advanced Western economies in future will require all workers to be 'brain' workers. A new business culture was born out of Japan, by the USA. World-class organizations of all kinds, airlines, car manufacturers, government departments, railways, etc, have all recognized that the customer is 'God', and that only a Total Quality approach to Management will do. In this scenario organizations have had to recognize that their most important resource, and investment is their people. Schools must not be afraid of this culture change. It is completely compatible with the good teachers' view of her professional relationship with the child.

How then would a commitment to TQM require a change in the culture of the school? The answer is that it would, but not in the direction which teachers commonly assume a 'management-led approach' would require. Our original 'agenda' would now look something like this.

A new set of values

- All children want to learn, and must be encouraged to do so.
- If some refuse to do so, or find the process difficult, they must be helped to overcome the problem, not be labelled as 'stupid' or 'difficult'.
- All children have the capacity to learn. The aim must be continuously to improve their performance and self-esteem, not measure their failure in order to place them on a normal curve.
- Positive achievements must be recognized and celebrated.
- Competition is natural, but cooperation is more effective in achieving goals. The two are not irreconcilable.
- Teaching methods are not sacrosanct. There is a place for all methods.
- Teachers in the classroom are facilitators and coaches, not merely managers, supervisors or instructors.

Our aim must be to create an atmosphere in which the precepts below are followed.

- Children are respected, and heard, as being one of our 'customer' groups.
- Where children, and the aspirations of children, should be unlimited.
- Where the search for the improvement of understanding, knowledge and skill is endless, and fostered by the teacher.
- Where children are encouraged to believe that they can and should get work 'right first time'.
- Where fear has no place.
- Where the parent is encouraged to play an active role in the process.
- Where the school creates strong bonds with its surrounding community, which contains the ultimate 'customer', the employer.

Most teachers would probably claim that this is exactly how they proceed. But on reflection we would all recognize that we have indulged in labelling and stereotyping and all that flows from this. We have all at times felt that our best efforts have been undermined and undervalued by the headteacher, a difficult child, a parent, or the media. All of us have expected too little from young people.

The young are not innocent: they are anarchistic, they are difficult to manage. But they have enormous reserves of energy and talent if we do not stifle them. We must develop a 'corporate culture' in which they feel valued and heard. This is the secret discovered by companies which have had the courage to adopt a TQM philosophy.

Listen to the people

Toyota manufactures cars worldwide, in many different cultural and social settings. It encourages all workers, at every level, to take part in Quality Circles on a voluntary basis. These self-run, voluntary groups of workers meet once a week in company time to discuss ways of improving the performance of their department or workstation. Their suggestions are passed to management, which considers them for implementation. In a recent year they had a total of 5,000 suggestions, no less than 98 per cent of which were implemented by the management.

When did anybody last ask you to offer ways in which the school might be improved, and then implement your suggestions?

The application of TQM principles to a school will make it more effective, serve its external customers better, use its resources more efficiently. But first the culture described here must be put in place. In essence the teachers and other staff are no different from the children. They have enormous reserves of talent and energy, and will use them if they feel valued.

The culture of a school is set within an organizational structure, through which it is transmitted and made operational. In extreme cases where the school has lost sight of (or never thought through) its 'mission', the organizational structure may in a sense become the culture. In this case the structure becomes the greatest impediment to change. The structure must therefore be reconstructed. This is a painful process which threatens long-established fiefdoms. It must be done however, and in Appendices 1 and 2 the training programme sets out ways in which it might be done.

By now I hope that the reader is convinced of the importance of switching to TQM culture. It cannot be stressed too often that commitment from the top is the essential ingredient. It does not matter what brought about the recognition of the need for change, whether success or failure, provided the the commitment is total, and the Head is prepared to lead by example. Whatever the mission which you have set out for your school, I hope that you will now recognize that what follows is the route by which the mission should be pursued.

The continuous improvement journey

- Seek continuous improvement in all activities.
- Focus intently on 'customer' requirements, both internal and external.
- Create a system through which to measure and eliminate 'waste' in all areas of school activity.

- Insist on the importance of team-work.
- Insist on open communication systems, top down, bottom up and laterally.
- Empower all colleagues, academic and ancillary, by constant training.
- Recognize and celebrate achievement, and avoid blame and scapegoating.

At this point it is important to consider in what ways the organizational structure of a school might need to be changed before it is possible to create a TQM culture and system. Is it possible to identify some common characteristics of most kinds of organizational structure used in schools? Do any or most of the following appear familiar to you?

Organizational failure

- Departmental imperialism in pursuit of resources and promotion.
- Lack of cooperation across departmental boundaries, and between academic and ancillary staff.
- Secrecy in decision making and lack of communication.
- Isolationism and fear of cooperation amongst classroom teachers.
- Excessive and proliferating bureaucracy.
- Absence of coherent training and staff development programmes.
- Appraisal systems designed to manage by fear, rather than increase self-esteem and skill.

If you recognize all or most of these characteristics as being present in your school, then you can be sure that, from a TQM perspective, it is not an efficiently functioning organization. You can also be sure that the morale and motivation of your staff will be at an unnecessarily low ebb. If these features are present, and your management style is excessively authoritarian, or *laissez-faire* (see Table 6.1) then you have got serious problems, of which you have been unaware until now.

Table 6.1 *Four management systems*
Source: R. Likert, Human Organization, *McGraw-Hill, New York, (1967).*

System 1	System 2	System 3	System 4
Exploitive/ Authoritative	Benevolent/ Authoritative	Participative	Democratic
Manager has no confidence and trust in his subordinates.	Manager has condescending confidence and trust, as a master might have of a servant.	Manager has substantial but not complete trust and confidence. Still wishes to keep control of decisions.	Manager has complete confidence and trust in all matters.
He seldom gets ideas and opinions of subordinates in solving job problems.	He sometimes gets ideas and opinions of subordinates in solving job problem	He usually gets ideas and opinions of subordinates and tries to make constructive use of them.	He always asks subordinates for ideas and opinions and always tries to make constructive use of them.
Subordinates do not feel at all free to discuss things about the job with their boss.	Subordinates do not feel very free to discuss things about the job with their boss.	Subordinates feel reasonably free to discuss things about the job with their boss.	Subordinates feel completely free to discuss things about the job with their boss.

Two true stories

Thirty years ago a famous independent school was run by a Head, supported by a Second Master who undertook all day-to-day administration and discipline, as well as teaching half a timetable. Ten heads of departments, chaired by the Head, constituted an academic board, which was responsible for all planning recommendations. This group operated as a team, and was proud of its important role in decision making. There were only two secretaries, and the bursar did the accounts with a fountain pen in a large ledger. The school ran like clockwork.

Eventually a new Head decided to add an extra layer to the hierarchy by appointing a Director of Studies, amongst whose responsibilities was chairing a now less frequent heads of department meeting, whose recommendations were filtered before reaching the Head, and were largely ignored. This simple change to the structure of the organization had dramatic effects on the status and self-esteem of heads of department, on the way decisions were made, and on the communication system. The bureaucracy in the administrative side of the school then grew exponentially. Teamwork and cooperation went in to decline, and the school as a community was diminished by the loss of a collegiate approach to decision making and management.

The exigencies of LMS recently caused the Head of a large London comprehensive to look very carefully at his organizational structure in the light of the need to reduce expenditure on salaries without weakening the teaching function. He did not adopt the standard response of inviting everyone over fifty to take early retirement, cut out part-time posts, cut supply cover, cut training, etc. Instead he looked afresh at the school and concluded that the least useful people in the organization were his two deputy heads and another senior manager. They were invited to leave. The administrative functions undertaken by them were handed to a collegiate team of heads of department, and shared out. All were paid a little more, and the overall financial saving allowed the employment of an extra 1.4 teachers, rather than a reduction in the number of teachers. Naturally there are cries of 'unfair, go to the industrial tribunal'. One has to admire the courage and determination of the Head to put education before administration.

You must find a way to do the following:

Organization for success

- *Flatten the hierarchy*.
- Create *teams*, permanent and temporary, across departmental and functional boundaries to solve specific problems.
- Turn middle managers into coaches rather than organizers, directors, controllers and supervisors.
- Empower everyone to make decisions – delegate.

The spurious 'management' posts – head of year, coordinator of this that and the other – must go; so must senior management jobs which have no discernible educational function. The old collegiate model which existed in the old-time grammar school was

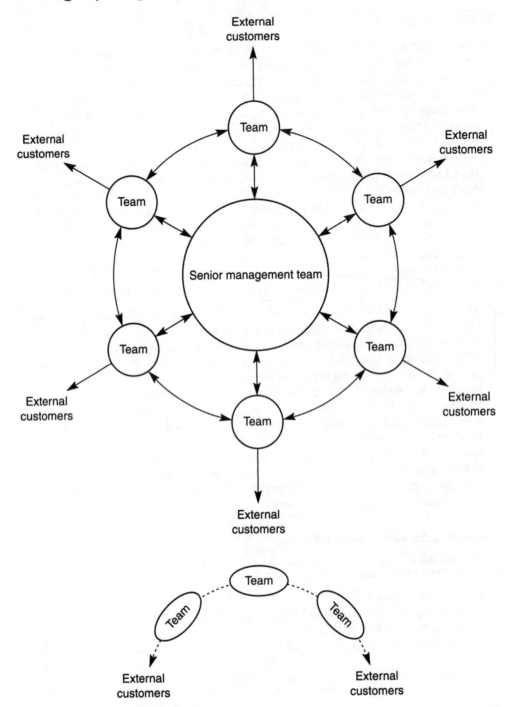

Figure 6.2 *A quality-based organizational structure.*
Source: West-Burnham (1992)

much closer to a TQM model than the bureaucratic monstrosities which have been created in recent years. Incidentally, your staff (apart from the managers) will worship the ground you walk on.

In his recent book, John West-Burnham has represented this flattened school hierarchy, created to be responsive to customer requirements, as shown in Figure 6.2. The teams in Figure 6.2 may be traditional subject departments, or teams responsible for age or ability groupings. The most significant feature of this form of organizational structure is the freedom for teams to communicate laterally, and their immediacy to the customer, internal or external. They may in some cases be cross-functional or cross-departmental teams, with membership which may include people from all parts of the organization – academic, management, technical, administrative and maintenance. They may be set up for specific short-term projects (e.g. establishing a new IT system) or on a more permanent basis (for example, a Health and Safety Committee). They may, of course, be set up to plan specific improvements to the internal processes in the organization as part of the never-ending search for continuous improvement.

A task for the reader

You might at this point find it helpful to construct a traditional tree diagram describing the organizational structure, reporting and accountability in your school. If you do not have the time, ask your sixth form to do it; they will find it great fun. Consider how you might flatten the hierarchy, reducing the number of levels and introducing a team-based structure to break down departmental barriers. You may be surprised when you discover who contributes least to the organization's mission.

Chapter 7

Transform Your People

Drive out fear, so that everyone may work effectively for the organisation.

W.E. Deming

In a recent book,[1] Tom Peters, the American management guru, tells how he asked a management consultant the secret of his success. The consultant replied, 'It's simple, I visit my client's place of business, speak briefly to the boss, I then wander round the works, from department to department, pausing to chat to people as I go. I ask them how things are going, if anything is wrong, and what they would do about it. They tell me, and I tell them to fix it. They do, and later I collect a fat cheque from the boss.'

The point of the story is that the boss could have done it himself if he had created an atmosphere of trust in which workers were confident that they were not going to be blamed for something which was out of their control. Remember that in Chapter 1, we saw that once a process is in statistical control and major random causes of variance have been eliminated, then the remaining variance can only be removed by improving the system – and the system is the responsibility of management.

Have you (or your headteacher) got the confidence to trust totally in the professionalism of your people? What happens when something goes wrong in your school? Is the first reaction to search for someone to blame? Or was a serious attempt made to identify the causes of the problem, rather than reacting to the symptoms?

The captain of a cricket team has steered his team into a winning position. Suddenly an apparently simple catch is spilled. The crowd shout derisive comments. Colleagues express their disgust in verbal and body language, tension rises. The captain reprimands the guilty player, who promptly puts down another catch in the next over and the match is lost. The captain is hauled over the coals by the committee. Suppose the captain had responded to the first miss by commiserating with the fielder, and raising the heads of the rest of the team by verbal encouragement. The second catch might well have been held, and the match won. Which style of leadership are you familiar with in schools?

Is your school driven by fear, or led by encouragement and reinforcement? Does your school encourage people to 'fail fast', that is, take chances, experiment? Or is initiative and experiment crushed?

A parable

A young biology teacher with 'green' tendencies approaches you anxiously. She is very unhappy about having to use dissection in practicals for A level, since it offends her, and a number of pupils refuse to take part. She explains that she is sure that she can teach what is necessary by using an interactive video which she has recently seen advertised. It costs £200. Do you tell her to go ahead, order it, and then report back to you on its effectiveness, or tell her not to be squeamish, and get on with the job?

Another parable

You are receiving complaints from the staff and parents that the central heating system is inadequate. You are anxious about your budget, since the unusually cold winter has caused the heating account to overrun the projected budget. How do you respond? If your response would be to admonish the caretaker for poor management of his resources, and to tell staff and pupils to wear an extra jumper and keep the windows closed, then you have not got the TQM message. If you sent for the caretaker and asked him to call a meeting of his team, in order to search systematically for possible causes of the problem, brainstorm possible solutions, evaluate the most useful-looking alternative, produce an implementation plan with costings, then you have got the TQM message.

Keith Blanchard in his book *The One Minute Manager*, sums up neatly what I am saying:

Catch people doing something right and tell them so, criticise behaviour, but never undermine the person.

I have tried to hint at the basic management style which it is essential to have in place if a TQM culture is to be created. But it is important to consider the present state of mind of the people you have to lead. This will obviously differ from one school to another, but I suggest that the following propositions would hold good in many or maybe most schools at present.

- Teachers feel that they have been unfairly blamed for many of society's ills – increased crime, illiteracy, innumeracy, vandalism, etc.
- Teachers feel that they have been unfairly accused of being left-wing agitators.
- Teachers have been said to be overpaid, underqualified and underworked. They feel that the opposite is the case.
- Teachers feel that they have been unjustly accused of irresponsibility and incompetence.

Whether or not all this is true does not matter, it is enough that they feel it to be so. As a result, the general mood of teachers is resentful and unmotivated, with an increasing incidence of stress-related diseases. The battery of reforms with which they have been expected to cope since 1985 has greatly increased their workload, and reduced their confidence in what they are doing. They have neither been encouraged nor trained to be able to manage these changes in such a way as to make them tolerable, and preferably enjoyable. All organizations are now living in a volatile environment, and *must* learn to love change. Self-esteem and confidence are essential for this to happen. Since the changes experienced in education are externally imposed, we have to learn to live with them. A TQM approach is essential.

The organizational impact of recent reforms so far has been to cause a switch from something like a collegiate structure to something more akin to the old-fashioned managerial model now rapidly being superseded in British business. The features of this old model can be summed up as follows:

An obsolete management paradigm

- An emphasis on direction and control.
- A short-termist view, stressing immediate profit rather than long-term development.
- A confrontational approach to manager–worker relationships.
- Concentration on shipping out product in volume, at lowest unit cost, with quality inspected in after the event.
- A failure to develop partnership with customers and suppliers.
- A preference for mechanization, and the treatment of workers as an extension of the machine.
- Organization by function.

It is possible with a little thought to see how this model might be transferred to a school environment. The reader might perhaps at this point translate these features into his or her own context. A mechanistic approach to management based on driving the organization by fear is very demotivating. Thus if your school has a steep and long hierarchy, with no upward communication; with a total emphasis on 'results', SATS, GCSE, A level, or simply attendance and behaviour, and with teachers treated as dispensable cannon fodder, then it will be an unhappy and ineffective school. What is required is an organizational structure which encourages 'ownership of the job' by the 'workers'. Perhaps I can explain what I mean most effectively with yet another parable.

Yet another parable

Tressell's hero, Owen, is one of a group of housepainters who are engaged on the renovation of a property owned by Sweater, the capitalist villain. He has chosen to embellish one room in Moorish style, with friezes and stencils. Rushton, the owner of the painting firm, asks Owen to produce some designs. He offers no extra pay, even though he knows that Owen is much more gifted artistically than any artist he might hire at great expense. Owen agrees, provided he is allowed (reluctantly) by Rushton to work at home. He becomes totally obsessed with his task, and gains enormous satisfaction from the chance to 'own' his work, and express himself through it.

The moral of the story is clear. If a worker is allowed to obtain personal satisfaction from his work, and a sense of ownership, then it is not necessary to pay him more, or offer performance-related inducements to persuade him to give of his best.

There is much evidence available from psychological theory to support this view. Elton Mayo in the famous Hawthorne experiments,[2] demonstrates that what really motivates workers is not just (as he had thought) improved working conditions, but positive attention and interest shown by an important 'other'. Maslow's model of a hierarchy of human needs stresses the importance of self-actualization and self-esteem. These intangible factors are far more important than the fulfilment of basic needs of a biological kind (food, sex, shelter, comfort), through improved basic pay. Herzberg makes similar observations. Skinner and the Behaviourists (who deny the existence of feeling and meaning, and concepts such as freedom and dignity) nevertheless stress the importance of 'secondary reinforcement' of desired responses to contingencies of the environment. Teachers, like any other worker, will feel good about themselves and what they are doing if someone they see as being important openly and publicly values what they are doing. Moreover, they will perform the task better as well. However, this alone is not enough. They must not only have a sense of ownership of the job, and be valued for their contribution, they must also be enabled to achieve that state by constant access to the possibility of training and self-improvement, with a clearly defined career path. This means that they need to be taught certain skills and encouraged to bin many cynical habits and attitudes developed under the old regime. We must enable them to banish fear.

What sort of 'fear' do I have in mind?

Drive out fear

- Fear – of loss of control, of children, of workload, of own time, of personal life.
- Fear – of management's power to punish, by giving the worst classes or pupils, by blocking promotion, by assigning unpleasant duties, by failing to give support in disciplinary matters, by using appraisal as a weapon of control.
- Fear – of curriculum change, and its possible exposure of lack of competence or knowledge.
- Fear – of loss of self-esteem and confidence due to low public esteem.
- Fear – of physical or verbal assault by pupils or parents.
- Fear – of change of all kinds.

All of these causes of stress are present in the working life of every teacher in any kind of school to some extent. In many cases the stress is sufficiently intense to bring on physical or mental breakdown. Yet many of the causes of stress can be reduced or eliminated by good management.

One powerful weapon against these demotivating stress factors is positively directed training. Not training seen as a 'punishment' for inadequacy, but training as a powerful tool to enhance the confidence and ability of the teacher. Nor should it be used as a means of papering over the cracks in the system, to conceal the inadequacy of the school and its management. Its purpose must rather be to empower the teacher to not only do her job better, but to feel a genuine sense of ownership of the job.

Empower teachers

The teacher must be:

- Encouraged to use initiative.
- Given adequate equipment, physical and mental.
- Be trained to use it effectively.
- Have achievements, however small, recognized by management.

The question now is, 'How are we to achieve this objective?'

TRAINING FOR CAREER DEVELOPMENT

All teachers will possess professional and degree qualifications. However, if performance is to be subject to 'continuous improvement', which must be the aim of the Total Quality fanatic, training and more training must be provided, financed and regularly undertaken. The following pattern would ensure professional development.

A training agenda

- In-service/in-house activities, curriculum or classroom management, weekly or monthly, team or group based – the educational equivalent of Quality Circles.
- Short subject-based courses, to bring subject knowledge up to date, LEA, DES or university sponsored.
- Short professional courses on particular activities for which a teacher has a special responsibility, e.g. records of achievement, or timetabling.
- After a long period of continuous service, a sabbatical term to be spent in a university, or possibly a company, to recharge the teacher's batteries and widen his/her horizons. Once or twice in a career.
- In addition to the above, all teachers should be positively encouraged to undertake ANY programme of an educational nature, be it a PhD or a course in flower arranging. All such activity will create a fresher, livelier and, in many ways, better teacher.

Any system of staff appraisal should be based upon a developmental approach – thus emphasizing the importance of training. This book is not the right place to pursue the matter of professional training any further in general terms. All we are trying to establish is the overriding importance of training of all kinds if we are to improve our performance as teachers – in line with the TQM philosophy which we are setting out here. Training is not an optional bolt-on extra, it is a vital first-priority investment in your most important resource, your people. This means all staff including teachers, administrators and ancillary staff.

There are, however, also some specific training matters which must be dealt with if a TQM culture and system is to be put in place in your school.

Training for TQM

At this point in the book we would like to establish some basic principles. These will be developed into a specimen training programme model later in the book. We are concerned to develop a specific cast of mind, a way of looking at the world, and a model for problem solving. This involves five key elements.

Five key training elements

- Logical problem-solving techniques.
- Simple statistical techniques and measures.
- Lateral thinking.
- Team-work skills.
- Communication skills.

These techniques will provide a 'toolkit' for not only your teachers, but all members of your staff at all levels. This is necessary if a culture of continuous improvement to meet customer requirements is to be undertaken.

Logical problem solving

The essential steps in this process are set out in Figure 7.1.

Lateral thinking

We are all trained by our own educational experience to think in a straight-line sequence of logical reasoning. This can quite often produce a wrong diagnosis and inappropriate solution. For example, 'most misbehaviour occurs during the lunchbreak, the break is 1.5 hours long, thus encouraging bad behaviour, therefore we should solve the behaviour problem by reducing the length of the lunch break'.

Edward De Bono has suggested a technique which he calls lateral thinking. This is basically a systematized version of what might be called the act of creativity. This is a skill usually thought to be the privilege of a gifted minority. He suggests that it is in fact a skill which can be learned and developed by practice. The process of learning the skill is both fun and a prerequisite to the development of successful team-work for problem solving.

Try it first with a small group, up to ten maximum (pupils or colleagues). If possible use an experienced team leader. Start with a warm-up exercise. Ask the team, working as individuals, or in pairs, to write down in five minutes as many alternatives as they can to a door handle. They should be able to produce between them twenty or so. Give

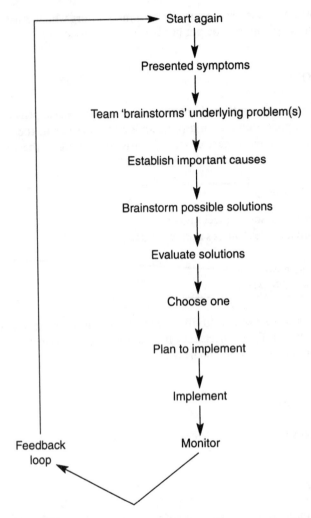

Figure 7.1 *Logical problem solving.*

Brownie points to anyone who suggests the most radical solution – for example, doing away with the door. Then ask them to work on the problem of lunchtime misbehaviour mentioned above, using the following sequence of stages.

A lateral thinking session

Stage 1 Each member to spend three minutes writing down as many solutions as possible, without any consideration of feasibility, or any evaluation of relative merits.

Stage 2 Each in turn to offer one alternative solution to the team leader, who should produce a list on a flipchart or blackboard. Continue until all alternatives have been exhausted.

Stage 3   Ask the team to work in pairs, each pair to produce a short list of three solutions which appear to be possible, in five minutes.

Stage 4   Each pair to decide on one preferred alternative, team leader to list the preferred alternatives offered.

Stage 5   Whole team to discuss the pros and cons of the short list of three or four generated in Stage 4. Seek to reach agreement on ONE most feasible alternative.

It is vital that the team leader quash any attempts to evaluate choices before Stage 3. We are trying to encourage an open mind, in order to permit the really innovative alternatives to emerge.

Simple statistical techniques

We shall in Chapter 7 identify various simple statistical devices which might be used to calculate the 'costs of quality'. We shall attempt to apply them to areas of school activity where such 'costs' might occur. Teachers are often less numerate than they would like to think, and have a particular fear and suspicion of statistics, which they see as organized lying. Nevertheless we need to find a painless way of introducing all colleagues to the essential methods used for the collection, collation and processing of information in the attempt to quantify a problem. They need to understand how processes in an organization work. Detailed explanation of these simple statistical techniques will be found in the Training Programme in Appendix 1 and also in Chapter 8, on 'The costs of quality'.

The team should be taken quickly through these methods in the first session and then, having had time to digest them, be asked in the next session to work in three groups of three or four. Each group should take on a particular and topical 'problem' which they are all aware of as relevant to their school. Each group should decide which methods are appropriate to their problem, and produce a report for the plenary session. Why not try the lunchtime behaviour problem as a warm-up exercise?

It is very important to avoid labelling symptoms as problems. In this example symptoms might be: damage to public and personal property; complaints from parents or members of the public; theft; and so on. The problem is likely to be more deep-seated.

Team-work skills

Team-work skills should already be developing as you take the team through the previous two exercises. The skills which should be emerging are as follows:

- Constructive, open and positive discussion, instead of defensive posturing.
- Willingness to listen to all the contributions of others.
- A systematic approach to problem identification and solution.
- Cooperation and consensus rather than conflict and competition.

There is a Samurai saying which is used by Japanese managers to justify their insistence on consensus-based decision making:

> A man may take an arrow in both hands and easily break it. But if he takes three arrows together, he cannot break them.

If decisions are taken by a team of equals, after reasoned discussion, it is much more difficult later, should a solution to a problem not work, to scapegoat and blame an individual.

Communication skills

This is not the place to discuss the important features of human communication systems. Sufficient to say that one or two important points should be borne in mind in any meeting.

- Seventy per cent of communication is non-verbal.
- The layout of furniture influences the possibility of cooperation, or probability of conflict.
- Listening is the most difficult communication skill.

Further discussion of these issues may be found in Lita de Alberdi's book on the psychology of business.[3]

The purpose of this chapter has been to offer some ground rules for the conduct either of training programmes or of serious management meetings. We believe that it is important to develop the skills discussed above in all members of the organization, from top to bottom. They are as important to a group of caretakers discussing ways of reducing the heating bill as they are to senior managers discussing ways of delivering the National Curriculum.

Appendix 2 offers an example of a TQM training programme used in the business world, adapted for use in school. If the headteacher is not confident of her ability to run such a course, she should perhaps attend one of those offered by IFS and others for business people in order to acquire the skills, and then adapt the programme to meet her needs. The objective of doing so is:

- To empower your people to do a better job.
- To transform your school through a programme of continuous improvement.

Whatever problem is tackled by teams of colleagues (after the training), you should be confident that they are able to answer the following questions:

- Are we capable of doing the job properly?
- Do we continue to do it properly?
- Have we done it properly?
- Could we do it better and more consistently?

The power of teamwork

Why should team-work be a better way to achieve these objectives?

- More problems can be tackled.
- By the people closest to the problem.
- Greater diversity of skill and knowledge is applied.
- Frustration is removed, and morale improved, if people think that their contribution is welcomed.
- Cross-functional/interdepartmental problems can *only* be dealt with in this way.
- Solutions produced are more likely to be implemented.
- This will be especially true if contributions and solutions are recognized and celebrated.

Once the training programme has been completed, then you can consider what teams might be set up. It does not matter what you call them, provided they are a recognized and permanent feature of organizational life, in which all colleagues have a chance to play a role. Of course it will be a waste of time if you do not implement solutions offered by your teams, or at least explain personally why it is impossible to do so. The next chapter develops this theme by suggesting ways in which these techniques may be applied to produce a programme of continuous improvement.

NOTES

1. T. Peters, *Thriving on Chaos*. London: Pan, 1988.
2. F.J. Roethlisberger and W.J. Dickson, *Management and the Worker*. Cambridge, Mass.: Harvard University Press, 1939. Cited in C. Handy, *Understanding Organisations*. Harmondsworth: Penguin, 1993.
3. L. di Alberdi, *People, Psychology and Business*. Cambridge: CUP, 1990.

Chapter 8

The Costs of Quality

Cease dependence on inspection to achieve quality. Build quality into (the process) in the first place.

W.E. Deming

WHAT IS A PROCESS?

A process is the transformation of a set of inputs, which may include materials, actions, methods, people and operations, into desired outputs, in the form of products, information, services, skills or – generally – results.

Any process can be analysed by an examination of the inputs and outputs. This will determine the action necessary to improve quality.

At every supplier–customer interface there is a transformation process and every single task throughout an organization must be viewed as a process in this way.

Defining the scope of a process is vital, since it will determine both the required inputs and the resultant outputs. When it has been defined, the inputs and suppliers, outputs and customers can also be defined, together with the requirements at each of the interfaces.

Figure 8.1 shows some of the inputs and some of the outputs to processes. They are by no means comprehensive.

In Figure 8.2 we can see that education is a process. All processes, whether in a factory or a school, have certain common characteristics.

- The quality of the outputs is a function of the quality of the inputs, plus the management of the process.
- The process will contain variation around a mean (average).
- The degree of variation is measurable.
- The range of variation around the mean is the *variance*.
- The process is a system which is likely to be stable and predictable.
- The predictability of the system may occasionally be broken by extremes of variance.
- These extreme examples of variance are the consequence of 'special' causes from outside the system.

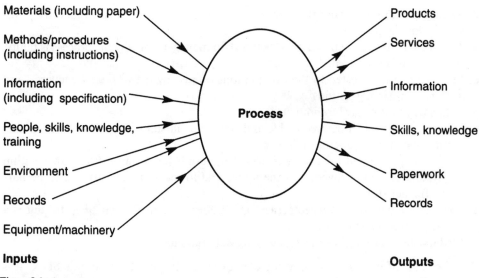

Inputs

Outputs

Figure 8.1 *A process.*
Source: Oakland (1989)

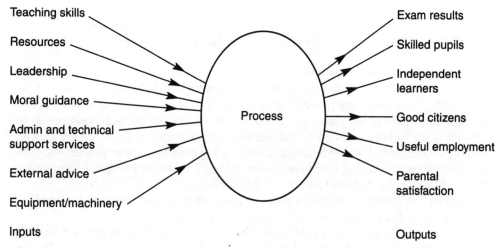

Inputs

Outputs

Figure 8.2 *Education is a process.*

- These 'special' causes may be identified by problem-solving techniques, and possibly eliminated.
- The remaining variance, within measurable upper and lower control limits (see later explanation), is the result of 'common' causes, which are the consequence of faults in the system or process.
- These faults are the faults of the management of the process, since they, not the workers, create the system.

- Management must ensure that the workers (teachers) are trained to identify problems inside the process.
- The workers (teachers) understand better than management why the process is faulty, since they are closer to it.
- Management *must* listen to the explanations offered by the workers (teachers), and implement their suggestions.
- In this way faults may be eliminated.
- The process will then be predictable and stable (i.e. in statistical control) within narrower upper and lower control limits.
- Further improvement programmes may then permit the 'mean' performance within the system to be improved, and the upper and lower limits of variance to be narrowed further still.
- The target must be 'zero defects' (perhaps 100 per cent A–C at GCSE). But this is a *journey*, not a destination.
- Medium-term targets must be challenging but attainable.

The above set of points constitutes the core of the argument set out in this book. It is very tightly reasoned, and your understanding of it in full will depend on your careful reading of the remainder of this chapter, in which the statistical explanation of the concept of variance is set out. Illustrations of its use as a means of processing historical data about the performance of a school will be found in Chapter 9.

THE CHANGING EDUCATIONAL ENVIRONMENT

Regardless of whether we are talking about profit- or non-profit-making organizations, in manufacturing or in service industries, all organizations, if they wish to succeed, are now finding that they have to monitor customer requirements continuously and strive to satisfy customer needs. Issues of quality are the major management concerns for all organizations, as is exemplified by the recent glut of 'Charters' with which we are continually confronted. The NHS, which is undergoing changes similar to many of those taking place on the educational scene, has recently produced the Patient's Charter along the same lines as the Parent's Charter, a DFE publication.

Independent schools have always had to manage their own resources and be accountable to parents. State schools are no longer an exception to this rule.

A series of Education Acts, culminating in the Education Reform Act (ERA) 1988, has meant that the service provided by schools has moved nearer to the client. Its aim, says the government, is to improve the quality of teaching and learning in schools by the introduction of market forces, choice and competition into the education system.

In the past, state education has been producer led. Politicians, bureaucrats and teachers have decided what is best for children and for most of the population it has been a take-it-or-leave-it state monopoly, a far cry from a free market. We are moving away from that monopoly.

The Education Act has made schools more accountable (via the formal publication of examination results, staff appraisal and the introduction of a national assessment system); furthered democratization (via the reconstitution of governing bodies, local management of schools (LMS), open enrolment and opting out); and introduced the National Curriculum.

By the end of 1993, LEAs had delegated responsibility for the management, including control of finances, to all secondary schools and primary schools with more than 200 pupils. LMS requires governors, working with the Head and staff, to arrange delivery of the National Curriculum from within a delegated budget determined largely by pupil numbers. The overall aims of LMS are to enable the most effective and efficient use of the resources available to the school. Schools have to be marketed, administrative procedures have to be established, senior management roles have to be reviewed and full responsibility for staffing has to be assumed.

Publication of examination results and other forms of league table will lead to greater awareness of standards and variations from school to school. Assessment procedures, recording achievement and reporting academic outcomes will all have to be managed.

The introduction of staff appraisal will raise a number of issues: the objectives and aims of the school will have to be clear; managers will need to be trained in appraisal techniques; professional development will have to be managed; and the impact on time will have to be addressed.

The introduction of the National Curriculum means that schools will need extra resources (both staff and equipment) and that more money will be spent on examinations. Time will have to be managed so as to meet all the requirements of the curriculum. Staff will have to be deployed and developed in order to respond to new demands and maximize expertise.

Open enrolment means that parents will be able to indicate a preference for schools from authorities other than their own. Therefore parental choice procedures will have to be managed.

Choice implies competition which, in the mind of the government, leads to improved efficiency. Competition also leads to an increased awareness of the service. The introduction of LMS, the possibility of alternative institutions (grant-maintained schools or City Technology Colleges) and the reform of governing bodies are designed to give the customer a better deal and to improve the service.

> Schools under a market system should produce what the customers want. If parents are pleased with the product they will send or keep their children there and the school will generate income. If not, other schools will receive the children and the money that goes with them.
>
> P. Downes (1988)

A similar programme of reform is being undertaken in the USA with the same objectives of greater accountability both for academic performance and financial performance.

COSTS OF QUALITY

Manufacturing a quality product, providing a quality service, or doing a quality job, one with a high degree of fitness for purpose, is not enough. The cost of achieving that quality must be carefully managed so that the long-term effect of quality costs on the organization is a desirable one.

The analysis of quality costs is a significant management tool which provides: a method of assessing and monitoring the overall effectiveness of the management of quality; a means of determining problem areas and action priorities.

J. Oakland (1989)

Managers are often of the opinion that quality costs more. However, consider the steps which have to be followed in order to carry out a particular job. First, the time taken to plan and prepare what is to be done, if used effectively, will result in less wasted time later on. Secondly, if the appropriate equipment is used it will ease the task of doing the job properly. Even with the right equipment an incorrect step in the process will result in wasted time. Getting it right first time means that the objective is achieved at minimum cost.

It takes time, money, skill and effort to produce defective products and services. In the pursuit of quality we strive to achieve minimum defects, thereby using these valuable resources efficiently.

The costs of quality are no different from any other costs; they can be budgeted, measured and analysed and can be split into three different categories, namely *failure costs, appraisal costs*, and *prevention costs*.

Failure costs

Failure costs can be further split into those resulting from internal and external failure.

Internal-failure costs

Internal-failure costs occur when the results of work fail to reach the required standards and are detected before transfer to the customer takes place. Internal-failure costs include:

Waste – the activities associated with doing unnecessary work as the result of errors, poor organization, the wrong materials and so on.

Rework or rectification – the correction of defective material or errors to meet the requirements.

Reinspection – the re-examination of products or work which has been rectified.

Failure analysis – the activity required to establish the causes of failure of internal product or service.

Internal costs of quality in a school

The following are possible areas for investigating waste in schools:

Meetings:
Are agendas clear?
Are they arranged at the most convenient time for the majority?
Are conclusions reached?
Are positive outcomes achieved?

INSET days:
Is training relevant?
Are these days well attended?
Does change take place as a result?

Inappropriate textbooks:
Does this result in photocopying and further preparation for staff?
Are pupils working against the odds and lacking appropriate background reading material?

Underutilized resources (including staff, pupils, governors, parents, equipment and buildings):
Could school buildings be used by the local community in order to increase income and/or enhance the standing of the school within the community?
Is careful consideration made before equipment is bought to ensure that it will do the job properly, it will not become obsolete overnight and it is compatible with the school's existing equipment?
Do staff, governors and parents possess skills which could be exploited for the good of the school?
Are pupils used as ambassadors for the school when visitors are received?

The stationery store:
Is a check kept upon the amount of stationery used, and can those using it account for that which is used?
Is the school carrying stocks of stationery which are not being used as a result of having been purchased without careful consideration as to the requirements of those using it?
Who has the responsibility for deciding upon what is bought?

Parents' evenings:
Are parents aware of the dates?
Are parents encouraged to come into school?
Is time spent with parents spent effectively?
Do they achieve the desired outcomes?

Photocopying:
Is paper wasted?
Do staff waste time trying to use machines which are constantly not functioning properly?
Is the quality of communications emanating from the school via photocopied correspondence of the desired quality?
(Photocopying is necessary but teacher time spent photocopying is a waste.)

Timetabling and layout of the school:
Are lessons timetabled and rooms organized so as to minimize the amount of time wasted as pupils and staff move around the school between lessons?

As far as *rework, rectification* and *reinspection* are concerned it will be useful to determine how often tasks have to be repeated, how much time is spent in doing so, what other resources are wasted and what other tasks are omitted as a result (including students' set work, tests, exams, etc.).

External-failure costs

Costs resulting from external failure include the correction of products or services after delivery to the customer. External failure includes:

Complaints – all work and costs associated with handling and servicing of customers' complaints.

Liability – the result of litigation and other claims.

Reduced number of applicants – for both pupil places and staff positions.

Bad publicity – resulting in a poorer perceived image of the school from within the community.

Internal and external failures produce the 'costs of getting it wrong', or the 'costs of non-conformance'. For businesses probably the greatest single element in the 'cost of failure' is lost sales due to lost customers. Recent studies at Harvard Business School confirm this. They show that the retention of just 5 per cent more customers can often increase a business's profitability by 100 per cent. They have also shown that it costs five times as much to acquire new customers as it does to retain the loyal ones. In school terms, loyal customers are ones who will send each of their children to the same school if they have been satisfied with the education of the first child who went there. For a family with four children, an unsatisfied parent or pupil will mean that three other children will not put the school down as their first choice. Schools must be aware of the costs of getting it wrong. In a sense quality is free because, as the 'cost of failure' drops to zero, there are no additional costs in doing things 'right first time'. It is having to repeat work which increases costs and negatively affects people's morale. There will always be some 'prevention costs'.

Appraisal costs

Cost of appraisal is the cost incurred to determine conformance with quality standards. Examples include:

Inspection checks – include checking that product and/or service standards match the agreed specifications. In a school, the marking and correction of work is the greatest appraisal cost.

Quality audits – to check that the quality system is functioning satisfactorily.

Vendor rating – the assessment and approval of all suppliers, both of products and services.

Appraisal activities result in the 'costs of checking it is right'.

Prevention costs

Prevention costs are the costs of activities that prevent failure from occurring. They include training employees, quality awareness programmes, planning and so on.

There is presently very little empirical research on waste in schools. The figure for manufacturing industries in the UK is between 15 and 30 per cent of their sales revenue, and for the service sector the DTI figures show costs at an even higher level of 40 per cent. This inability to get it 'right first time' accounts for a staggering £15 billion per annum. At £14 billion, the government's public sector borrowing requirements for the tax year 1991-92 was £1 billion less than the 'cost of failure' in Britain. Even if costs amounted to only 10 per cent of staffing costs in schools then they would still represent a highly significant amount.

The relationship between the costs of prevention, appraisal and failure costs and the ability of the organization to meet customer requirements is illustrated in Figure 8.3.

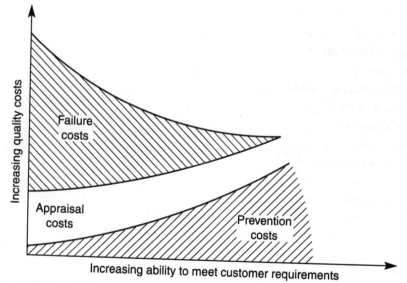

Figure 8.3 *Costs of quality.*

Where there is little ability to match the needs of the customer, costs are high, and failure costs predominate. As ability is improved, by investment in prevention and possibly appraisal costs, failure costs are reduced. However, investment is not necessary in order to improve quality. The management of processes is necessary and is indeed essential. It is understood that most schools will not have unlimited funds available to them for the improvement of quality, therefore the management of processes will be the area upon which to focus.

It may take many years to see the results of working to eliminate waste. However, there are many areas where direct benefits will be almost immediate.

An activity for the reader: understanding the costs of non-conformance

Select a short time span (a week or a fortnight) and identify the number of times you have had to do each activity by writing the number in the boxes provided.

Doing the same task twice ☐
Having work retyped ☐
Postponed a meeting ☐
Asked for clarification of a document ☐
Reset deadlines ☐
Provide on-the-spot training ☐
Seek more information ☐
Modify printed material ☐
Ask for an agenda ☐
Clarify the purpose of a task ☐
Ask for work to be repeated ☐
Seek confirmation of a verbal agreement ☐
Explain documentation ☐
Ask for more time ☐
Find spare accommodation ☐
Confirm an order ☐
Change a timetable ☐
Duplicate information ☐
Get equipment repaired ☐
Leave a job half finished ☐
Take over a delegated task ☐
Redefine specifications ☐
Return wrongly ordered/supplied goods ☐
Cut corners to complete a task ☐
Abandon agreed procedures ☐

Source: West-Burnham, (1992)

If you estimate the time taken for completion of all this 'rework' of jobs which could have been done right first time, and multiply it by your hourly rate of pay and then by your number of working weeks in the year, you can arrive at a reasonable guesstimate of the cost to your school of inefficient processes related just to yourself. Multiply it again by the number of staff and you have a guesstimate of the cost of what in industry would be called 'scrap, waste and rework'. I think you will find that this figure is close to or above 25 per cent of your annual school budget. Think what you could do with these resources if you could save them by improving the process. This is what we mean by the costs of 'non-conformance'.

HOW CAN WE IMPROVE OUR WORK PROCESSES?

There are many methods available to us to refine work processes. Some are quantitative; others are qualitative and can be useful in analysing complex situations. In any event it is important to view them as tools which facilitate a team-based approach. Some of the techniques which are described here have already been mentioned, and will now be explained in more detail. The techniques described here are:

- Benchmarking
- Process flowcharting
- Tally charts
- Histograms
- Pareto analysis
- Cause and effect analysis
- Scatter diagrams/correlation
- Control charts
- Cusum charts

These are all basic tools which can be used to interpret data fully and derive maximum use from them. They offer the means to collect, present and analyse data.

Benchmarking

AIM To improve upon best practice.
MEANS By benchmarking the following:
Products and services delivered to the internal and external customer.
Processes in all departments and functions.
Organization, culture and calibre of people.

Benchmarking is essentially about finding good ideas and ways to improve existing practice by looking at the operations in organizations which are seen as leaders in their field. West-Burnham (1991) explains that it can be structured in the following way:

STEP 1 Review:
        Identify the product or process to be improved.

Identify the organizations which do it better, by monitoring performance and practice of key competitors.
Gather hard data to inform analysis.

STEP 2 Analysis:
What factors contribute to their success?
Is their product/approach right for us?
What are the implications of adopting their approach?

STEP 3 Planning:
What can we achieve?
How are we going to achieve these outcomes?

STEP 4 Action:
Implement specific actions.
Monitor progress against norms.
Go back to the original and review.
Consider ways of extending improvement further.

The process can be used to compare good practice in different schools but is more likely to be effective within a school in looking at, for example, how different departments work and how effective different teaching methods are.

In focusing upon competitor schools questions such as the following may be relevant:

- Are they better? If so, how much?
- If they are better, why are they better?
- What can we learn from them? How can we apply what we have learned to our school?

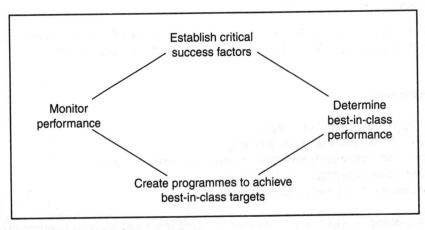

Figure 8.4 *The Benchmarking Cycle.*
Source: Banks (1992)

The diagram (Fig 8.4) illustrates a simple approach to benchmarking called the benchmarking cycle.

Process flowcharting

Any processes, whether they relate to administrative, managerial, teaching or ancillary activities, can be examined in detail using the method of process flowcharting.

Five standard symbols are used, which together represent all the different types of activity or event likely to be encountered. These are shown on a detailed flow process chart and a flow diagram which together give a complete picture of the flow and its component.

The symbols are as follows:

◯	Operation	Indicates the main steps in a process.
▢	Inspection	Indicates a check on quality or quantity.
⬠ ⬇	Transport	Indicates movement, of people, information, materials, paper etc.
D	Delay	Indicates a temporary storage, delay or hold-up between operations.
▽	Storage	Indicates a controlled storage, such as filing, which is not a delay.

It will be very rare for one person to be able to complete a flow chart alone. The very act of flowcharting will, therefore, improve knowledge of the processes and help to develop team-work.

The charts and diagrams may be of four basic types:

- Recording what people actually do.
- Recording how material is handled or treated.
- Recording how equipment is used.
- Recording how information flows and to whom or where.

Figures 8.5 and 8.6 illustrate how process flowcharting was used to save the valuable time of a school's IT expert (based in one building of a school) and reduce the time which teaching staff had to wait for computer-printed notes. A critical examination of the two figures together shows how much time is taken up by this particular process. This is time in which the IT expert could be carrying out jobs for which he or she alone is qualified. In any analysis of this type certain types of question need to be asked (see p. 91).

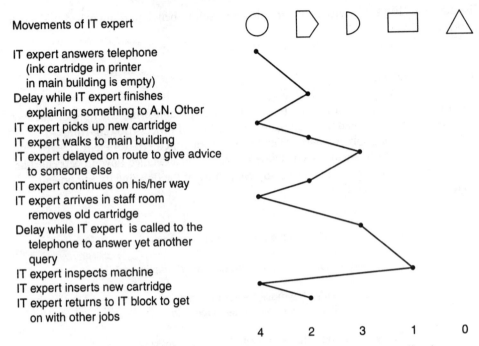

Movements of IT expert

IT expert answers telephone
  (ink cartridge in printer
  in main building is empty)
Delay while IT expert finishes
  explaining something to A.N. Other
IT expert picks up new cartridge
IT expert walks to main building
IT expert delayed on route to give advice
  to someone else
IT expert continues on his/her way
IT expert arrives in staff room
  removes old cartridge
Delay while IT expert is called to the
  telephone to answer yet another
  query
IT expert inspects machine
IT expert inserts new cartridge
IT expert returns to IT block to get
  on with other jobs

4   2   3   1   0

Figure 8.5 *Flow process chart: method for inserting new cartridge into computer printer in staff workroom.*

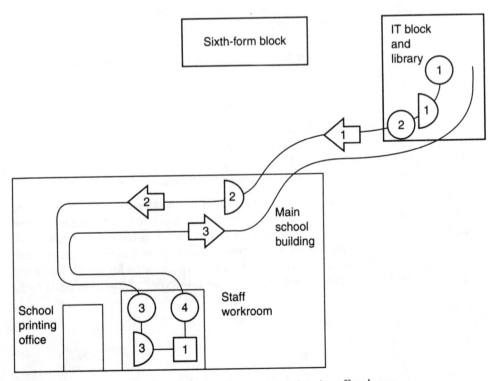

Figure 8.6 *Flow diagram: inserting new cartridge into computer printer in staff workroom.*

| Purpose | What is actually done?
Why is it necessary?
What else might be done? |] Eliminate unnecessary
parts of the job. |

Place · Where is it done?
Why is it done in that place?
Where else could it be done?

Sequence · When is it done?
Why is it done at that particular time?
When might, or should it be done?

People · Who does it?
Why is it done by that particular person?
Who else might, or should do it?

] Combine wherever
possible and/or
rearrange operations for
more effective results or
reduction in waste.

Method · How is it done?
Why is it done in that particular way?
How else might, or should it be done?

] Simplify the operations.

Questions such as these, when applied to this particular problem, raise many points demanding an explanation, such as:

Question Why is it that only the IT expert can insert a new cartridge into the printer?

Answer Because nobody else has been shown how to do it.

Question Who else could be asked to do it?

Answer The secretary who is in charge of photocopying and is in a room just along the corridor from the staff room.

No doubt there are other questions which could be asked. There is evidently room for improvement. This is a real-life example of what happens when a series of activities is started without being properly planned.

The solution arrived at by this school can be seen in the Figures 8.7 and 8.8.

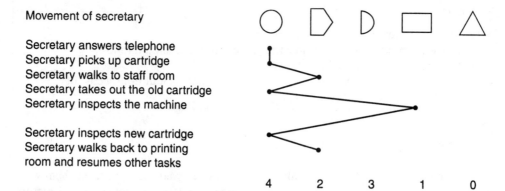

Movement of secretary

Secretary answers telephone
Secretary picks up cartridge
Secretary walks to staff room
Secretary takes out the old cartridge
Secretary inspects the machine

Secretary inspects new cartridge
Secretary walks back to printing
room and resumes other tasks

4 · 2 · 3 · 1 · 0

Figure 8.7 *Flow process chart: improved method for inserting new cartridge into computer printer.*

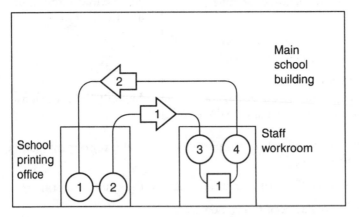

Figure 8.8 *Flow diagram: improved method of inserting new cartridge into computer printer.*

It will be seen from the summary on the new flow process chart that the number of delays has been cut by three. The flow diagram shows the much shorter distance which has to be travelled by the secretary in comparison with the distance travelled by the IT expert. Both the IT expert and members of the teaching staff saved much valuable time as a result of this change in the process. It should also be remembered that the cost per hour of secretary time will be much lower than the cost per hour of teacher time.

A task for the reader

Summary:

- Draw a flowchart of the existing process.
- Draw a second chart of the flow the process could or should follow.
- Compare the two to highlight changes.
- Work out costs and savings on basis of assumptions about hourly cost of employing expert and secretary.

Tally charts, frequency distributions and histograms

When data are collected it is difficult for us to draw any conclusions from them when they are in their raw form. However, if we convert the data into some kind of picture, we immediately reach a certain degree of understanding.

Consider the following example which shows the marks, out of 100, obtained by 101 pupils in an examination.

```
47 62 61 60 69 34 37 46 81 62 74 62
65 53 47 52 38 25 42 40 70 63 62 83
59 26 59 49 53 52 88 91 51 52 24 80
69 59 32 33 27 58 22 73 59 36 34 31
21 63 72 54 18 71 44 71 43 44 18 93
12 55 60 71 82 13 61 64 25 63 82 71
11 58 64 39 56 23 10 92 83 75 36 74
43 29 85 65 42 57 70 63 54 55 49 81
47 72 65 63 60
```

The tally chart and frequency distribution are alternative ordered ways of presenting the data. In this example it is necessary to group the marks together; here we have used intervals of width 10. First list the intervals in a column. Then go through the data and each time you come to a figure put a score in the appropriate interval. For convenience, each time you reach five in an interval, score through the other four using a horizontal line. This simplifies the calculations.

Class boundary	Tally	Frequency
10 – 19	JHT I	6
20 – 29	JHT IIII	9
30 – 39	JHT JHT	10
40 – 49	JHT JHT III	13
50 – 59	JHT JHT JHT III	18
60 – 69	JHT JHT JHT JHT I	21
70 – 79	JHT JHT II	12
80 – 89	JHT IIII	9
90 – 99	III	3
		Total 101

In the preparation of a grouped frequency distribution and the corresponding histogram it is advisable to:

1. Make the intervals of equal width.
2. If a central target is already known place it in the middle of an interval.
3. Preferably choose the interval boundaries so that they lie between possible observations.

The histogram derived from the data in this chart is shown in Figure 8.9. The somewhat confusing data, as originally presented, are now in the form of a picture which shows central tendency, the spread and the form of distribution.

Figure 8.10 illustrates a set of data which is approximately symmetrical about a central value. This is not always the case. For example, a histogram of the salaries within a normal company will peak towards the bottom of the range, reflecting the fact that

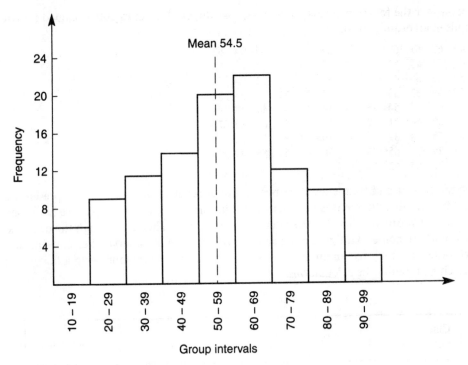

Figure 8.9 *Marks out of 100 for 101 pupils in an examination.*

most employees are paid salaries towards the bottom of the range. A histogram of the outcomes on the throw of a dice should have no peak as all outcomes are equally likely. Histograms of data concerning efficiencies, examination results and such like are often skewed, reflecting the fact that higher values are more difficult to achieve.

Pareto analysis

If the symptoms or causes of a particular problem are identified and recorded, it is possible to determine how much importance to attribute to each of them, thereby identifying the vital elements which should be addressed.

Pareto analysis is an approach which was developed by the Italian economist Pareto who put forward the '80/20' hypothesis. This states that 80 per cent of the problem can be accounted for by 20 per cent of the causes. The approach is a means of identifying the major contributing factors to the problem so that they can be prioritized and addressed in order of priority.

The analysis is done in the following order:

1. Identify the causes to be compared by brainstorming and/or use of cause-and-effect analysis. Appropriate units of measurement should be identified and a time period should be specified for collecting data.

2. Gather the results and display them on a histogram. The histogram is then reordered so that it displays declining frequency from left to right.
3. Label the right-hand vertical axis to show the cumulative percentage of the total.

The following example shows how a simple Pareto analysis was used to determine the main reasons why pupils in a particular school chose not to stay on in the sixth form of the school, but chose instead to go to the sixth form of another school or on to a Sixth Form College.

A Poor reputation for discipline.
B Poor preparation for FE/HE.
C Poor provision of careers advice.
D Lack of choice of appropriate courses of study.
E Lack of links between business/community and the school.
F No sixth form block/commonroom.
G Teaching methods. Lack of opportunity for students to research ideas for themselves.
H Poor facilities.

Results are shown in the frequency table below and in Figure 8.10.

Reason	Frequency	Cumulative percentage
D	77	38.5
H	39	58.0
F	24	70.0
G	16	78.0
E	15	85.5
B	12	91.5
C	10	96.5
A	7	100
Total	200	

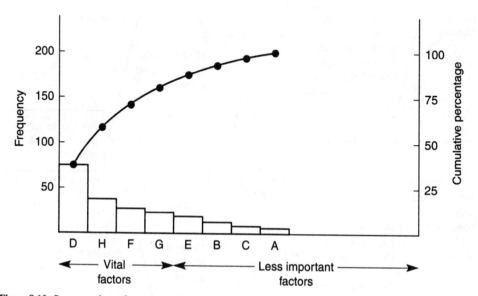

Figure 8.10 *Pareto analysis: factors contributing to pupils not being retained in sixth form.*

In this example it can be seen that three factors account for 70 per cent of pupils who leave the school to study elsewhere at 16+. It is, therefore, possible to identify appropriate solutions to these problems, in accordance with the resources available to the school.

Cause-and-effect analysis (and brainstorming)

A cause-and-effect diagram, also known as an 'Ishikawa' diagram (after the originator) or 'fishbone' diagram (after its appearance), is a useful way of mapping the inputs which affect quality.

The systematic use of cause-and-effect diagrams can:

- help to identify all the causes of a particular problem;
- distinguish causes from symptoms;
- analyse the relative significance of related causes.

Method

The effect is shown at the end of a horizontal arrow (Figure 8.11). Potential causes are then shown as labelled arrows leading on to the main arrow. Each of these arrows may, in turn, have other arrows leading on to them showing possible contributing factors.

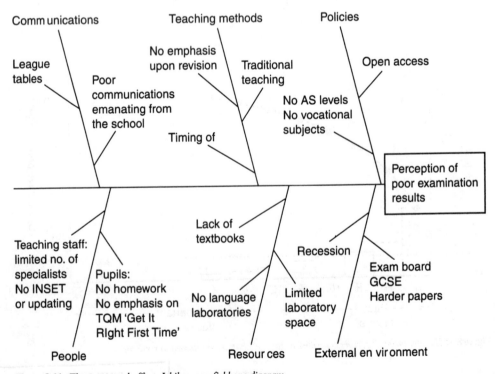

Figure 8.11 *The cause-and-effect, Ishikawa or fishbone diagram.*

The causes and/or contributing factors are brought out by the process of brainstorming. Brainstorming involves members of teams putting forward any ideas which they may have regarding the possible causes. At the brainstorming stage no ideas are dismissed as unreasonable. The main objective is to create an atmosphere where people feel enthusiastic and are willing to contribute. All ideas are recorded for future analysis. The process is continued until all conceivable causes have been included. Ideally the chart should be displayed for a few days after it has been drawn up, so that people have the opportunity to add further ideas as and when they come to mind. The proportion of which each factor contributes to the effect may then be calculated or estimated and a simple Pareto analysis can be used to identify the major causes, i.e. those worth investigating.

Typical project sequence

This sequence of activities is vital to the establishment of a successful *Continuous Improvement Programme*. We take the view that this method of problem solving can be taught to employees at all levels, and (if simplified) to pupils of any age. See Figure 8.12.

Scatter diagrams and correlation (evaluating data)

We may wish to compare two sets of data, *X* and *Y*, to decide whether there is any relationship between them. For example:

X	Y
Pupil's mark in mathematics	Pupil's mark in English
Number of absences of a pupil	Position in class of that pupil
Number of pupils late for lessons	Subject of lesson
Age of pupil	Number of absences of pupil

If the values of *Y* are plotted against the values of *X*, then a scatter diagram is obtained. The three diagrams shown in Figure 8.14 are examples of what a scatter diagram may look like.

(a) shows two variables which appear to be directly related to each other.
(b) suggests that there is no association between the variables.
(c) suggests that there may be some kind of relationship between the variables.

We must, however, remember that common sense is needed when interpreting scatter diagrams. For example, we may find that there is an increase in the number of bank robberies and the number of health food shops in a particular town, giving a scatter similar to that in A, but to look for a relationship would be foolish.

The two factors may not be linked by a direct causal effect, but they may be separate and independent causes of some other behaviour.

Simple steps for setting up a scatter diagram are outlined below:

1. Select the dependent and independent factors. The dependent factor could be a cause from a cause-and-effect diagram, while the independent factor is selected because of its potential relationship with the dependent factor.

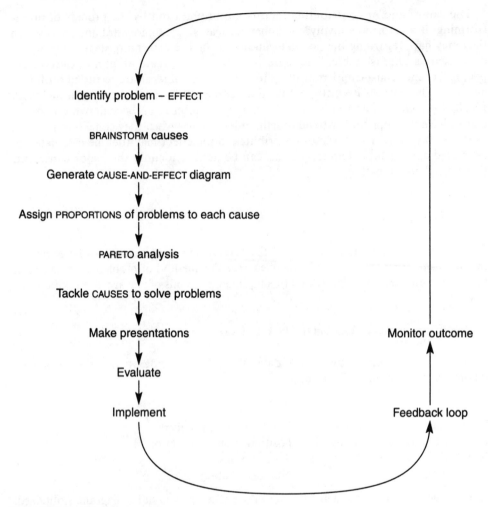

Figure 8.12 *Typical project sequence.*
Source: Oakland (1989)

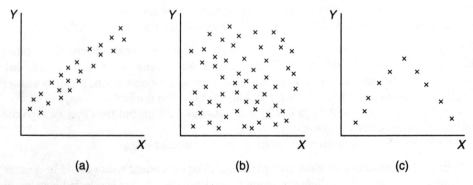

Figure 8.13 *Scatter diagrams.*

2. Either use existing data, or collect the required data.
3. Decide upon the time interval for which the data is going to be collected.
4. Once the data has been collected plot the points on a scatter diagram. Convention says that the independent variable should be plotted on the horizontal axis, while the dependent variable is plotted on the vertical axis.
5. Read and analyse the diagram.

A very simple correlation test may be applied to a scatter diagram for which there are at least seven points plotted. This can be done in the following way:

1. Divide the scatter diagram, in turn, with two lines, one vertical and one horizontal, so that there are an equal number of points on either side of each line.
2. Count the total number of points in each of the four quadrants and add together the numbers falling in diagonally opposite quadrants. This gives two numbers; call the larger N and the smaller n.
3. Apply the test:

Is N greater than $0.6n$?

4. If not, then it is safe to assume that a significant correlation has not been found. If the answer is 'Yes', it is worth proceeding to a full-scale analysis to establish the significance of the correlation. (This type of analysis is beyond the scope of this book.) In the meantime, examine the scatter diagram and ask what the relationship between the two factors means, and how you can make use of this knowledge to aid quality management.

Control charts

For successful quality management it is essential to understand variation and how and why it arises.

In order to determine whether or not a process is in control a series of measurements is taken from the process over a period of time. The results are then grouped into samples of size four to ten ($n = 4$ to 10). A total of 50 individual results, taken over a 'recognized' period of stability, is the minimum requirement for a capability study. The mean and range of each group of five results are calculated and the grand mean of means (process mean $\bar{X}$) is determined, together with the mean of the sample ranges $\bar{R}$.

Mean charts

The means of samples taken from a stable process will vary with each sample taken, but not as much as for the individual results. This is illustrated in Figure 8.14 where it can be seen that the spread of the sample means is much less than the spread of the individual measurements.

In setting up a mean chart, where samples of a given size n are taken from the process over a period when it is thought to be in control, the sample mean is recorded on a control chart. Provided that the sample size is $n = 4$ or more, the mean values will

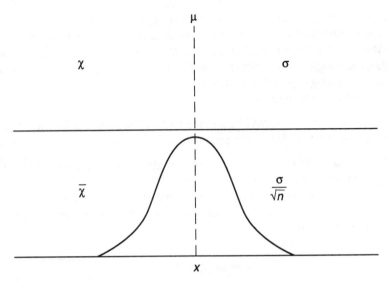

Figure 8.14 *What happens when we take samples of size* n *and plot the means.*

be normally distributed even if the original population itself is not truly normal. The standard deviation of the sample means, called the standard error to avoid confusion with the standard deviation of the parent population, is smaller than the parent standard deviation:

$$\text{standard error of the sample means} = \sigma / \sqrt{n}$$

where σ is the standard deviation of the parent population.

Figure 8.15 shows the principle of the control chart for sample mean. If the process is running in-control, we expect all the means of successive samples to lie between the lines marked upper action (UAL) and lower action (LAL). These are set at a distance equal to $3\sigma/\sqrt{n}$ either side of the process mean. The chance of a mean falling outside either side of these lines is about 1 in 1,000, unless the process has altered. If a point falls outside, this indicates the presence of an assignable cause and the process should be investigated or the setting appropriately adjusted.

Figure 8.15 shows warning limits that have been set at $2\sigma/\sqrt{n}$ either side of the process mean (UWL and LWW). The chance of a sample mean plotting outside either of these limits is about 1 in 40, i.e. it is expected to happen once in every 40 samples. When it does happen, however, there are grounds for suspicion and the usual procedure is to take another sample immediately, before making a definite decision about the setting of the process. Two successive sample means outside one of the warning lines indicate that action should be taken to adjust the process immediately.

In process control of variables, the sample size is usually less than ten, and it becomes possible to use the alternative measure of spread of the process, the mean range of samples $\bar{R}$, to calculate the control chart limits. Use may then be made of Hartley's conversion constant (*dn*) for estimating the process standard deviation: $\sigma = (\bar{R}/dn)$.

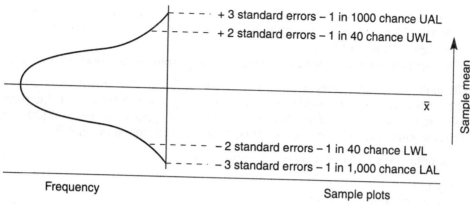

Figure 8.15 showing labels:
+ 3 standard errors – 1 in 1000 chance UAL
+ 2 standard errors – 1 in 40 chance UWL
X̄
– 2 standard errors – 1 in 40 chance LWL
– 3 standard errors – 1 in 1,000 chance LAL
Sample mean
Frequency
Sample plots

Figure 8.15 *The principle of the mean chart.*

Range charts

A process is only in control when both the accuracy (mean) and precision (spread) of the process are in control. A separate chart for control of process variability is required, and the sample standard deviation could be plotted. More conveniently, the ranges of samples are plotted on a range chart which is very similar to the mean chart, the difference between the highest and lowest values in the sample being plotted and compared to predetermined limits.

If a range chart is plotted in conjunction with a mean chart, similar action and warning lines can be drawn to indicate trouble.

Steps for setting up the mean and range charts:

a. Select 20 or so random samples of size n ($n = 4$ to 10).
b. Measure the variable for each of the sample items.
c. Calculate each sample mean and range.
d. Calculate the process mean X and mean range R.
e. Calculate the action and warning lines for the mean and range charts.

The detailed methods and constants for calculation of the control chart limits may be found in *Statistical Process Control* by John Oakland and Roy Followell (1990).

Process 'in control'

Before the charts are used to control the process, the initial data are plotted on the mean and range charts to confirm that the distribution of the individual items is stable. A process is 'in statistical control' when all the variations have been shown to arise from random causes and none attributable to assignable or special causes. The randomness of the variations may be shown by the plotted mean and range charts when there are:

• No mean or range values lying outside the action limits.
• No more than about 1 in 40 values lying between the warning and action limits.

- No incidences of two consecutive mean or range values lying in the same warning zone.
- No runs of more than six sample means or ranges which lie either above or below the average control chart line.
- No more than six values of mean or range which are continuously either rising or falling.

The data plotted on the mean and range charts in Figure 8.16 clearly demonstrate a process which is in control, since all the above requirements are met. If the process examined in this way is not in statistical control, the assignable causes should be ident-ified and eliminated. The process may then be re-examined to test for stability.

Some of the general types of assignable causes are:

People:
Fatigue, illness, state of health
Lack of training/novices
Inadequate supervision, lack of discipline
Lack of knowledge of the requirements
Lack of motivation, attitudes
Changes/improvements in skills

Process/methods:
Changes in inspection/test methods

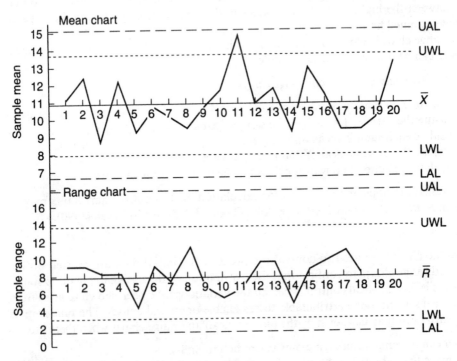

Figure 8.16 *Mean and range charts from samples of* n = 5.
Source: Oakland (1989)

Machines:
Lack of adequate, scheduled preventive maintenance
Badly designed equipment
Worn machinery or tools
Differences in test or measuring devices

Environment
Gradual deterioration in conditions
Seasonal daily, weekly changes
Variations in temperature
Variations of noise

An example: process control applied to absenteeism

Absenteeism can only be measured in terms of two criteria, namely present or absent. It is, therefore, only a case of deciding which decision is appropriate. The sampling process of then governed by the laws of the 'binomial distribution'.

If the proportion of absentees is p, when samples of size n are taken, then the average number of absentees in each sample is np. The control chart for number of absentees, or np chart, operates in a similar way to those for variables, with warning and action lines. These lines are again set by reference to the average and standard deviation of the number of absentees on the samples.

Figure 8.17 shows a control chart for number of absentees (np) for a situation in which the sample size is $n = 20$, and the proportion of absentees is 0.1.

Cusum charts

A cusum (cumulative sum) chart is a type of graph which takes a little longer to draw than the conventional control chart, but which gives a lot more information. It is particularly useful for analysing a trend, and enables the eye to separate true trends and

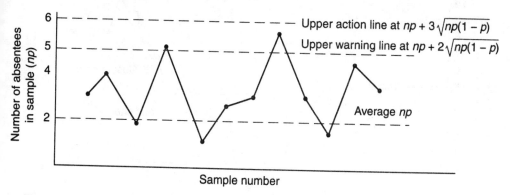

Figure 8.17 *An* np *chart for number of absentees.*

changes from a background of random variation. Cusum charts can detect small changes in data very quickly. In essence, a reference or 'target value' is subtracted from each successive sample observation and the trend results cumulated. Values of this cumulative sum are plotted and 'trend lines' may be drawn on the resulting graphs. If this is approximately horizontal, the value of the variable is about the same as the target value. An overall slope downwards shows a value less than the target, and if the slope is upwards it is greater.

Figure 8.18 shows a comparison of an *np* chart and cusum chart which have been plotted using the same data. The change, which is immediately obvious on the cusum chart, is difficult to detect on a conventional control chart.

> Reducing the variation of key processes about their target values is the primary objective of a quality improvement programme.

The practice of stating specifications in terms of upper and lower limits suggests that the customer is equally satisfied with all values within these limits and is suddenly not satisfied when a value slips outside these limits. In any process there will be a variety of sources of variation which all combine to give the total variation. If it is desirable to reduce variation then the factors which contribute to variation should be measured. A Pareto analysis will enable determination of those factors which account for most of the

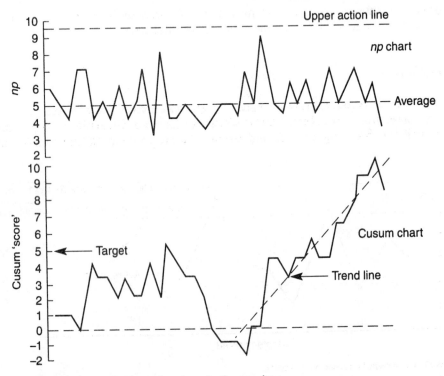

Figure 8.18 *Comparison of cusum and np charts for the same data.*
Source: Oakland (1989)

variation. It will then be necessary to minimize the effects of these contributing factors so that variation can be reduced. In this way the process is refined and the upper and lower limits are adjusted in order to reflect these improvements.

Conclusion

The reader should realize that these particular techniques of statistical process control (SPC) are as applicable to a service organization, such as a school, as they are to a manufacturing organization. In fact they can be applied to any human activity as long as it can be regarded as a process.

All types of process are inherently stable, have random and assignable causes of variation present, have control procedures which add to the variation and have a common objective of perfection. Failure to recognize, investigate and eliminate assignable causes of variation means that they go on needlessly adding to total variation.

Non-conformance occurs when outputs from a process are not what was accepted. Evaluating process capability from existing data leads to the identification of any major problem areas, and introduces the concepts of variation, stability and their management to process operators and managers. Data obtained from processes must be analysed quickly so that continual reduction in the variety of ways of doing things will lead to never-ending improvement.

Other examples of the use to which SPC techniques have been used in 'non-manufacturing' include:

Process capability studies in banks.
Tracking sales and profits in airlines.
Forecasting income.
Activity sampling.
Monitoring absenteeism.
Checking errors on invoices.
Examining injury data.

Summary
All work is a process.
Managing quality is about refining processes.
School processes can be measured.
The aim is to get things right first time, i.e. cut out inspection.
This is achieved by refining operating procedures.
Techniques for doing so are readily available.

Action
Measure the costs of non-conformance.
Analyse work processes in your school and consider ways of improving them.
Determine areas of 'waste', calculate their costs and improve the processes which give rise to such waste.
Analyse your own behaviour in terms of the following:

clarity of the instructions which you give;
the amount of 'hassle' in your life;

the amount of time you spend re-doing work;
the amount of time you spend dealing with problems and complaints.

This chapter is the core of our argument, and if you found it difficult to follow, do go through it again. It is critically important. When you have grasped the principle of variance, and the ways in which this sort of management information may be collected and processed, you will want to know how you might disseminate it through your team of colleagues, and get them to put it to work in the search for continuous improvement of product and process. One possibility is to adapt the Japanese concept of the Quality Circle.

THE QUALITY CIRCLE

Quality circles are a means, developed by Japanese manufacturers such as Toyota in the 1960s, of 'empowering' their workers to involve themselves in continuous improvement activities for the benefit of the whole organization. In more recent years quality circles have been used amongst white-collar workers as well as shop-floor workers.

Groups of workers from a workstation or department are invited, on a voluntary basis, to use one hour per week of company time (or in some cases out of working hours) to identify problems affecting their workstation. These problems may overlap into another workstation, in which case a joint group would be set up to address the problem. In order to be effective in this activity, the workers are first trained to use the tools which we have described in this chapter.

Quality circles have been found to be very successful only where the voluntary principle is followed. Peer-group pressure may well eventually ensure wider participation. The groups are usually permanent, but may vary in membership. The other critical factor, if such groups are to be effective, is that management listen personally to presentations of their findings and recommendations, and then act on them. Where action is totally impossible, management must explain to the group why this is so.

Success is much more likely to be achieved if management institutes the circles solely with a view to developing their workforce's skills and motivation, rather than in the search for financial savings, which should be a by-product of the activity.

It should be noted that it is more difficult to develop quality circles in a white-collar environment, even though it might be supposed that such workers would be more likely to understand the statistical techniques than shop-floor workers. This may be because there exists a stronger tendency to defend established positions and practices, as well as departmental boundaries. On the other hand it may be that this kind of team-work is already well established amongst white-collar workers, and the point of learning these new skills of statistical process control is seen as less relevant to them.

However, there is no reason why this approach should not be attempted in school. Many schools are already collegiate and cooperative in style at line management level, but existing working parties and groups would certainly benefit from training in statistical techniques. Otherwise they will (as Deming stresses), be likely to 'tamper' with the process and conceivably make things worse rather than better. Quality circles should certainly be a useful device to try with technical, ancillary and maintenance workers.

Chapter 9

Statistical Process Control in the Classroom

We need knowledge for the study of variation because we live in a world which is full of variation.

W.E. Deming

So far we have considered the use of statistical process control (SPC) largely in the context of the general management of a school and its resources, human and physical. At this stage we would like to consider the use of SPC in the classroom. How can it help the teacher and pupil in the quest for continuous improvement which must, in our view, be the main objective? All teachers have been in the habit of collecting large volumes of numerical information about the work performance of their pupils. This is no longer just a matter of best professional practice, it is required by law. The National Curriculum, Standard Attainment Tests and Pupil Records of Achievement have produced what many teachers see as an information and bureaucratic overload. This requirement to collect and collate vast amounts of information would be less of an irritation to them if it could be seen to have an educational purpose. At present it does not appear to do so.

Our contention is that this information could be used by teachers and pupils as a vital component in our quest for continuous improvement. This is the message from both Theresa Hicks in Ohio and Larrae Rocheleau in Alaska. Deming taught us the critical importance of gathering, processing and analysing data. The identification of special and common causes of variance is the first step towards improvement of both 'product' and process. From the teacher's point of view, the identification of the causes of variance both of her class and of the individual pupils within it is the first step towards helping individuals overcome their particular problems. The teacher and her colleagues may use the data in order to reduce the common causes of variance in the system, the process by which they deliver and monitor their course materials.

At present the information about pupil performance is usually collected in the form of raw data – marks for test work done at home or in class. The processing and analysis of these data rarely go beyond the calculation of termly or yearly percentage marks, and the construction of a rank order of pupils by 'merit'. Where several sets are doing parallel work, a matrix may be constructed to demonstrate the relative performance of sets and also of teachers. In schools where external examinations are undertaken, departments are likely to be required to summarize performance of sets, and the whole group. These data are usually expressed in terms of percentages obtaining each grade, A, A plus B, A plus B plus C, and percentage pass rate. In the UK this information is now used to construct national league tables for both state and independent schools. It may also be used at internal level for inquests into the performance of a department and its members. This may be a very threatening process since it takes no account of special causes of variance. Analysis of results over a long period of years is rarely undertaken. Outcomes may be used to scapegoat unfairly and lay blame in order to sharpen up performance next time. This is a classic example of 'driving by fear', and is in line with the classic Taylorian 'scientific management' styles that have wrecked British industry.

The impact of this approach to data is damaging not only for the teacher and his morale, but also for the pupil. It amounts to what I have referred to elsewhere as 'the tyranny of the normal curve', which dominates the examination system in the UK. More stress is laid on the identification of the rank order of merit than the standards actually achieved. In other words, the first objective is to label 25 per cent as failures. This is done constantly through a child's life. Is it any surprise that so many pupils fall by the wayside having undergone such a negative experience in school?

We feel that the information can be used in a more constructive and positive way for the benefit of both teacher and pupil. In Chapter 8 we identified a number of statistical techniques which might be useful, and which are non-threatening even to the non-mathematician. These were:

Process flowcharting	**What is done?**
Tally sheets	**How often is it done?**
Histograms	**What do variations in performance look like?**
Pareto analysis	**What are the big problems?**
Scatter diagrams/correlation	**What are the relationships between the factors?**
Control charts	**Which variations from the norm should we control and why?**
Fishbone diagrams	**What causes the big problems?**
Cusum charts	**How should we chart continuous improvement?**

Some of these techniques may help us to be more effective as teachers, and our pupils to be more effective as learners. It should also improve morale of both teacher and pupils. We would now like to consider some ways in which the sort of information which we collect as a matter of course might be put to constructive use. The data used here are all 'real' information drawn from the experience of one of the present authors (M.S.G.) in running a large (mainly sixth form) department over a period of thirty years.

HISTORICAL ANALYSIS: THE PERFORMANCE OF BRADFORD GRAMMAR SCHOOL CANDIDATES IN A-LEVEL ECONOMICS, 1966–92, AND BUSINESS STUDIES 1990–92

The purpose of this exercise is to identify trends over the long term in the performance of Bradford Grammar School's Economics and Business Studies Department. The same approach could be used to analyse the long-term performance of a whole school, or to produce comparative statistics for several departments. Once trends are identified, it is possible to seek reasons for any change in trend for better or worse. It is also possible to make comparisons with national trends, or with world-class schools which you are 'benchmarking' as examples of best practice. On this basis it may be possible to set attainable targets for improvement in the next time period as part of a continuous improvement programme.

The basic data for this analysis are taken from departmental records over the period 1966–92. These data are set out in Tables 9.1 to 9.3 and are expressed graphically using statistical process control methods in Figures 9.1 to 9.6. The following conclusions may be drawn from examination of the data.

1. That an improvement occurred between 1966 and 1973, provided that we assume that there was no lowering of the national marking standards during that period.
2. That during the period 1987–92 this improvement continued.
3. That throughout both periods performance exceeded national norms, as is to be expected in a highly selective school.
4. That by applying upper and lower control limits for the period 1987–92, it can be demonstrated that the pass rate (E grade and above) was in statistical control, but that possibly 'special' causes led to wide variations in the percentage of A, and A plus B, and A plus B plus C.
5. That in two years out of the six, performance was well above our own norm, whilst in one year it was somewhat below. This is obviously to be expected. In any data of this kind, there will be a distribution of 50 per cent above the average, and 50 per cent below.

Table 9.1 *Comparative analysis of 1991/1992 A level Business Studies*

	1991	1992	Diff
A	20%	38%	+18%
A/B	70%	69%	−1%
A/B/C	90%	85%	−5%
A/E	100%	100%	=

On limited evidence the 'process' for producing A level Business Studies would appear to be in statistical control. Our attempts to remedy the 1991 'problem' of insufficient A grades would appear to have been successful.

Table 9.2 *Comparative analysis of Economics Department results 1966/73 mean against 1987/92 mean against 1992*

	1966/73		1987/92		1992
A	18%	(+9%)	27%	(+17%)	44%
A/B	41%	(+12%)	53%	(+24%)	77%
A/B/C	54%	(+20%)	74%	(+13%)	87%
A/E	80%	(+14%)	94%	(+4%)	98%

Our efforts over a long period to produce 'continuous improvement' in A level Economics results would appear to be successful, with a 'process' which is again in statistical control.

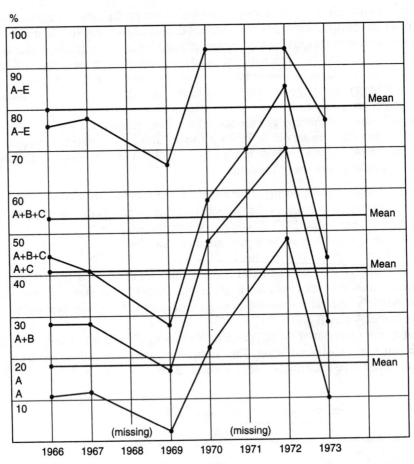

Figure 9.1 *A level Economics results, 1966-73 (slow streams only for 1973). This time series graph suggests that in term of A to E passes, the process is in statistical control. The percentage of passes at A, A + B, A + B + C are more prone to variation. This is explained by 'special' causes: for example, (a) 1969 was a very weak cohort of students; (b) 1972 was a very strong cohort of students; (c) in 1973 entry to the sixth form was from 'slow' streams only because on abolition of 'accelerated' streams that year.*

Table 9.3 *The best four years between 1966 and 1992*

	1972	1980	1990	1992	Mean 4 best years
A	49%	50%	40%	44%	46%
A/B	70%	75%	74%	77%	74%
A/B/C	86%	85%	87%	87%	86%
A/E	94%	100%	97%	98%	97%
Oxbridge	8	6	11	6	(+2 1993)

The occurrence of unusually good years at random intervals suggests 'special' causes at work; possible causes might be exceptionally high ability intakes, or some aberration in marking procedures by the Board.

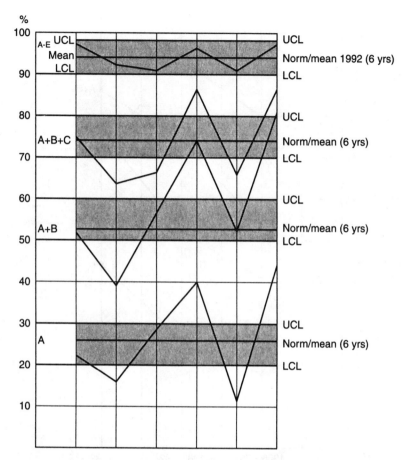

Figure 9.2 *A level Economics results, 1987–91. The shaded areas indicate acceptable performance band, and the thick lines indicate the upper control limit (UCL) and the lower control limit (LCL). More recent data suggest that the process is more tightly under statistical control, particularly A to E pass rate. As before, the higher grades are much more subject to the effects of 'special' causes.*

The 'common' causes of variance are usually variations in the academic ability of the intake of students, since the performance of the whole school cohort year on year suggests that some 66 per cent of the cohort are capable of A or B grades at A level. The distribution of this most able section of the cohort between subjects will vary from year to year, but seems in most years to break unevenly, with a majority taking Science A level courses. In the occasional year when the majority of most able pupils head for the Arts side, Economics results tend to peak. More detailed analysis of this hypothesis might have been undertaken on an added-value basis, correlating GCSE points score with A-level results on scatter diagrams.

If the GCSE points score of candidates for A level Economics is below the school average by say 20 per cent, then it would be expected that scores in A-level Economics would be 20 per cent worse than the school average. If they are not worse to that degree, then it could be that either Arts subjects are easier than sciences, or teaching methods in

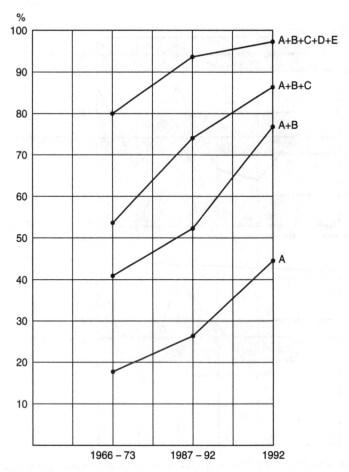

Figure 9.3 *Continuous long-term improvement of pass rates (unless it is to be argued that A level standards have been steadily falling).*

the Economics Department are better than average. If the results at A level are worse than the GCSE score suggests, then either Economics is harder than sciences, or teaching methods in the Economics Department are less effective than in other departments. In this case some action is required. This would be especially true if this pattern of results was apparent over several years.

The use of histograms and frequency distribution curves for grades in comparison with national averages, other things being equal, provides a useful measure of performance. It may suggest areas in which improvement might be sought. It is also possible to 'target' performance levels against which an improvement programme may be monitored. For this department in this school, a reasonable 'target' may be identified from Figures 9.5 and 9.6 as being 'To achieve 100 per cent A plus B grades in A level Economics and Business Studies'. This is fine so long as we see this as a journey direction, not an immediate goal; there are ways in which the target might be reached which are the antithesis of good educational practice, and unethical. For example, one could exclude from the course

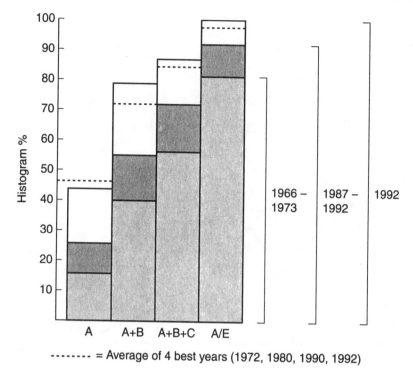

------- = Average of 4 best years (1972, 1980, 1990, 1992)

Figure 9.4 *Long-term performance of the department as shown by A level results. The histogram demonstrates the same point as Figure 9.3.*

all applicants who have not reached a GCSE score which suggests on past data that they are 90 per cent capable of reaching grades A or B at A level.

Conclusions of analysis of Economics Department data

1. The pass rate is in statistical control in the range 94–98 per cent (national average 75–80 per cent). It is unlikely that much can be done to improve this, short of refusing to enter candidates who appear likely to fail.
2. The percentage of candidates obtaining grade A for Economics is 27 per cent, which is 15 points above the national average and (on a much shorter sample period) in Business Studies the rate is 25 per cent above the national average. It is again unlikely that this can be pushed much higher without erecting barriers to entry to the course.
3. The biggest area of potential improvement is by seeking to improve the performance of the 15 to 30 per cent of candidates who score grades C, D or E.

    The point of this analysis is not to establish the degree to which this school is performing above the national average – it should be doing so. Rather the point is to establish where in this department is the most room for improvement. It seems that we should seek new and better ways to teach basic principles of the subject, and exam techniques, to the minority who end up with middling grades.

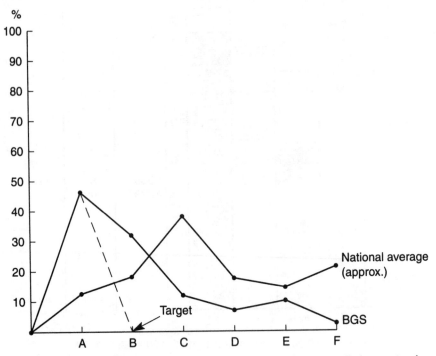

Figure 9.5 *A level grades, Economics, 1992. Skewed distribution = performance well above national average. But, is it better than (a) school average, or (b) best UK school average? The target must be to bring C, D, E candidates up to B grade standard, i.e. 100 per cent A + B.*

STRATEGY FOR AN IMPROVEMENT PROGRAMME

We have used historical data to establish where there is room for improvement in this department of the school. We have decided that, given the highly selective nature of the school, too high a percentage of our A level Economics candidates are scoring grades C, D or E. This may then be a symptom of something wrong with professional practice in the department. We need to consider what it might be that needs changing. In Figure 9.7 we have generated an Ishikawa cause-and-effect (fishbone) diagram containing as many possibilities as we could think of.

We should now consider areas which could be brought under control, and improved by the head of department and his team in the short term. There will be some factors which may be important, but over which the team has no control (management creates the system). These clearly include the following:

- Student basic ability levels.
- The physical facilities available to the department (which are not ideal).
- The timetabling system in operation.
- Textbooks available. If they are inadequate this can be remedied by the head of department provided he has sufficient funds.

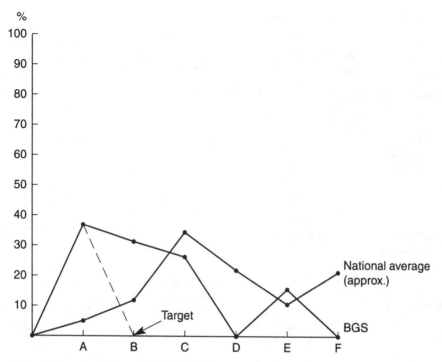

Figure 9.6 *A level grades, Business Studies, 1992. The same comments apply as to Figure 9.5. The two figures illustrate the relationship between the performance of this school's entry and the national average in the two subjects. The relationship is as would be expected given the highly selective nature of the school. The data are, however, useful in indicating the area where improvement might be sought, i.e. raising the performance of candidates in the 'middle' ability range who tend to score C, D or E to a more acceptable B grade.*

- Wrong teaching methods. This can be remedied. It would be possible to review techniques which have proved especially effective with the middle ability range, and increase their use. This might be, for example, self-teaching via computer program.
- Weak analytical skills. This may be remedied by greater attention to developing better ways of teaching basic theoretical concepts.
- Low skill levels. More individual attention may help here, as will an increase in the number of practice exercises set and monitored.
- Lack of organizational and time management skills in the students. It may be possible to help in this area be offering well-tried tricks, and suggesting and making available suitable reading matter.
- Lack of motivation. This is perhaps the commonest problem, and the most intractable. Only patient attention to individual student needs, combined with a supportive attitude, will help. The use of positive secondary reinforcement by encouragement and praise for right responses will work better than carping criticisms and punishment regimes. If an atmosphere of team-work in the group is developed, stronger students will help weaker ones, who will then be less likely to lose heart and give up.

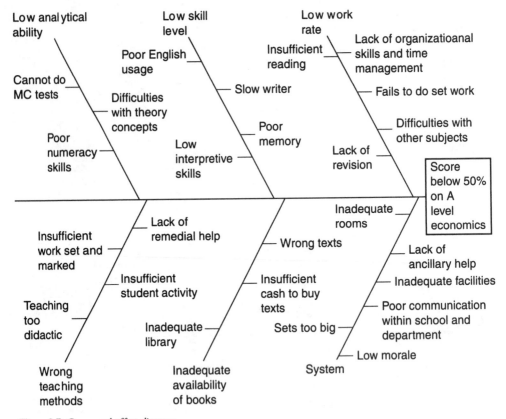

Figure 9.7 *Cause-and-effect diagram.*

- Variability of performance of teachers within the department.
- Effects of change in departmental personnel.
- Effects of excessively large sets (above 13 pupils).
- Weaknesses in planning and delivery of the course.
- Poor communications within department.

All of these may be addressed by the head of department and his team. If possible, a Pareto analysis should be used to identify the most persistent problem. This should be the first to be tackled by the team.

There may well be special causes of variance which are outside the control of either the head of department and his team, or the senior management team. These may cause variation around the long-term trend. These might be:

- Variations in the difficulty of the exam set by the Board.
- Variations in the quality of the national intake of students into this subject, which may make it appear that our results are worse than they actually are.
- Variations, accidental or deliberate, in the marking standards of the Boards.
- Politically induced shifts of grade boundaries.

We cannot influence these factors, but we should be watching out for them when conducting long-term analysis of results.

Statistical process control and classroom management

The argument in this chapter so far has centred around the use of SPC as a tool for senior management (headteachers) or middle or line management (heads of department). The aim was to look at ways in which long-term trends might be established in the quantifiable aspects of school performance, with a view to seeking to establish a programme of continuous improvement. We now need to examine ways in which the classroom teacher might use SPC to improve his own performance, and that of his pupils.

Our example in this case is a group of 16-year-old boys, studying GCSE Economics in the fourth and fifth years. This is an optional course which is only available to the 'bottom band' pupils (i.e. less able) in a very academic school. It competes with Latin, Biology, German, Technology and Art, and inevitably picks up some of the weakest and least motivated students. In this particular experimental group, 33 per cent were to produce an overall GCSE result amongst the worst five in the year in the group.

In the opinion of the teacher the supposed weakness of the group lay at least as much in motivation as in ability. Low motivation was the result of a sense of failure after being at the bottom of the year group for four years, a classic case of the 'labelling effect'. Yet all had successfully passed a very difficult entrance exam at 11 years, and should be in the top 20 per cent by ability of their cohort over the whole district. In some cases this problem of motivation was compounded by disciplinary problems, and problems at home. It is of course not clear which came first.

In an attempt to create a climate in which the pupils felt that they were capable of improved performance, and were making progress as the year went on, the teacher decided to use a combined control and cusum chart. This is illustrated in Figures 9.9, 9.10 and 9.11 which were created from the raw data in Figure 9.8. Each pupil had his own chart, and all ten were permanently displayed on the noticeboard. Two examples are shown here, for the strongest and weakest members of the group. The chart begins from the score obtained in the summer exam at the end of the fourth year. From there on, each month's accumulated test scores are added to the percentage score at the end of the previous month, and the chart is then marked up to date. The mark for the mock exam in March is entered separately in order to indicate where exam techniques might be a problem.

The purposes of the charts were as follows:

- Both teacher and pupils were able to *see* the degree of progress made, and to spot any adverse change of trend in order to take remedial action.
- It was hoped that pupils would be motivated by signs of progress to seek further improvement. They could see how they were performing in relation to each other, and national standards. They actually found the exercise great fun.
- The teacher was enabled accurately to forecast probable outcomes of the year's work.
- The pupil was enabled to set himself an attainable target grade.
- They provided useful information for discussion with parents at the parents' evening in January.
- The teacher received a greater sense of control over the process by using more effectively the raw data collected as a matter of course in his mark book.
- By plotting the average score for the group at the same time, the teacher was able to establish whether the process was in statistical control.

5ths GCSE Economics	Student: student no	Test Set: 1. Production DR	Estimated grade 9/9/91	2. Public spending DR	3. Taxation DR	4. M/C Pub spending/Tax	Cusum % score (Oct)	Est. grade (1/2 term)	5. Money	6. Money	7. Banking	8. Saving	Cusum % score (Nov)	Estimated grade	Rank order	9. Inflation	10. Inflation/Unemployment	11. Unemployment	Cusum % score (Dec)	Estimated grade	12. Protection/Free trade
		20		20	25	20	%	est	20	20	20	20	%	est	pos/10	20	20	20	%	est	20
Names omitted	1	12	C	13	14	18	67	B	8	17	14	15	73	A	5	9	13	14	67	A	15
	2	13	C	10	16	17	66	B	6	6	9	15	62	B	8	6	5	10	51	C	13
	3	15	B	14	15	17	72	B+	12	17	16	17	81	A	2	14	13	12	72	A	13
	4	12	C	16	17	17	73	B+	8	16	17	17	79	A	3	14	12	11	71	A	19
	5	11	C	10	ND	15	42	E	11	12	12	14	55	C	10	13	15	7	60	B	6
	6	14	B	10	9	21	63	B	5	9	18	13	65	B	7	20	16	11	66	B	13
	7	19	A	13	16	20	80	A	11	11	18	17	83	A	1	16	ND	8	75	A	17
	8	18	A	16	11	18	74	B+	9	14	16	16	78	A	4	ND	17	8	72	A	14
	9	13	C	15	17	11	66	B	3	8	19	13	66	B	6	8	ND	12	60	B	ND
	10	12	C	9	11	10	49	D	8	10	14	16	57	C	9	8	6	9	51	C	3

This material is reproduced direct from the teacher's mark book

Figure 9.8 *Typical raw data from a teacher's mark book.*

13. Exchange rates (20)	Cusum % score (Jan) (%)	14. Bal. of payments (20)	15. Bal. of payments (20)	16. M/C test 1988 (40)	17. M/C test 1989 (40)	Cusum % score (Feb) (%)	Exam paper 1 M/choice (40)	paper II (100)	Exam % (%)	Rank order (pos/10)	Coursework (1) (25)	Coursework (2) (25)	Overall exam % (%)	Rank order (pos)	18. D/R test 1988 (20)	19. D/R test 1989 (20)	20. Trade unions (20)	21. Income/Wealth (20)	Cusum % score (Mar) (%)	Rank order	Estimated grade (est)	22. D/R test 1990 (20)	23. D/R test Business (20)	Cusum % score (April) (%)	24. M/C test 1990 (40)	Estimated grade	Actual grade	Plus/minus
13	71	12	19	28	26	66	31	52	62	4=	19	21	64	4=	nd	11	17	13	70	3	A	20	11	72	35	A	A	=
5	53	11	9	19	27	51	26	39	45	10	9	12	46	10	10	9	nd	8	49	9	D	16	nd	54	31	D	D	=
8	75	20	14	32	34	74	29	64	65	3	14	16	67	3	13	15	16	13	72	2	A	14	16	73	36	B	A	+1
13	57	20	15	30	29	70	36	68	75	1	19	22	77	1	9	14	19	14	77	1	A	20	13	74	33	A	A	=
3	53	6	9	26	27	55	25	61	60	6	10	16	59	6=	6	15	12	11	51	8	C	10	9	53	28	C	C	=
5	69	14	19	32	32	68	31	73	72	2	15	13	74	2	12	13	15	10	67	4	B	17	13	67	37	B	B	=
13	79	18	12	30	29	73	31	52	58	7	12	18	59	6=	10	10	nd	9	66	5	B	18	13	60	37	B	B	=
6	77	11	9	29	20	66	30	56	62	4=	14	16	64	4=	10	13	nd	12	57	7	C/B	16	13	64	32	B	B	=
12	64	13	13	27	27	61	28	48	54	8	11	17	54	8	5	10	nd	11	58	6	C	14	8	48	28	C	C	=
3	48	9	9	30	14	47	23	38	47	9	14	17	49	9	9	2	nd	10	44	10	D	16	10	47	27	D	D	=

Figure 9.8 *Continued.*

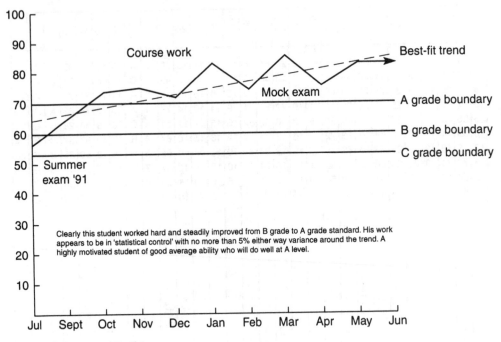

Figure 9.9 *Progress of Pupil 4.*

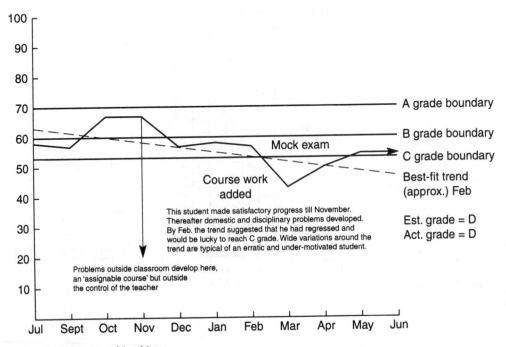

Figure 9.10 *Progress of Pupil 2.*

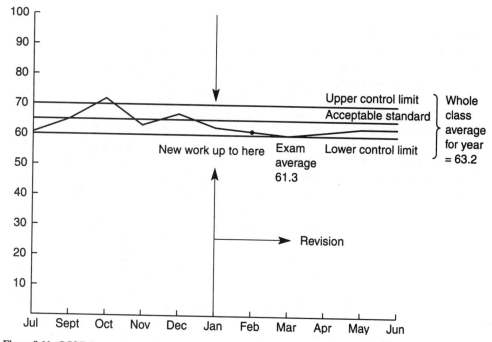

Figure 9.11 *GCSE Economics results. An average of 65% – midway between A and B boundaries – is acceptable. On this basis the process appears to be under 'statistical control' for the group as a whole, but not necessarily for individuals within the group.*

This experimental programme proved to be very useful and effective, and will now be extended to A-level students, who will, however, be invited to maintain their own records.

The accuracy of the final forecasts of grade outcomes which were derived from this exercise reflects in part the manner in which the data was collected as much as the way it was used.

- All test materials used were from past papers of the Board to be used.
- All tests were unseen, and done in supervised conditions, against the clock.
- All marking was against the Board's criteria, or where available, marking schemes.
- The mock exam was the previous year's paper in its entirety.

The advantage to the student of the use of this sort of cusum chart is that he knows exactly where he stands, and cannot harbour any illusions about his prospects. He is made aware of the amount of work he needs to do to reach his personal and realistic target grades.

As it stands, the charts cannot tell the student *what* he needs to do to reach his target. It is however possible to elicit clues from the raw data in consultation with the teacher. The pupil may himself be able to offer 'special' causes of variation of which only he could be aware. For example, a pupil who has weakness in Maths may at some point start to have extra tuition in that subject, at the expense of the time allocated to Economics. Another may have been advised to drop one of his subjects, and so have more time to spend on Economics. Another might have been traumatized by the serious illness of a parent, or by the divorce of parents. From the data themselves the teacher may be able to elicit reasons for variance which stem from within the process, i.e. are 'common' causes. These might include, for example, a point in the course where new material proves to be particularly difficult for some but not all students; or, when revision of a particular skill is being undertaken, a particular pupil may find this extremely difficult.

In our examples Pupil no. 4 has obvious problems with two topics, inflation and unemployment. He also performs erratically on data response questions. In the latter case closer examination may reveal that it is numerical stimulus material, rather than verbal, which causes problems. We were able to point the student to specific material to improve his understanding of the two topics, and give him appropriate extra practice on data response questions on those topics. The whole exercise was also helpful in advising the student as to whether to study Economics or Business Studies in the sixth form. He chose the latter.

In the case of Pupil no. 2, performance was clearly erratic in all sections of the course. It is, however, clear that certain specific sections of the course caused particular difficulty. These were those on money and the financial services sector, inflation and exchange rates. The overall impression developed as the year progressed that when he put in some time and effort, he could cope with the course, but that he lacked motivation. This would seem to be a 'special' cause of variance so far as the teacher is concerned, but to be a 'common' cause (i.e. stemming from overall school system) when seen in a wider context. Clearly the pastoral care and disciplinary system had failed to pick up and deal with problems outside the direct control of the school. Arguably the school had failed the pupil, not the other way round.

At the end of the year, Pupil no. 4 obtained very good passes overall, including an A grade in Economics, whilst Pupil no. 2 failed four out of the eight subjects attempted. He reached only a D grade (fail) in Economics. The notable thing is that both he and no. 4 started the year at the same point on the chart, and in the teacher's view they were roughly equivalent in natural ability. This outcome should remind us of the limitations of SPC in the classroom. We are working not with stable 'raw material', but with volatile human beings. Some special causes of variance will be outside the control of the teacher, and are in fact 'common' causes when the whole school is seen as a system or process. The 'common' causes of variation within the one classroom are sometimes, perhaps always, outside the control of the class teacher (for example, poor classroom conditions, or lack of textbooks, ancillary help, materials, etc.). This is the reason why SPC can be fully effective as a tool for the achievement of continuous improvement only if it is adopted by senior management for use in the school itself as a system, or process. The single teacher can nevertheless make use of these techniques as we have shown, even if the school has not 'bought' the Total Quality paradigm.

We hope that you will be encouraged to experiment in your classroom, remembering that Theresa Hick in the USA has used these same techniques successfully with 8-year-olds. One cautionary note should be added. Remember Deming's hatred of ranking and grading. Emphasize always to your students that they are *not* competing against each other, but collaborating to improve against some absolute standard, despite the requirements constantly laid on us by authority to rank and grade our students.

Chapter 10

Planning for Quality

Institute a vigorous programme of education and self improvement. Remove barriers to peoples' right to pride in workmanship.

W.E. Deming

A brief training course along the lines outlined in this book should convince all, or at least key management personnel, of the vital importance of a quality culture. It is to be hoped that the obvious commitment of senior staff, and especially the headteacher, to the TQM principle will reinforce and sustain this conviction. The question then is what is the next step forward? We have to find some way of reinforcing the commitment in principle, without a Quality Improvement Programme becoming just another bandwagon to be climbed on by the ambitious, and cynically dismissed by the old pros. The answer must be a systematic quality programme which is not overwhelmingly bureaucratic and time consuming, and is fun. It must also bring to light quite quickly and dramatically some quantifiable evidence that it is worth doing, from the point of view of both the teachers in the front line and the customers – the children.

Deming remarked that 'what gets measured, gets done'. It does not really matter where you start, but the more important the 'problem' is that is tackled, the more likely are the results to spark off enthusiasm for a wider-ranging programme to develop a quality system. What matters most for the external 'customer' is results. The introduction of SATs throughout the school age range, combined with GCSE and A-level results, has provided a mass of raw data, which has been seized on by the media. The government has insisted on a legal requirement that schools publish results, the aim being to enable parents to exercise a more informed choice of school for their children, thus forcing schools to respond to the pressures of the market-place to succeed or go under. The effect has been the production in the media of 'league tables' of A level results, compiled in an unscientific fashion by the media. Schools have been frightened into thinking more carefully about what might be revealed or concealed by different means of measuring results. The concept of 'added value' has emerged as a means by which initial differences in the quality of raw material may be discounted in the attempt to produce a more accurate representation of a school's success or failure to serve its customers well.

The positive effect of this pressure to quantify results in a meaningful way has been apparent in one or two institutions. Being obliged to think about ways of measuring performance in a school is perhaps the first step to recognizing that it is essential to measure 'the costs of quality'.

A school is not a factory, but there are identifiable 'costs of quality' in the 'production process', producing 'waste scrap and rework', just as might be seen in an old-fashioned factory. There is no reason why the approach to measurement of quality costs used in industry cannot be adapted for use in a school. Moreover it is generally recognized by quality gurus that there is much more waste to be found in the service and non-production functions of a manufacturing business. According to Philip Atkinson, as many as 80 per cent of problems in manufacturing sector businesses are to be found in non-production areas like sales or accounts. In a manufacturing business as much as 25 per cent of turnover may be found to be wasted; in a service sector business the figure may rise to as much as 40 per cent. A little mental arithmetic will quickly show that in an average-sized secondary school with a turnover (budget or fee income) of £1.5 million, we are talking about releasing for more productive use anything up to £500,000. A saving of this magnitude would give a school an enormous advantage over its competitors, and allow it to deliver a much richer curriculum.

Example of saving via costs of quality

Take a small organization with a turnover of £1 million
Suppose it makes a profit of 10 per cent after tax
If the costs of quality are 20 per cent of turnover
Profits in year 1 are £100,000
Reduce costs of quality, via a Quality Improvement Programme, by 50 per cent
This saves £100,000
Thus the Quality Improvement Programme has had the same impact on profit as
DOUBLING TURNOVER

Do not be put off by the reference to 'profit', which you may have seen as an unjustified surplus extracted on the backs of the workers by greedy capitalists. It is much more sensible to see profit as Tom Peters does, as 'the price of staying in business'. By this he means that profit is needed, not just to satisfy shareholders by rewarding them for risking their capital, but as the means by which the business is able to to invest in its future. Perhaps at this point we should apply this reasoning to a school example?

Savings in a school via costs of quality: Case A

Take an independent (day) school of 1,000 pupils, charging fees of £3,000 per annum
It has no endowment income, and no access to government funds
Refurbishment and development have to be undertaken out of fee income
Major building programmes are undertaken out of funds raised through appeals to parents and old pupils. Now apply the same reasoning as before
Turnover of fee income £3 million per annum
Surplus for contingencies 10 per cent
Surplus available for development in year 1 is £300,000

Costs of quality are 20 per cent of turnover
Reduce costs of quality by 50 per cent
Saves £300,000
THIS LEAVES AS MUCH IN THE DEVELOPMENT FUND AS YOU WOULD HAVE HAD WITH
TWICE AS MANY PUPILS, OR FEES AT DOUBLE PRESENT LEVELS

This might well convince the doubting Thomas in an independent school, but what of the average maintained school?

Savings via costs of quality: Case B

Total budget funds under LMS of say £400,000 for a school of 200 pupils
Surplus in year 1 is zero
Costs of quality 20 per cent
Reduce costs of quality by 50 per cent
Savings £40,000

The figures are less dramatic at a glance, but even more important in their impact in the school. Suddenly you do not need to do without two part-time teachers, a replacement computer, and repairs to the leaking roof. You have enough to deal with all these problems.

The truth is that a school cannot afford to ignore the costs of quality. But so far you are not convinced that the figures make sense. Is it possible to make savings of this magnitude? Surely you have already made every economy possible in order to survive? Is it possible that there are serious amounts of saving which can be achieved?

In Chapter 8 we have indicated some of the kinds of 'costs' of quality which may be identified, quantified and eliminated. Also in Chapter 2 we have looked at one or two real cases of schools which have pioneered this approach. What we are trying to do now is to convince you of the need for a Quality Improvement Programme, and indicate how you might plan for quality – incidentally, not just for mercenary reasons but because it is important for its own sake.

There will always be people who will find reasons why a Quality Programme will fail. Recent research work suggested that of UK companies which have introduced a Quality Programme, only 20 per cent have achieved success.

The search for quality is a never-ending process, not something which is done once then forgotten about. This is why we have stressed (as does Atkinson) the importance of culture change. It is not enough to have an impressive system in place which becomes an end in itself. Quality must be a 'mission' for all members of the organization. Excessive concentration on the system, and number crunching, may be dangerous. It can lead to inter-departmental competition and just the kind of defensive and uncooperative behaviour which we are trying to eliminate.

Your programme for the introduction of a quality system must be planned with the same precision which you would apply to planning a new £1 million building. You may want to use a GANNT chart, or even Critical Path Analysis to aid the planning process. Whatever you use, the plan must both structure your efforts and inspire continued commitment. It will also help if you bear in mind Atkinson's seven S's:

The seven S's		
Hard S	Strategy Structure Systems	can be changed *without* effect unless
Soft S	Staff Skills Shared values	you have in place the soft s

At this point perhaps we should remind ourselves of the key features of the quality culture which we are trying to put in place, partly through our quality system, but without which our quality system will certainly fail.

A quality culture

Management must stop allocating blame
Management must lead by example/celebrate success
Management must empower people/encourage champions
People must be self-directed
Middle managers must become coaches and facilitators, not bosses
Customer requirements come first, every time
Manage horizontally/flatten the hierarchy

If once your quality system is in place, and to your astonishment you find that it is breaking down, these are the reasons why it has happened:

Reasons for failure of a quality programme

Fear of the unknown/and of retribution for failure
Loss of control/security
Personal sense of inadequacy
Past resentments and barriers
Fear of commitment to more work
Cynicism about top-down reforms
Lack of commitment from the top

The last of these is the most likely reason for failure. Of course there will be setbacks, as is confirmed by the experience of all organizations who have taken this step forward. Leadership commitment from the top is vital at key points on what Atkinson calls the 'transition curve' (Figure 10.1).

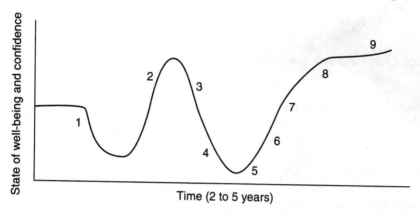

1 = Shock
2 = Denial
3 = Strong emotion
4 = Frustration
5 = Acceptance
6 = Frustration
7 = Experimentation
8 = Fuller understanding
9 = Integration

Figure 10.1 *Transition curve.*
Source: Atkinson (1990)

Now we have seen why we must have a quality programme, and looked at some of the possible pitfalls of the journey, we can go on to develop a model for a system which might be applied in a school.

QUALITY SYSTEMS: A MODEL FOR SCHOOLS

A quality system for a school should contain two elements:

1. A system to ensure that the organization carries out its function of delivering all aspects of 'education services' to its immediate customers – parent and child – and its external customers – employers and institutions of higher and further education. It must ensure that every department within the organization is aware of the imperative need to deliver a quality service to all its internal customers.
2. On a second level, the system must be developed to ensure that a consistent approach is taken by all teachers to the delivery of a quality service to their pupils. It

must also be capable of creating a culture of 'continuous improvement' in the minds of all pupils. This aspect is dealt with separately in Chapter 8.

In fulfilling element 1 above, a number of elements must be in place.

Key elements of a quality system

1. A quality policy
2. An appropriate organizational structure
3. A quality system
4. Regular customer surveys
5. An appropriate curriculum design
6. A minimal documentary system

A quality policy

This constitutes a restatement in quality terms of the school's perceived mission. It may be produced as a separate document, or be incorporated in a well-produced replacement for the school prospectus. Such a document should contain the following:

a. A restatement of the mission, e.g. 'to provide an education based on academic excellence, but catering for the needs of the whole person'.
b. A clarification of the meaning of the term 'quality' e.g. 'satisfying the educational and personal needs of the child in every respect'.
c. A statement of quality intent, e.g. 'to promote continuous improvement in every aspect of educational provision'.

We have included in Figure 10.2 an example of such a quality policy statement, which happens to be the one produced by British Steel's Middlesbrough plant. We have then adapted it into a form which might be used by a school. The purpose of such a document is to pronounce to all members of the organization and its customers a firm pledge by headteacher and governors of their commitment to the quality ideal. It is, if you like, a statement of belief in a set of values.

An appropriate organizational structure

We are accustomed in the UK to organizations, whether public or private sector, which have a steep organizational structure, with many layers, and a directive top-down communication system. This model owes much to the experience of the military over several hundred years, and to Weber's late-nineteenth-century model for bureaucratic organization for public sector activities. Figure 10.3 shows an example of this sort of model in an educational context. This form of organizational structure is totally inappropriate for the model which we are trying to develop.

In total contrast we offer an example of best practice from the world of business. This is a small Japanese-owned textile company in West Yorkshire, called Minova textiles.

Teesside Works TQP Objective

Teesside Works will be a profitable, efficient and ENVIRONMENTALLY AWARE innovative leader in the international volume steel market.

Our aim is to provide all customers, internal and external, with quality products and services and to strive for continuous improvement.

This will be achieved through harnessing the capabilities of safety conscious, high calibre, technically aware and well trained employees.

**Teesside Works
TQP Objective**

The key words of the Objective have been chosen carefully as being essential in the maintenance and improvement of Teesside Works as a successful business both now and in the future.

We all know what it means to be non-profitable – a business will die without the means to pay wages, purchase raw materials and services and to INVEST in new plant and equipment.

Only by operating in the most COST EFFECTIVE way will we be able to produce the necessary PROFITS.

We must continually strive to break into NEW products and designs and forever search for BETTER methods and equipment.

We have proved we can be the BEST in many of the things that we do – we need to be WORLD LEADERS in all aspects of our business.

Whilst our home market is essential for our continued success, our export orders are VITAL to us achieving the VOLUME of business necessary for the EFFICIENT operation of our plants.

Without EXTERNAL CUSTOMERS we have no business at all – our objective must be to CONTINUALLY satisfy AGREED Customer requirements at all times.

We can only satisfy our EXTERNAL CUSTOMERS if everyone at Teeside Works makes sure that our INTERNAL CUSTOMERS can rely on QUALITY service and products.

If we stand still there is nothing so certain that our COMPETITORS will catch and pass us. We can only avoid that happening by CONTINUALLY IMPROVING every part of our operation.

We must ensure that we make our place of work as SAFE as possible and encourage SAFE THINKING AND ACTION to become an integral part of our daily activities.

Only by investing in TRAINING can we be certain that we are all capable of meeting the changing demands and knowledge required to do our jobs effectively.

Figure 10.2 *Quality policy statement for British Steel's Teesside Works.*

TQP
The Key Principles

So just what is **Total Quality Performance**?
Let's start with some definitions.

QUALITY is continually satisfying agreed customer requirements

TOTAL QUALITY is to acheive Quality at lowest cost

TOTAL QUALITY PERFORMANCE is achieving Total Quality by harnessing everyone's commitment.

TQP follows seven guiding principles:

> Prevention is the only way of ensuring that our customer does not receive defective goods and substandard service. Investment in the prevention of failures in Quality will protect the customer and produce substantial dividends in the form of reduced costs of waste, errors, rework and checking. A Policy that allows inspection to take a larger share of quality costs often creates an unquestioning acceptance of the inevitability of Quality failure. A policy that is tolerant of Quality failure is likely to be extremely expensive.

> The initiative must come from management. It must encourage others by example and guide the actions that follow, through successive levels of the company.

> Making people resonsible for Quality is less effective than creating a climate in which people are willing and able to take responsibility themselves. Creating a single department 'responsible for Quality' takes away at least some of the incentive for other people to do Quality work. You can't inspect Quality in.

> The total costs of Quality are usually not visible in company records. Most accounting systems fail to isolate them, yet Quality can be measured. There are three elements to the cost of Quality – prevention, appraisal and failure. Prevention is the cost of getting it right first time. Appraisal is the cost of checking and inspecting whether we have done it right. Failure is the cost of not doing it right.

> It is costly to compromise on Quality. Right first time is the standard by which we evalute Quality performance. We must aim for 'zero defects'. Why settle for less?

> Opportunities for Quality improvement abound in every part of any company. Quality is needed in marketing, in personnel, in administration – indeed, in every department – not only in manufacturing.

> There is no instant solution. Lasting improvement in Quality takes a sustained effort over years to create a climate of continuous improvement.

Figure 10.2 *Continued.*

It is owned by a multinational Japanese company, and was established from scratch in the UK in 1980, in the teeth of recession and deindustrialization. It has neatly combined best practice from Japan with sound Yorkshire common sense, and has been very successful. Moreover it is a very happy company, with low labour turnover. Like all Japanese companies (including the largest such as Nissan in Durham), it has only three levels in the hierarchy, and its operation is based on team-work, and what the Japanese call the 'tile' system; that is, each functional department is expected to overlap the others, creating flexibility of response to customers, and shared responsibility. Teams of workers and managers in the departments operate in what is best described as a collegiate style, where the manager is *primus inter pares*, and functions as a coach and facilitator rather than a controller.

Those who have taught for a long time will remember that in the now distant past, schools, especially grammar schools, operated on a model not too dissimilar this.

The past twenty years or so have seen the development in larger schools of an ever more complex and deep hierarchy, with more and more division of responsibility and function. The key to promotion has increasingly been to escape from teaching as such into bureaucratic activities such as pastoral care, exam administration, etc.

The exigencies of local management of schools and ever tighter budgets have already caused one or two headteachers to look afresh at the organizational structure, and

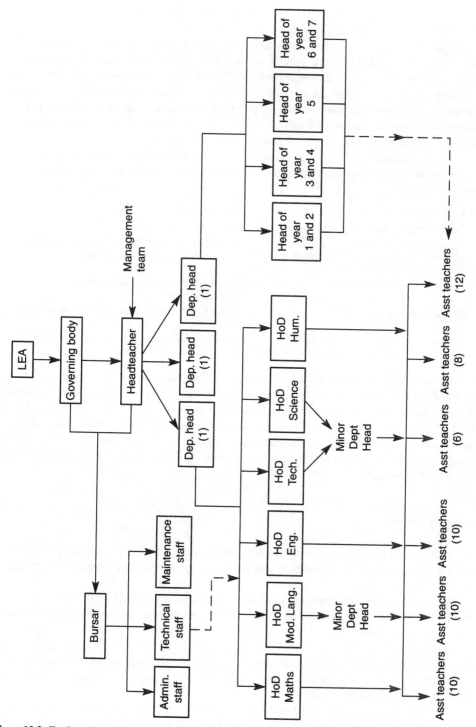

Figure 10.3 *Traditional organizational structure of a school. Note the following: (a) the complete separation of 'line' management from 'staff'; (b) the steep hierarchy (at least six layers of accountability; (c) the separation of academic from pastoral; (d) 'top-down' communication; (e) 'bottom-up' accountability.*

make radical changes with startling results. The experience of one such school is described in the Postscript, Chapter 14.

Smaller schools, such as most primary or elementary schools, already possess a flat hierarchy. The head and deputy head teach a full or near-full timetable, and special responsibilities are spread across a number of staff. There are few status distinctions, and team-work is the norm. In such an environment the introduction of a quality management paradigm and system should not be too difficult. All that is needed is the recognition and acceptance of a new set of values, centred on the concept of continuous improvement, rather than the preservation of the status quo.

In larger schools and colleges a much more complex structure will have evolved, which is likely to be inimical to a quality culture. It will be essential to institute the following features:

Old structure	New structure
Deep hierarchy with up to seven levels	Reduce to three levels
Strict functional boundaries between academic departments, and between academic and ancillary staff	Remove boundaries, institute cross-functional teams – the Japanese 'tile' system
Top-down communication	Replace by horizontal, and bottom-up communication
Vertical accountability	Replace with lateral accountability to internal customers
Proliferation of supervisory middle managers, with control and direct functions	Retrain to be coaches and facilitators, team leaders rather than bosses

If these changes are not made, the culture of the organization (whatever leadership style the Head adopts) will be defensive of departmental boundaries and privileges, and confrontational in the struggle for resources in a zero-sum game. No one will hear, let alone respond to, the needs and opinions of the front-line worker in the classroom. Not only should hierarchies be demolished and reduced to three levels, but equal status should become the rule, as in the case of Minova Ltd. Power and status games make team-work impossible.

A quality system

By 'quality system' we mean 'a systematic mechanism for collecting, collating and interpreting data of all kinds, in order to deliver a quality service, to all customers, internal and external'.

This system could be developed gradually 'in house', or it could be introduced over a period of one or two years with the assistance of a consultant. In the latter case it would be possible to focus the development of the quality system around a formal accreditation process such as BS 5750. This is now available to service as well as manufacturing organizations, and one or two higher education and further education institutions have gone down this road. Information about BS 5750 may be obtained from the Department of Trade and Industry.

It should be stressed at this point that the achievement of B5 5750 is *not* in itself symptomatic of a quality culture being in place. It is a possible first step in the right direction. Our own feeling is that it is necessary to achieve the culture change then seek BS 5750, as a programme to implement that culture. BS 5750 is, however, neither a necessary nor a sufficient condition for achieving a quality organization. We should remember that it is seen by the Japanese as irrelevant. Quality is simply the way they do business, not a bolt-on extra.

Regular customer surveys

You cannot know whether or not you are satisfying your customer requirements if you never ask them. This may seem self-evident, but when did your school ever systematically ask your parents, or children, what you should be providing for them? I think we tend to follow the producer-led or expert-led model, and define for our customers what we think they ought to want. To some extent this is necessary but only in collaboration with the customer. At present the teacher sees himself as the 'gatekeeper' of the educational service, just as doctors have tended to see themselves in this way in the NHS. It is being belatedly admitted in both services that the customer has an increasingly sophisticated awareness of what he wants from the system. This may match your view, but it may not. Can you afford not to listen?

There are various ways in which customer responses may be elicited:

- survey techniques;
- panel interviews;
- investigation of customer complaints;
- responses invited from school reports, and Records of Achievement

These methods are dealt with and illustrated in more detail in Chapter 4. You may be rather surprised at the responses which you receive. The data generated from these activities *must* then be fed into the management decision-making process, at every stage.

Curriculum design

The 'product' which you provide for your customers may be thought of primarily in terms of the curriculum. The design process will be influenced by various factors:

- availability of resources;
- dictates of the National Curriculum;
- needs of higher education, further education and employers;
- educational balance;
- capabilities and desires of pupils and parents.

Beyond this, so far as the external customers are concerned, the product is more than a bundle of academic subjects, and is better thought of as a whole person. In terms of the needs of employers, the person produced by the school should possess certain characteristics. These are not always recognized by the school as being important.

Important 'product' characteristics

- Smart personal appearance, as appropriate for work and other social circumstances;
- Good oral presentation, confident and clear speech;
- Reasoning abilities, problem-solving skills;
- Social skills, appropriate manners;
- Integrity, honesty;
- Staying power;
- Team-work skills;
- Independence, self-sufficiency and self-respect;
- Cooperativeness;
- Confidence and self-esteem.

These should have been developed through the media of curricular and extra-curricular activities. But they may not, perhaps because of the nature of the curriculum offered in a particular school, and its general ethos. The schoolteacher's perception of what should be expected of children does not always match the needs of the external customer. Every school must decide what it is setting out to achieve in the personal development of its pupils, but must do so with the external customer's needs in mind. For example, if children are encouraged to attend school in casual leisure clothing, by teachers who see cords and pullover as suitable professional apparel, then the children are being done a disservice. Employers expect young people to recognize what the business and working world sees as appropriate for the daily routine. If children have been driven by a highly didactic teaching system in order to achieve high academic results, they may lack some of the intangible but highly necessary characteristics of independence, self-motivation, team-work skills and so on. If the school has a philosophy which denies the value of competitive instincts, the pupils may appear to be too lethargic and easygoing for the needs of the commercial environment.

Documentary control system

Perhaps more than any other organization, schools tend to become plagued by enormous quantities of bureaucratic paperwork. Some of this is imposed on the schools, e.g. Records of Achievement, truancy returns and so on. Some is internally generated. Tom Peters recounts the story of the chairman of a major company who killed off paperwork by binning every memo which he received. Perhaps this is going too far. Winston Churchill insisted that memos from his staff should never be longer than one page of foolscap. We tend to grumble at new bureaucratic impositions but then to get on and deal with them. Management rarely steps back and considers whether we need to undertake a particular task, and whether there has developed an overlap which can permit the removal of one bureaucratic imposition. For example, if the sixth form parents are invited to meet the teachers in mid-March, and are then sent a school report in late March, do they need yet another report in June, when there have been only two or three weeks of revision teaching before the start of the exams in May? Arguably not, but no doubt many schools continue to send one without considering whether or not it is useful.

One way of both reducing the 'costs of quality' and simultaneously improving our capability to offer what the customer actually wants may be to look afresh at all documentation and internal communication systems:

- Why do we do it?
- Who does it help?
- Can we do without it?

If the answers are:

- Do not know.
- No one.
- Think so.

then abolish it. With a flatter hierarchy, Quality Improvement Programme and quality circles in place, people will be talking to each other cooperatively, not writing defensive memos, or filling in forms with spurious information.

Documentation should be limited to that which fulfils the following criteria.

Basic documentary requirements

- That which has an essential purpose – conveying information, or interpreting it, for customers, whether internal or external.
- That which is required by law, e.g. Records of Achievement, registers and school reports. Even these items should be subjected to scrutiny and redesigned where necessary. For instance, a good first project for the quality improvement team might be to redesign school report forms.
- That which is required for purposes of accountability (who did what, when, for what purpose?), e.g. medical inspection, punishment, travel indemnity for school trips.
- That which is required for process control. Work and job dockets for ancillary staff, markbooks and other recording systems for process and progress management in the teaching programme, e.g. cusum charts, etc.
- That which is needed for relationships with suppliers, e.g. book order, equipment order.
- That which is required in relationship with customers, e.g. registration of pupils, entrance exam details, personal data, university applications, pupils' testimonials and references.
- That which is needed to set in motion, record and subsequently monitor action programmes, e.g. minutes of meetings, requests for specific information, correspondence etc.
- That which is required to maintain records of all relationships with suppliers and customers, e.g. filing systems, databases.

Much of this data could be computer-generated and stored, thus reducing the amount of manual record-keeping required. It is important, however, to be aware of the requirements of the Data Protection Act in setting up such a system. A model of such a system is set out in Figure 10.4.

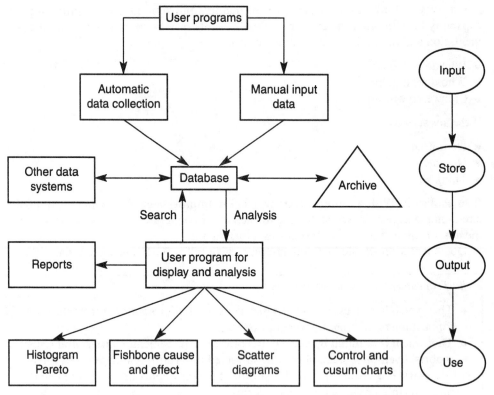

Figure 10.4 *Quality information: a computerized system.*
Source: Oakland (1990)

Desirable, even essential, though this system may be, it will only be acceptable and useful if it is developed in such a way as to reduce bureaucratic overload, not increase it. It must be remembered that its efficiency depends on people, who must be trained in its use, and given precise instructions. For example, a teacher appraisal scheme is in our philosophy undesirable, but if it is required by law, it must be introduced on the basis of serious training for everyone. If not, it will not just be a nuisance, it will be a disaster. Teachers are intelligent people who must see a reason why they are required to do something, if they are to do it well.

Chapter 11

If Japan Can, Why Can't We?

People must work as a team.

W.E. Deming

When asked recently how Rover Group plc had made such a remarkable recovery in recent years, the chief executive commented thus, 'We have been talking to Honda for ten years, and for the first seven years we did not understand a word they were saying.' I hope that by this point we have established the importance for all organizations, including schools, of the philosophy for quality, as set out by Deming. It is not, however, an easy route to excellence. Various recent research projects have established that some 80 per cent of total quality initiatives in companies and public sector organizations in both the UK and the USA have failed to deliver any improvements and in many cases have been abandoned. The result has been a strong reaction against the quality paradigm amongst executives, and in the management journals. TQM is seen by many as just another management 'fad' which we can now ditch in favour of the next.

At this point it may be helpful if we summarize the reasons which have been advanced for the success of TQM in Japanese companies, and in some Western companies which have successfully emulated them.

R.G. Hannam, in his recent book *Kaizen for Europe*, points to the impact of historical experience on Japanese attitudes to their economy. In the nineteenth century Japan was humiliated by the West's superior military strength, and retreated into isolation whilst seeking to acquire from the West the industrial technologies which they needed to avoid such military inferiority in the future. Their defeat in even more humiliating circumstances in 1945 led the Japanese to set out on another search for outside inspiration and know-how, which is where Deming and Juran came into the story. Japan was greatly aided by large-scale assistance and investment from the USA, which stimulated its manufacturing base and allowed it to develop world-class companies in steel-making and shipbuilding. To these basic industries were added motor vehicles and consumer electronics. Growth was remarkable in the 1960s.

The commercial history of Japan in the nineteenth century had been built on the activities of a handful of large trading organizations which dominated not only trading but also banking and manufacturing. In this century these powerful companies were interdependent with the institutions of politics and government. The Ministry of Industry and Technology (MIT) played a coordinating role in the long-term strategic planning of the economy. This interdependence within the macro- and micro-economy prevented the economic system from being bedevilled by crises brought on by the short-termism of investing institutions which owned the greatest stake in industry and commerce in the West. A strong sense of loyalty to all things Japanese in tandem with this system of government has brought about an effective protectionism against imports, and this has enabled the Japanese manufacturers to pursue export-led growth unaffected by loss of market share at home. This contrasts sharply with the experience of the UK and USA, and causes many commentators to see the Japanese approach as 'unfair trading' or even corruption.

A third important general factor in Japanese success is the cultural basis of their society. Based on a Confucian ethic, the strongest feature of Japanese society is an unshakable bond of loyalty to a group identity. As P. Wickens of Nissan puts it in his introduction to Hannan's book: 'The Japanese people value group harmony more than individuality – it is not [therefore] surprising that group-oriented ideas have been adopted into management practices.' Writing of the transplanting of Nissan to the UK Wickens remarks, 'The key to Japanese success lies in ... the managers and the managed, and how they relate to each other.'

A fourth important factor is the absence for these historical reasons of the steep hierarchical format with downward control which characterizes Western organizational structure, and which itself derives from the historical experience of Western government and military structures which predated the industrial revolution.

Stemming from the Confucian culture, the tradition of group loyalty and the flat hierarchies which prevail in Japan are two other linked factors. These are the system of life-time employment of core workers, with promotion by seniority, and the strong emphasis on long-term training and education of all employees.

Dale of (UMIST) and Allan (of Nissan) have in a recent article identified the more specific impact on the operation of Japanese companies of these general factors. The fanatical pursuit of quality is seen by them as the dominant reason for Japanese success. Quality Improvement Programmes are not, as so often in the West, a bolt-on extra, but are fully integrated into everything which the organization does. More specifically, this involves a constant process of listening to what customers say about the product or service offered in terms of product attractiveness, the company's response to market needs, reliability, and conformance to requirements. Constant benchmarking of best practice worldwide is combined with long-term planning for development, and rapid new product development cycles. On-going continuous improvement programmes are the central theme of management practice. Statistical process control, simultaneous engineering, and Just in Time inventory management are standard practice. Waste is eliminated throughout the process, and the vehicle for this is a constant flow of information about processes.

All of this is perfectly accessible to Western companies; indeed, much of it originated in the West. The critical factor is the addition of a human dimension to these mechanistic procedures. People are seen as the only really important resource. Life-time employment, wide experience, education and training throughout life, and promotion by seniority all underpin a management style which is participative. It calls on the employees at all levels to be responsible for the quality of their work, operating in self-contained teams. Leadership is by example and coaching rather than direction or control. The abilities of all workers are called upon in a climate where prevention is seen as more sensible than constant firefighting. Arguably the culture change required in a Western organization to achieve this format is extremely difficult.

At this point it might be helpful to look at two examples of relatively small Japanese subsidiaries, operating in West Yorkshire, which we recently visited. The fact that they had successfully implemented in a UK environment the sort of culture change which we have just described may encourage us to believe that it can be done in any organization, whether it be a factory or a school.

TWO CASE HISTORIES OF CULTURE CHANGE

1. Minova Ltd

A subsidiary of a multinational company, Minova was established in Morley (near Leeds,) 12 years ago. There are three Japanese senior executives, but the rest of the staff are local workers and managers, recruited from the ailing West Riding textile industry.

The company manufactures high-quality worsted suitings, 85 per cent of which are exported, mostly back to Japan and Far East. Minova undertakes the design of the product, buys in yarn (from Germany, sadly – local product is not good enough), twists the warp itself on very expensive machinery, then subcontracts the weaving to several Huddersfield firms, before preparing the cloth itself for subcontracting for the finishing processes before dispatching to customers.

The features which struck us on our visit to this company were:

- Single status – senior executives and directors shared offices with middle managers; the managing director was to be seen on the shop floor talking with the operatives, the canteen was partitioned off from the shop floor, well furnished, and used by everybody.
- Everybody had an absolute commitment to produce a first-class product, and seek continuous improvement.
- The workforce at all levels were obviously happy, highly motivated and confident.
- The directors took a long-term view, and were committed to investment on a large scale – they had just spent £600,000 on new machine (since replaced by an even more advanced machine). They had been allowed by the main board in Japan to plan to work for ten years before they took a profit. This would be unheard of in a British-owned firm.

As we left, the production director, an old-time West Riding textile man, said, 'Moving here was the best thing I ever did in my life.'

---

2. *Toyota Industrial Equipment Ltd*

A wholly owned subsidiary of Toyota, but previously British-owned from 1972 to 1989. Acts as sole main distributor for fork-lift trucks in the UK. Run by three Japanese directors and one British one. With 75 employees, it is engaged partly in sales and marketing, and partly in customizing fork lifts for specific customer requirements in its own large workshop. It has been working very hard for three years to introduce a Japanese TQM style of management. The features of the transformation of this company which struck us forcibly were:

- The rationalization of the parts store (which serves all UK distributors) on a Just in Time inventory basis, saving virtually a whole warehouse area, and reducing the cost of excess stock.
- The fact that the employees in the workshop had been invited to reorganize the operations and processes in there. They were invited to rewrite the rules on clocking in, first-aid, health and safety provision, lunch breaks, times of starting and finishing work, and, even more significantly, had been invited to calculate standard times for every job themselves. The only criterion imposed was that every worker should be able to do at least five tasks instead of one, and that the machines move from workstation to workstation, rather than worker to stationary machine.
- The fact that work study and piece-rate payments had been abolished. Every man to be on a standard wage, plus an extra £750 per annum for every course of training undertaken, with no limit to the number or types of course attended.
- Despite the dramatic change in management style most workers had 'bought in to the changes'.

WHY TQM PROGRAMMES MAY FAIL

At the present time there is in the literature of management, and amongst executives, something of a backlash against the quality paradigm. It is already being seen by some observers and managers as a management fad which has had its day, and which must now be replaced by the latest buzz concept emerging from the business schools and management consultancies. This backlash probably stems from the perceived failure of many TQM initiatives in Western companies. As many as 80 per cent of such initiatives have been revealed as failures in recent research. We would argue that this failure is the result of the mistakes of those responsible rather than because the paradigm is fundamentally flawed. However, in the interests of balance perhaps we should seek to point to some of the reasons why these initiatives are seen as failures.

The decision to undertake such a TQM programme must stem from a decision by senior management. They may choose to do so for a number of reasons which will in themselves make it likely that the initiative will fail. Obviously if the choice is made simply because TQM is the flavour of the month, and with no serious knowledge of the paradigm or commitment to its development, failure is almost inevitable. If the choice is made simply because a downstream customer insists on it as a condition of doing further business, as often happens in the car industry, then failure is probable. If it is undertaken only because of an edict from Group HQ, it is likely to be seen as getting in the way of business and it will fail. If a company seeks to be accredited with the

BS 5750 Quality standard, and supposes that this means it has become a quality company, or if BS 5750 is sought simply as a marketing tool, the initiative will fail. If being seen to undertake a quality programme is seen as a public relations exercise, it will fail. If the company is unable to translate the costs of quality measurements into data which can be accommodated in standard accounting procedures, no 'bottom line' advantage will be seen and the quality programme will probably wilt.

Even where top management is clear as to what TQM means as a concept, and is totally committed to its introduction, the initiative may well fail if the basic mechanics of its adoption are inadequately addressed, and both middle management and work-force trained in their new and expanded roles. Thus if a company does not know what it wants to do and be (have a mission), know where it is starting from (undertake a quality audit), set up a comprehensive continuous improvement programme, involving everybody, and constantly monitor and review progress, it will fail.

In a recent article an American consultant, Greg Boone, has identified a futher reason for failure which may come into play even if all the above essential matters have been dealt with. This is the 'politics of quality'. This occurs where the persons placed in charge of the quality improvement programme seek to use it as a power base for them-selves, to improve their own career prospects or security. He uses two true stories to illustrate his point. One concerns the appointed manager of quality in a software com-pany which was losing market share. She turned herself into an instrusive, domineering high guru of quality who used her 'knowledge' (which was very limited) as a tool for the criticism of other people's work. The second story concerns a former public sector agency, now privatized. This new organization was to be run by a top manager who was knowledgeable about quality, and committed. The hierarchy was to be very flat, team-work across functional boundaries was to be the norm. The management style was to be participative. However, the quality team which was set up was unable or unwilling to 'give away' its knowledge, or establish any rules for action, These volunteers, who had set out with the task of establishing a few ground rules which would enable the rest of the staff to develop their own quality initiatives, had in fact become a little bureaucracy. They were the biggest barriers to spreading the quality gospel. It had become their vehi-cle for power and influence.

In Boone's view, the greatest dangers to the development of quality programmes are: the evangelists – the bright misfits who see this as a means of disrupting a system which they dislike and substituting anarchy; and the popularity seekers, whose leadership skills are minimal.

In the context of the school system, or the health services, we have all seen the ambi-tious careerists climb on any new band-wagon as a vehicle for promotion. They often combine the slippery flexibility of the Vicar of Bray with the authoritarianism of a Hitler. In one hospital trust in the UK, in a recent year, a considerable budget shortfall (resulting from bad management) led to a decision to reduce a group of paramedics serving the community by one third. All were invited to apply for their old job back (in some cases at a lower grade). The procedure which was to be used to screen the candidates and short-list for the team-leader positions was the requirement to produce a 750-word presentation on methods of introducing a Quality Improvement Programme into their department. On the basis of this document they would be interviewed. None of them had been offered any training on quality management, and they were given only ten days in which to prepare themselves for the interview and write the presentation. Many could not even understand the 'jargon' and were not at all clear what they were being asked to do. This is a blatant example of the use of the quality paradigm as a tool to enhance management power. In this climate the trust concerned is bound to fail in its quality initiative. Cases of this kind can only bring the whole paradigm into disrepute. In such a climate as we have described above, it is easy for pseudo-Marxist critiques to flourish.

Delbridge *et al.* recently published just such an article. In the interests of balance, we offer you the chance to consider their point of view. They are particularly concerned with the application of Japanese management methods in a manufacturing context, and have nothing to say on developments in service-sector organizations. Their perspective and language are essentially Marxist. 'The system is ultimately intended to ensure 60 minutes of useful labour from every worker in every hour, thereby leading to *a more efficient extraction of surplus value from labour and therefore the more efficient accumulation of capital*' (emphasis added). This is achieved in their view by a devolution of responsibility to the workers which does not actually empower them, but rather ensures a much stricter control through constant surveillance and monitoring of workers' activities. This ensures that peer pressures are harnessed within 'teams', who have a joint responsibility for all outcomes from their workstation. Overall it represents an intensification of the labour process, creating even greater subordination of worker to capital than ever before. Furthermore, it involves great pressure on workers to input their ideas for the benefit of capital. Close and constant surveillance through statistical process control creates a very stressful situation for the worker through peer pressure contained within the group bonus systems which replace the individual bonus which was characteristic of the old methods of scientific management based on work study and individual bonuses (piece rates). Worse still, the system of Just in Time inventory management, which has removed buffer stocks from the system, has also as a result removed the workers' power to create an informal system by which to manage the process, giving the possibility of slowing down the pace of work, or speeding it up, through custom and practice. The workers become '*preoccupied with surviving the system*' (emphasis added). The result is not a humanized workforce, with real autonomy, but rather 'a highly regulated and regimented labour process with many of the characteristics of bureaucratic control'. In Delbridge's view, 'For TQM we should read Total Management Control.'

I think that this is an extreme view, which flies in the face of the evidence from Rover and many other companies where TQM has been a success. However, it does provide us with a warning note of importance. There is a danger in any work environment that a total quality initiative may be used by an unscrupulous management as a means of exercising greater control over the workforce. This danger is more obvious in a factory environment, but still exists in a service-sector environment such as a school. This is why from the start of this book we have stressed the importance of culture change, and top-management commitment rather then the importance of mechanistic quality control systems, especially in a sensitive human organism like a school. Perhaps headteachers should follow the example of the managing director of a Japanese battery company, K. Murato, who from the day the plant opened in Wales insisted that he and his three fellow directors spend every Tuesday morning on the shopfloor. First they mop out and clean the workpeoples' cloakroom, and then they go down the line seeking ways, however trivial, in which they might help the workers.

Perhaps at this point it would be helpful if we summarize the contrasting aspects of traditional management and total quality management. This summary has been adapted from comments by Ed Baker in his address to the W.G. Hunter Conference on Quality in 1989. You might like to use this comparison in Table 11.1. as a checklist to audit the style of management which prevails in your organization, school or classroom. This will tell you (if you are honest with yourself) how far you will have to travel to match Deming's ideal organization. Better still, ask your colleagues, employees or pupils to undertake the exercise; this will give you an even better picture.

Table 11.1 *The contrast between traditional and quality management*

Traditional management	Quality management
Enterprise seen as a *collection* of specialized individuals, linked within a functional hierarchy.	Enterprise seen as a *system* of interdependent processes; linked laterally through a *network* of internal and external customers and suppliers. The system is a hierarchy of processes and subprocesses.
People viewed as *commodities*, interchangeable; *passive* contributors, with little autonomy, doing no more than they are told.	People seen as vital; given *opportunities* for growth and personal development. Encouraged to learn and grow in self-esteem, becoming *active and creative contributors*. Each person owns and manages his part of the process.
Quality defined as *adherence to specifications and standards*, based on what has been done in the past. Quality measured by absence of defects and is inspected in after the event. Innovation discouraged.	Quality defined as *products and service, beyond present customer requirements*. Innovation for improvement is important.
Functional departments defend parochial interests in a *zero sum game*. People discouraged from cooperation across boundaries.	Everyone wins where self-interest and good of the organization are served by delighting customers, internal and external.
'Quality' is an issue only for production managers.	'Quality' is an issue applicable in all parts of the organization.
Managers manage departments as *collections of individuals*, without recognizing interdependence of both.	Managers both manage and *lead interdependent systems and teams*, through participative management.
Failure is seen as the fault of people or departments.	Failure is due to systems, not people, and is the responsibility of management, which must seek continuous improvement through team-work.
An *internally competitive environment reinforces individualism.*	Rewards and recognition systems reinforce both individual and lesson contributions, and so *encourage cooperation*.
'Performance appraisal, recognition and reward' systems maintain this culture.	
A *formula for apparent success is regarded as permanent.*	*Organization responds to a constantly changing environment.*
Management aims to *maintain the status quo*, prevent change, and squash challenges.	Management leads *improvement, change and innovation* in product, process, and system, seeking to shape rather than respond to, the future.
An *adverserial relationship* exists between management and followers, with restricted communication and much secrecy.	Management and followers *act in partnership* and collaboration, recognizing a common interest in survival and success. Training and involvement of employees seen as critical.
Hierarchical functional or departmental organization structure – creates internal competition and conflict – over resources etc.	*Formal and informal mechanisms* to encourage cross-functional, cross-departmental collaboration.
Adversarial relationship with suppliers, who compete on price.	Suppliers seen as *partners*, long-term relationships developed.
Control achieved through complex and inflexible *rules and procedures.*	Control achieved by *shared beliefs*, values and sense of mission.
Motivation achieved by *fear of punishment*. Driving by fear makes people feel like losers.	Managers lead by *empowering individuals*, creating a sense of having made a contribution. People feel like winners.

Table 11.1 *Continued*

Traditional management	Quality management
Manager *plans* subordinates' work and *inspects* for failure.	Manager seeks to give people capability to *manage their own contribution.*
'Customers' are outside the organization, and to be dealt with only by sales and marketing people.	*Everyone is both customer and supplier*, both inside and outside the organization.
Competition is inevitable and inherent in human nature.	Competition is not inevitable between people. *Cooperation enables positive competition*, to please the customer, or eliminate waste.
Business is a 'game' with winners and losers in an arena of conflict.	

Adapted from Ed Baker, 'The chief executive officer's role in Total Quality', Proceedings of the W.E. Hunter Conference on Quality, Wisconsin, 1989.

Perhaps another parable will reinforce the points we have been seeking to make in this chapter?

Another parable

Many a True Word Spoken in Jest?

The following is a contribution from ex-BDA employee Fiona Henderson, now in Belize. It was sent to her office by one of her company's suppliers in Miami.

Once upon a time an American steel company and a Japanese company decided to have a competitive boat race on the Monongahela river. Both teams practised hard and long to reach peak performance. On the big day both felt as ready they could be.

The Japanese won by a mile.

The American team became very discouraged by the loss, and morale sagged noticeably. Corporate management decided that the reason for the crushing defeat had to be found. A continuous 'Measurable Improvement Team' was set up to investigate the problem and recommend appropriate corrective action. Their conclusion was as follows:

The problem was that the Japanese team had eight people rowing and one person steering, whereas the American team had one person rowing and eight people steering. The American corporate steering committee immediately hired a consulting firm to do a study on the management study on the management structure. After some time and millions of dollars later, the consulting firm eventually concluded that 'too many people were steering and not enough were rowing'.

To prevent losing to the Japanese again next year, the team management structure was totally reorganized to four steering managers, three area managers, and one staff steering manager, and a new performance system for the person rowing the boat to give more incentive to work harder. 'We must give him empowerment and enrichment; that ought to do it.'

The next year the Japanese won by two miles.

Humiliated, the American corporation laid off the rower for poor performance, sold all the paddles, cancelled all capital investments for new equipment, halted the development of a new canoe, gave a 'high performance' award to the consulting firm, and distributed the money saved as bonuses to the senior management executives.

Source: British Deming Association

Chapter 12

Deming's System of Profound Knowledge

Experience is insufficient for theory. Theory means prediction. Theory means we think we understand. Without theory there is no knowledge.

W.E. Deming

You may have gathered from what has gone before that Deming's vision extends beyond merely producing a blueprint for the better management of an organization or business. That is how it began, but the inexorable logic of mathematics led to the development of what amounts to a complete philosophy of life, or at the least of social organization. I would like to end this short account of the principles of what has become known (perhaps misleadingly) as Total Quality Management by summarizing the key elements of that philosophy, as seen by Deming and his followers.

CORE VALUES

The essential features of Deming's thinking are summarized in Table 12.1. His original interest in statistics led him to study the work of Walter Schewart on variance. From there he recognized the crucial importance of the understanding of the theory of variance. This led him to the recognition that any process is a system, within which there will occur variance, some caused by 'special' causes, other by 'common' causes. The latter are the consequence of the structure and mechanics of the system, which is the responsibility of the management, not the operatives. Moreover, such a system must have an aim or objective, and this must be based on a value judgement. The objective or mission creates the system, not the other way round.

Prediction and optimization are central to his theory of knowledge. Appreciation of the nature of systems led Deming to see that the management of any system must be based on prediction, which requires systematic analysis and problem solving to enable 'optimization' of the system's capability. This is what he means by a theory of knowledge, a 'clear perception of facts and truths'. This level of prediction may only be achieved by empirical methods, rigorous experiment and analysis, interpreted for the prediction of the consequences of changes in the condition of the system. This required level of prediction can only be achieved when a system is brought into statistical control; that is, when 'special' causes of variance are eliminated, and only 'common' causes remain. We 'appreciate' a system when we understand these characteristics of systems.

The recognition that systems are the result of human decisions, actions and visions led Deming to see that knowledge is only possible given some appreciation of psychology, since it is people who must be taught and motivated to improve any system.

Table 12.1 *The core values, the cornerstones, and the 14 points*

The core values of Deming's Theory of Profound Knowledge	The Four Cornerstones	The Fourteen Points
		1. Establish constancy of purpose
		2. Adopt the new philosophy
		3. Cease dependence on mass inspection
1. Appreciation for a system	→ The purpose of a business is: →	4. End the practice of awarding business on price tag alone
2. Some knowledge of the theory of variation	1. to stay in business and to create jobs	5. Constantly improve every system
3. A theory of knowledge	2. to expand the market	6. Institute training
4. Some knowledge of psychology ←	3. to continually improve	← 7. Institute leadership
	4. to grow intelligently	8. Drive out fear
		9. Break down barriers between staff areas
		10. Abandon slogans
		11. Eliminate numerical quotas
		12. Remove barriers to pride of workmanship
		13. Promote education and self-improvement
		14. Take action to accomplish the transformation

Source: N.J. Mauro, 'A perspective on Deming's Theory of Profound Knowledge', British Deming Association, World Series Booklets (1992)

FOUR CORNERSTONES

The core values of Deming's Theory of Profound Knowledge were developed over a 60-year period, moving from understanding of systems to the recognition of the supreme importance of the human dimension. Much of that time was spent advising businesses, teaching them how to achieve a corporate culture based on the 'continuous improvement of product and process'. In doing so Deming dismissed the old models of business management, which were based on the twin pillars of 'scientific management' and the maximization of short-term profits. In their place he set out the 'four cornerstones' of good business practice:

- To stay in business and create (preserve) jobs.
- To expand the market (*not* just market share).

- To improve continually (product and process).
- To grow intelligently (long term, without endangering survival).

FOURTEEN POINTS

Out of this chain of reasoning there emerged Deming's 'Fourteen Points'. These amount to a blueprint for the management of any organization, whether business, public sector or voluntary sector. It centres, as to be expected, around the theory of variance. As Mauro has remarked, 'the ability to lead depends on one's ability to understand variation'. This sounds a little extreme, but without this understanding, a leader will never know what his system (organization) is capable of achieving, because he will never bring the system into statistical control, which is essential for the rational prediction and problem solving necessary for continuous improvement. Even more important, the leader will never recognize the capabilities of his people, since they cannot be expected to optimize their performance and understanding in a system which is out of control. The leader would always blame his people for faults and mistakes which are really his, not theirs.

This is why the first two of the points stress 'constancy of purpose' (commitment from top management), and the adoption of the new philosophy of 'profound knowledge' by the leader.

Points 3, 4, 10, 11 and 14 stem directly from the implications of variance. Points 5, 6, 7, 8, 9, 12 and 13 all stem from Deming's stress on the implications of profound knowledge for human beings as 'operatives' within any system, at any level.

Lack of understanding of two key points (lack of understanding of variance, combined with the power of the normal curve of distribution to shape our judgements of each other) has led to the diminution of the human spirit rather than its optimization. When asked one day how it was that his students all did so well on their course, he replied that he simply gave them all A grades, and they produced A-grade work. Deming's reply is devastating in its implications for workers in a factory, or for that matter your pupils.

Why does Deming refer to his ideas as 'profound knowledge'? It is profound in the sense that it is a holistic theory of knowledge which is capable of revolutionizing the performance and self-esteem of human individuals. Moreover, it is applicable in any sphere of human activity, including (and perhaps particularly) in schools. I have taken the liberty in Table 12.2 of adapting the Fourteen Points specifically for schools. I hope that you will see its relevance to what you are trying to do.

CONCLUSION

If I may quote Mauro again, 'Deming has changed the world, and anyone who doubts his legacy merely needs to examine the working models that exist currently in Japan and in South East Asia.' Deming's message was that his theory is macro in its relevance to economy and society. He argued that society cannot afford the waste represented by unemployment any more than a business can afford the waste implicit in a system which is not in statistical control.

Table 12.2 *Deming's Fourteen Points adapted for schools*

1. Pursue continuous improvement of curriculum and learning diligently and constantly.
2. Adopt the system of profound knowledge in your classroom and school as the prime management tool.
3. Build quality into teaching and learning and reduce the inspection of quality into work after the event.
4. Build a partnership relationship with colleagues, students, colleges and employers.
5. Constantly improve the system within which teaching/learning takes place.
6. Take every opportunity to train in new skills and to learn from your pupils.
7. Lead, do not drive or manipulate.
8. Drive out fear of punishment, create joy in learning.
9. Collaborate with colleagues from other departments and functions.
10. Communicate honestly not through jargon and slogans.
11. So far as possible create a world without grades and rank orders.
12. Encourage and celebrate to develop your students's pride in work.
13. Promote the development of the whole person in students and colleagues.
14. Wed your students to learning by the negotiation with them of a quality experience.

Source: W.E. Deming, 'Out of the Crisis', 1982 (adapted to school rather than manufacturing context by L. Richeleau and M. S. Greenwood)

His long-term strategy for a business, or for an economy, centres on the optimization of the human contribution, and the elevation rather than degradation of the human spirit. It is in this sense that Deming's theory of knowledge is truly 'profound'. It also speaks directly to the spirit which moved you and us to work with young people in the first place. That is why we owe a duty to our students to introduce them to 'profound knowledge'.

If we do so, we may go some way towards achieving two linked objectives: the survival of our society and economy in an increasingly competitive world, and the maximization within that society of the life chances of our students. We simply cannot afford to be left behind. Again let Professor Mauro express what I am trying to say: 'If America [and the UK] does not join those who have embraced already the "Theory of Profound Knowledge", they will surely join the group of Third World nations in the not too distant future.'

Chapter 13

Can the Deming Approach
Work in School?

*We must give back to people intrinsic motivation; for improvement, for joy in work, for joy in learning.
Then they will learn.*

W.E. Deming

Your first reaction to this book may well have been either (a) that the prescriptions of TQM are what you normally practise anyway, or (b) that it is too idealistic, or too commercial, to apply in either the classroom or in school management. If the former, it is likely that you have always been seen as a maverick. At least now you have a systematic justification for what you have always felt instinctively to be the right approach. If the latter, then I hope that we have convinced you that it is not so. In Chapter 2 we saw that TQM has already been applied successfully in both contexts by a handful of pioneers. In the Postscript to the book we have brought the story up to date so far as possible. We would love to hear from any other pioneers.

We have sought throughout the book to stress that this paradigm is applicable to both school management and classroom management. We stressed the importance of recognizing the continuous nature of the internal/external customer–supplier chain. The techniques of Total Quality Management which we have described must be understood and applied by senior management to the management process within the school as an organization if the school is to become one which is truly world class. However, even if that is not happening, it is possible for the teacher responsible for a department, or even just her own class, to apply 'profound knowledge' to the benefit of her pupils.

PROFOUND KNOWLEDGE IN THE CLASSROOM

How should the role of teacher and student change?

Key dos and don'ts

1. The material used is not in itself critical.
2. Transforming the attitudes and expectations of students is important.
3. Teaching methods adopted are important.
4. Students must be encouraged to choose, plan and organize, both their own work schedule and that of the group or class.
5. Team-based activities should be used where possible and appropriate.
6. Every success, however small, must be celebrated and recognized.
7. Blame and personal criticism which demeans individuals must not be used.
8. The importance of the search for continuous improvement must be constantly stressed.
9. All courses should where possible draw on real-world experience, and use the skills of interested outsiders, either parents or people from the community.
10. Students should be encouraged to monitor and audit the progress of the group regularly, and to suggest ways in which the course might be improved.
11. Information collected by the teacher about student progress should be the data used to apply statistical process control in the search for continuous improvement.

We may feel that we apply these precepts already, but I think if we are honest with ourselves, we allow the stresses imposed by the national system and its requirements to deflect us from some of the most important of them.

The role of the teacher

Above all, you as teacher must become facilitator and coach rather than director and controller. The TQM paradigm should underpin the way in which we deliver the course, and the way in which the students perceive the course. It should also determine the way in which you assess the contribution of individuals to the group and the process. The efforts and achievements of the students in the direction of continuous improvement as the course proceeds must be evaluated in terms of the objectives and goals which the students have to set for themselves. Each student should be assessed against these personal targets, not in terms of her performance in relation to the other members of the group.

We must remember that what we are doing here is to apply to a school and educational context a philosophy of management originally developed for manufacturing industry, but in recent years successfully used in a wide variety of service-sector organizations, public and private. The instant reaction of teachers is likely to be one of horror at the thought. This may be your reaction. What does a school have in common with a widget factory or an insurance brokerage? The answer is that they are all organizations, and all exhibit the same basic characteristics, whatever their objectives. The particular characteristics of a school may be summarized thus:

- A school is not a factory.
- Education is the 'product', but cannot be seen.
- The customers are pupils, parents, employers, society.
- TQM is in many ways a return to ideas developed fifty years ago, and since abandoned.

Remember above all:

> Students/pupils only get one chance.

Our aim must be to enable and empower students to take control of their own learning, and empower them to maximize their capabilities, and find 'joy in learning' (Deming).

We are suggesting that the best way to achieve this objective (with which I think most teachers would agree) is to adopt TQM. Two features of this paradigm seem to us to be especially important.

1. TQM is a collaborative process to improve what is done, the system by which it is done, and the people who do it.
2. It involves a significant change in the nature of the relationship between those who manage (teachers) and those who do the work (students).

The essential differences may best be summed up as in Figure 13.1. The quality-driven school may be described as follows (after Deming):

> *Headteacher, administrators, governors and teachers work in a system.* The headteacher works ON the system to improve it continuously with the help of others.
>
> *The teacher helps students to learn within a system.* The teacher works ON the system to improve it continuously with their help.
>
> *The student works in* (and on) *a system,* in order to become an independent self-motivated learner for the rest of his life.

We have commented that the student is a 'customer'. In what sense do we mean this? Products are bought as a result of having FEATURES, i.e. a range of added items or characteristics, and secondly as a result of having QUALITY, i.e. integrity of delivery of 'features'. We can put this into educational terms. The education product has 'features' which are the classroom equipment and resources which may be available, and possesses 'quality' in terms of the integrity of the teaching/learning process – which does *not*

Teacher	DO TO	DO FOR	DO WITH	ENABLE
Student	No choice – captive antagonist	Captive, passive, dependent	Dependent, accept follower	Independent investigator, seeker of knowledge
Student reaction	LET ME OUT!	I'M OK	IT'S OK	JOY IN LEARNING

DIRECTION OF INCREASING AUTONOMY →

Figure 13.1 *Role of teachers and learners.*
Source: After M. Trybus, paper given at the 1992 National Forum of the British Deming Association

depend on the 'features'. The students cannot influence the 'features' of their education which are available, although they should be consulted. They should, however, be actively involved in defining and refining 'quality'.

Teacher and student negotiate 'quality' on the basis of what conforms to the students' perceived needs from the educational process and system. This takes time to develop because of all sorts of established if unsatisfactory values and perceptions. It might best be established first in a non-examined course prior to the development of a programme to spread the paradigm to other areas of the curriculum, and hopefully the management style used in the school.

How shall we start?

Your students must be engaged from the start in negotiating a 'contract' which addresses these questions:

1. Why are you here?
2. What are you trying to achieve?
3. What does it mean to you to do well?
4. What should the teacher do to enable you to do well?
5. How will we all know whether we are doing well?

What should we as teachers expect of any course?

What it is not

- It is not solely outcome driven.
- Outcomes are not graded or ranked more than is required by external authorities.
- It is not driven by constant testing; testing is used for diagnostic, not judgemental, purposes.

What it is

- It measures only improvement from a starting point determined by teacher and student in collaboration.
- It validates the acquisition of various attributes and skills.
- It is a vehicle for creating 'joy in learning'.

What it should aim to deliver

- KNOWLEDGE which helps to make sense of and manage experience.
- SKILLS which put knowledge to work.
- WISDOM, i.e. the ability to decide what is important and set own priorities.
- CHARACTER, i.e. skill, knowledge and wisdom combined with motivation.

- MOTIVATION, of an intrinsic kind (as against extrinsic), built on self-esteem, gained by small successes continuously achieved.
- TEAM-WORK SKILLS, based on collaboration, consensus and mutual respect, which stem from all the above points when combined to achieve an agreed objective.

> The teacher becomes a coach, the student becomes increasingly autonomous.

The functions of the teacher

A. *Purpose*
Make possible the development process by:
1. Ensuring necessary resources are available when required.
2. Leading students to understand and apply 'profound knowledge'.

B. *Function*
1. Support the process of change in learning strategies and skills.
2. Promote coordination and cooperative strategies with colleagues, students and outside agencies.
3. Help students to coach each other.
4. Establish a method of recording the progress of groups and individuals.

C. *Personal skills required by the teachers.*
1. Be able to communicate: talk *and* listen.
2. Be persuasive.
3. Be assertive, but not aggressive.
4. Be able to build teams.
5. Be able to lead and motivate with understanding of intrinsic psychological needs of students.
6. Be able to understand and apply basic statistical techniques.
7. Be enthusiastic about the application of TQM to learning.
8. Be always willing to innovate, and learn, from and with your students.
9. Be resilient, tactful and self-motivated.
10. Be a team player but lead by example, always.

The following are the attributes which Deming believes to be required by a good leader.

Attributes of a leader

1. The leader understands the system within which she works.
2. Works well with others; she recognizes that her teamworks within a system.
3. Understands that people differ, but creates in all a desire to improve and learn.
4. Never stops learning herself.
5. Acts as coach/counsellor, not judge.
6. Understands what is meant by 'a stable system'.
7. Bases her power on knowledge and personality, not coercion and fear.

8. Creates trust by taking risks on people's capability.
9. Does not expect perfection, only continuous improvement.
10. Listens.
11. Understands the benefits of cooperation.

Some problems you will face

'Best Efforts' in Teaching

(Contributed by management consultant Henrik Giaever, who told this story at the seminar presented by the British Deming Association in Oslo, Norway in January 1993)

I would like to invite you to a classroom, some 10 years ago. I was appointed the teacher for the tenth-form students in Burfjord, north Norway. The school did not provide a tenth form every year – this was a special offer to students aged 17–20 years who had not been admitted to further education because of poor performance in the ninth form. My subject was Norwegian language and literature. I had not taught these pupils before.

Focus on short-term thinking

I decided my aim was to make them improve their results sufficiently to be admitted to further education.

Well, there was no other way to achieve this than by hard work, was there? With great enthusiasm, I rolled up my sleeves and designed a work-plan. By following this, the students would in 10 weeks repeat and learn properly all the grammar they should have learned in the ninth grade. They would also write an essay every week. Writing essays was very important since it is the most important part of the continuous evaluation and the exam.

They disappointed me. Some of them really tried their best, but they just did not improve.

The general level of knowledge and skills was alarmingly low. They would have to do a lot of hard work if they could even think of passing any exam. Their attitude to studying – and to teachers – was not the best.

Introduce inspection, encourage fear

Most of them did not even seem to make an effort. Obviously, there was a lack of discipline. So I made a speech to put them on the right track. I harshly criticized most of them, but praised those that had tried. Of course I put more work into their schedule. More tests. More grades.

After a few weeks it was impossible to see any signs of progress.

Study...

During that year I was also teaching the same subject in the fourth form. To my surprise, many of the 11-year-olds performed and progressed much better than 18-year-olds. I remember a heated discussion in the classroom, when one of the most hostile boys told me that the only books he had ever taken pleasure in reading were Morgan Kane (who is the main character in a Norwegian western series). These books are

very popular, but by no means accepted by literary critics. I had at the time never read any of them myself.

I discovered that many of the students in the tenth form hardly did any reading outside school, let alone writing. In many of their homes there were no newspapers and very few books.

The students became more and more hostile, spelling mistakes increased rather than decreased, the essays became even less readable than they had been at the beginning of the term.

The time had come for me to think. I realised that I had two options:

1. Give up (They obviously do not even try to make an effort) but keep up the facade.

2. Reconsider my basic educational approach. Why did all my best efforts produce the opposite of the desired results?

... Act

I decided to have a go at option 2. So I had to talk to them. Or rather I had to *listen* to them.

Communication was not easy. These students had for years learned not to trust teachers in general, and I had given them no reason to trust me in particular. We spent a long time discussing their situation and opportunities. Many of them had hardly any hopes for the future. They had very little self-respect. Most of them wanted to get a job 'to make a lot of money', some wanted further education; but they were all generally pessimistic about their chances. Nils, a boy of almost 20, was certain that he would be imprisoned before the age of 25 (he may well have had good reason for his fears ...).

I realised that I had focused on a short-term goal, and had created an atmosphere of fear. What these youngsters needed most of all was support to get some very basic training in the use of spoken and written Norwegian – not just to pass an exam, but to cope with life.

Break down barriers, drive out fear

We made an agreement. I promised to turn the curriculum upsidedown, to do my best to get the school's permission to introduce Morgan Kane and romantic love stories on to the timetable, and help them write applications for jobs and schools. The students promised to participate in working out realistic plans of progress, and to do the work we agreed on.

Some of my colleague teachers were sceptical about this new approach, but others supported it fully. I was allowed to buy class sets of 'Morgan Kane' and girls' books. I contacted Oslo University and got in touch with people who had produced scientific papers on 'trivial literature'. This helped give the project some educational status.

The students started reading. After a while they engaged in discussions, and they did some writing. I discovered that some of them were reading a lot more than we had agreed. I put more consideration into finding topics for essays that would interest them, and indeed relating all teaching to subjects of interest to them.

Win – Win

I started to look forward to the classes, and the attitudes of the students slowly turned from 'hostile' to 'indifferent' and even 'friendly' at times. They enjoyed the work when the requirements were on a level that they were able to meet. During the winter, some of them got quite good at expressing their thoughts and dreams, both verbally and on paper.

As I said earlier, they had a long way to go. Some of them showed very good improvement. I don't think any of them ever became masters of the Norwegian language, but they all reached an acceptable level to be admitted to further education. We had a lot of fun, and at least some of their fear of learning vanished.

Source: British Deming Association

1. A serious culture clash in style of teaching and learning with traditional approaches and methods. Students may have come to expect learning to be something done to them whilst they remain passive, not active.
2. A belief amongst students that anything not formally examined does not matter.
3. Objections, criticism or even rubbishing of the course by colleagues.
4. Or ditto parents.

We believe it to be essential that a training day be held for all staff before the commencement of the programme. They must know what is being attempted, and how.

Detailed training is also required prior to commencement for those who are to deliver the programme.

A 'champion' should be sought who is able to act as role model by immersing himself in the literature of quality. If necessary, bring in an outside consultant.

Improving the process

In delivering this course we must be conscious of our objective of 'continuous improvement', not just in relation to the 'product' (education of our students), but also the process by which we seek to achieve this objective. Students and teachers must be continuously engaged in a process of searching out opportunities for improvement of the process of learning, the quality of the learning experience, and of our delivery of it. It is very important that the contribution of students to the dialogue be recognized, treated seriously, and, wherever possible, implemented. Where they are impossible to implement, the students deserve a courteous explanation as to why this is so.

Conclusion

We would conclude by suggesting that if you successfully apply the Deming paradigm of 'profound knowledge', sometimes loosely called Total Quality Management, to your school, you should expect to see major changes to:

- What students are expected to do.
- What teachers are expected to do.
- What heads of department are expected to do.
- What headteachers are expected to do.
- What governors are expected to do.

The results which you might expect to see would be:

- Improved outcomes for students.
- More satisfied parents.
- More satisfied local employers.
- More places at college for your students.
- Happier and more productive teachers and students.
- More cost-effective use of scarce resources.
- Continuous improvement of 'product' and 'process' year by year.

If you are to make a start down this road, then first you must find your 'champion', to drive forward the programme for quality. He or she must possess rather scarce qualities:

- willing to learn
- open-minded
- self-confident
- a risk taker
- a creative and innovative thinker
- a leader who can inspire confidence and trust in others

Do you fit the bill? Why not give it a try? Help your people to drive out fear.

FINAL THOUGHTS

Much has been written about the impossibility of attempting to use in the West management methods which have worked for the Japanese. The reality, of course, is that we can see that it is possible from the example of Japanese companies which have successfully transplanted here, and British and American companies which have been able to amend these methods to work successfully not just with Western employees, but with Western managers. The story of the Japanese transplants is thoroughly documented by Peter Wickens in *The Road to Nissan*, whilst the success of the Rover company in recent years is common knowledge. What we have been trying to demonstrate here is that the methods originally taught to the Japanese by Deming are applicable in the UK in educational organizations just as much as in factories.

Deming's 'system of profound knowledge' is just that, a complete philosophy which goes far beyond its origins as statistical process control. We feel that there is enough evidence available already to show that the application of Deming's thinking in schools is capable of producing revolutionary change. But it does require champions who are themselves revolutionaries, willing to stand the conventional wisdom of fifty years on its head.

Perhaps the biggest obstacle to the application of these new management principles in any organization does lie in understanding one fundamental difference between Japanese and Western culture. In Japan the Confucian culture combined with historical experience has produced a strong preference for group consensus, and team-based approaches to any kind of problem solving, whether in politics, work or home. This has, however, meant that the need for individual self-expression has been partially suppressed at work. It finds its outlets in leisure-time activities, from golf to playing pinball machines. In the West, in complete contrast, the notion of competition, self-help and market forces, combined in the USA with the frontier spirit, has produced a highly individualistic and confrontational culture, in politics, work and home. The Western manager or worker finds expression of his need for team-based activities in his rugby club, male voice choir, community association and so on.

The fact is, we all need to develop both aspects of our personality, and, in the West, the trick in successfully implementing the quality paradigm is the harnessing of the basic desire of all of us to be part of a winning team, and the pleasure which we all derive from cooperative activities in our family and leisure time. Kazuo Murata of Yuasa Battery, saw this when he set up his battery plant in the Welsh valleys. A rugby fan himself, he noted the fanatical support for local rugby clubs, and the incredible management skills demonstrated by quite ordinary working men in running these complex organizations. He simply set out to make his workers feel themselves to be as much part of the company team as the rugby team.

Traditional Western management style, translated as it has been to the school and the classroom, truly does drive by fear. Deming, in contrast, constantly talks about 'joy in work' and 'joy in learning'. We believe that it is possible to improve the standards reached by all our young people, whilst still giving them a sense of ownership of their learning process, and true joy in learning.

Chapter 14

Postscript

No one, child or other, can enjoy learning if he must be constantly concerned about gradings and gold stars.

W.E. Deming

In Chapter 2 we began our account of the application of TQM principles in education with the story of Mt Edgecumbe High School in Sitka, Alaska, and the work of the Ohio elementary school teacher, Theresa Hicks. They had both been influenced by the work of W. Edwards Deming, and had successfully applied the principles of managing variance in processes to the problems posed, in the first case in managing a school and its work and resources, and in the second case in the management of the day-to-day work of a class-room. We would like to end our account by looking at two similar initiatives in a UK context. The William Howard School is a comprehensive school located in Cumbria in the far north-west of England. It is an area with serious problems of economic decline resulting from the process of deindustrialization which hit the UK in the 1970s and 1980s. It does therefore face similar problems to those experienced at Mt Edgecumbe High School. John Marsh is a freelance quality consultant who also works part-time for the Avon TEC, delivering in-service training courses to schools within the Avon Local Education Authority.

The critical influence on Roger Alston, headteacher of William Howard School, was not Deming, but the work of Malcolm Baldridge in the USA. In 1992 an officer from the Cumbria LEA attended a course at IBM UK. In the face of a rapid erosion of its market share in the early 1980s due to complacency and unawareness of either the work of its competitors or the needs of its customers, IBM has adopted a series of initiatives to improve quality and service offered to its customers. After initial successful attempts to improve manufacturing quality by using the Deming and Crosby models, it decided that these models did not work well in the service areas of the business, which constitute some 90 per cent or more of its activities. IBM therefore adopted the model for achieving 'customer-driven transformation' developed by Malcolm Baldridge and used for assessment of candidates for the highly prestigious Baldridge Awards, the highest accolade awarded in the USA for excellence in quality management.

The Baldridge model starts from the premise that transformation implies change. Change in turn implies that you understand where you are now (the current reality), and where you want to be (your vision). The essential features of the model are set out (courtesy of IBM UK) in Figures 14.1 and 14.2. The essential features of this model differ little in our view from the quality improvement programmes which are at the heart of the implementation of the Deming approach. These features are:

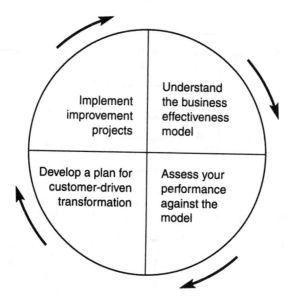

Figure 14.1 *Key elements of customer-driven transformation.*
Source: IBM UK Ltd (1993)

Customer-driven transformation is based on the Baldridge business effectiveness model and embraces the 'What worked?' elements of previous initiatives. It is a repeating cycle which has four closely-linked phases....

... Management teams review and analyse the model, using it to develop their own vision of a world-class organization;

... They then establish their own current reality and compare this with the model to identify strengths and improvement opportunities;

... Using the opportunities for improvement, they develop a 3–12 month implementation plan for the high priority changes. The plan includes objectives, delivered projects, responsibilities, organization, risk analysis and, most importantly, the process management system;

... The project teams design and lead the implementation of appropriate process, system and behavioural changes.

Let's look at these four elements in a little more detail...

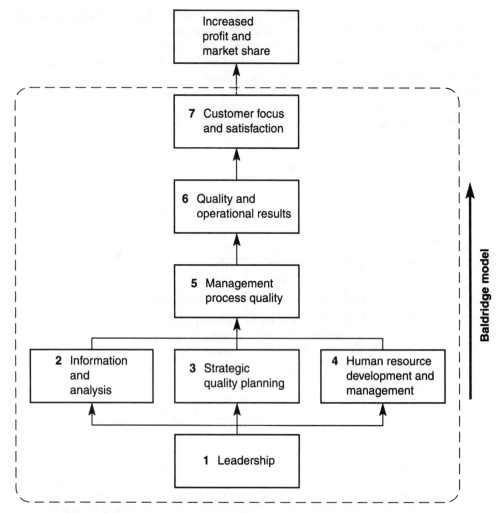

Figure 14.2 *The Baldridge business effectiveness model.*
Source: IBM UK Ltd (1993)

The Baldridge model describes a business, or any organization, which is highly *responsive to customers* and compares with the best in the world. Its only goal is customer satisfaction to world-class levels and it assumes, as do all models of this type, that managing the quality of the processes that deliver value to customers is of paramount importance. Prerequisites for this are well-formed information systems, highly motivated employees and quality planning/investment systems integrated with the organization's financial planning systems.

Without *leadership*, none of this will work – it is the *driver*.

The model has many feedback loops – some obvious, others less so. Understanding these loops and building simple management systems to drive continuous improvement is what it's all about.

The EFQM model is almost identical.

- responsiveness to customers
- the search for customer satisfaction
- benchmarking world-class practice
- managing processes for quality
- well-formed information systems
- quality planning systems
- well-motivated employees
- leadership from the top

A key difference arises in the operational delivery of the model. It rests on a results-orientated self-scoring system to be used by quality teams in assessing where their department or workstation stands a present. This is intended to allow teams to identify areas of strength and weakness in their activities which will lead to action programmes to bring about improvement. This assessment system is illustrated in Figure 14.3. It is used by IBM as a self-assessment system, but is also used by external assessors in measuring the performance of companies and organizations (which may include schools) for the Baldridge Award, presented each year by the President of the USA to successful companies. It is becoming as important in the US business scene as the Deming Awards are in Japan.

Both Deming and Baldridge would probably agree with the following comment (source unknown):

If you can't define it you can't measure it.
If you can't measure it you can't manage it.
If you can't manage it you will probably fail.

Charles Hobson, IBM(UK) Quality Manager, expressed an interest in acting as external consultant to enable a chosen school to apply the Baldridge model to its activities. He was interested to discover whether or not it would work in an educational context. William Howard School was eventually chosen for the experiment, and Roger Alston together with his senior staff attended a training session with Charles Hobson. This was held at an attractive venue in the Lake District, with no commitment initially on the part of the school. The main difficulty which emerged early on was (as we have suggested earlier) the incongruity of the commercial language in which the model is expressed. Fortunately the school had for some four years been developing performance indicators with which to examine the quality of teaching and learning in the classroom. As a result they were already talking in terms of 'mission statements' and 'quality control'. The language remains a problem in terms of obtaining 'buy in' from members of the staff. However, even the sceptics accept that the model is giving the school a structured method for identifying strengths and weaknesses and identifying areas for improvement. Roger Alston takes the view that the advantage of the Baldridge model lies in the absence of prescriptive techniques, such as SPC, to be used for improving quality. He believes that this makes the model more suitable for an educational context than the Deming model. We would not entirely agree with this, but accept that it is less important to use a particular model than it is to take on board the need to seek continuous improvement in everything we do in school, on the basis of team-work and measured data. Alston sees the model as used by IBM as being too dependent on rigid use of the scoring system. He intends to use it in a more flexible way.

William Howard School had been working along Baldridge lines, in collaboration with Charles Hobson, for one year. Already substantial progress has been made. A mission statement has been set out, which is reproduced overleaf.

APPROACH	DEPLOYMENT	RESULTS
Is there a management system and defined, repeatable processes for becoming market-driven?	Is the approach fully deployed, and in all areas?	Is the application of the approach getting measurable quality and market performance results?
100% • Fully effective prevention-based system of continuous improvement • Excellent integration across the business	• Fully deployed and used in all areas of the business and all support areas	• World-class results sustained in all business and support areas • Clear competitive advantage • Results obviously caused by the approach
80% • System well developed and tested • Excellent integrations in most areas	• Fully deployed and used in all major areas of the business and most support areas	• Excellent results in most areas of business and many support areas • Sustained, improving competitive advantage • Clear evidence that results are caused by the approach
60% • Well planned and documented with evidence of refinement through evaluation/improvement cycles • Good integration in many areas	• Deployed and used in all major areas and many support areas	• Good results in major areas of the business and positive trends in some support areas • Much evidence they are caused by the approach
50% • Sound, prevention-based system including evaluation/improvement cycles • Some evidence of integration	• Deployed and used in most major areas and some support (peripheral) areas	• Positive trends in most major areas with some evidence they are caused by the approach
40% • Beginning of prevention-based system • Methods, tools, techniques defined • Integration begun in some aspects of the business	• Deployed and used in many major areas of the business	• Positive trends in key areas of the business
20% • Reactive systems • Awareness of need for prevention-based systems and integration across business	• Beginning in some parts of the business	• Some results in areas where deployed
0% • No system or integration	• Not deployed or used	• No evidence that results are caused by the approach

Figure 14.3 *Assessment.*
Source: IBM UK Ltd (1993)

Associated with the model are a set of assessment techniques which enable management teams to measure the progress of their own customer-driven transformation programme against a 1000-point scale. This is a results-oriented approach, not an activity-based approach.

Assessment can be done by the team or by an external group who have an in-depth understanding of the model. Self-assessment is the recommended vehicle for the first and second cycles.

The assessment techniques learnt by the team enable them to distinguish between plans and processes and real, implemented changes. During this part of the cycle, teams arrive at a consensus on strengths and areas for improvement and also a numeric rating.

Achieving consensus can take a long time and generate vigorous discussion - but that's all part of the learning process.

The quality improvement plan so far has involved the establishment of four project groups on Communication, Reward and Recognition, Data Analysis and Customer Satisfaction respectively. These groups are overseen by a group consisting of several governors. The membership of the groups ranges from four to eight members, reflecting both the specialist interests of each group, and employees and governors from all levels in the organization down to administrative assistant. The groups have set out for themselves clear objectives and goals. They have also identified 'risk' factors which are likely to hinder progress. These include a level of scepticism amongst front-line staff. To them the quality programme may be seen as nothing more than the flavour of the month and as being divisive of staff and irrelevant to teaching.

We have set out below the essentials of the quality improvement plan in the form in which they were presented by Roger Alston at a seminar organized by Charles Hobson at IBM Training Centre, Warwick. We have also included two practical outcomes of the programme so far which have proved to be very useful. One is a complaints log. Systematic collection and collation of complaints from 'customers', be they parents or members of the local community, is a powerful weapon in the search for continuous improvement. Use of such data in a positive and constructive fashion contrasts with the more usual defensive and secretive approach to such matters in most schools. The other examples are two 'customer survey' questionnaires issued to students and parents. This is very similar to the example which we used in Chapter 4, which was used by Bradford Grammar School. Again, this is a very powerful instrument if a school genuinely wishes to improve its service to its 'customers'.

The William Howard School and Centre
IBM Quality Improvement Plan

Goal

We aim to:

- be responsive to the needs of all those involved in the school
- maintain commitment to continuing improvement

in order to provide the highest quality educational experience in our area.

Quality Projects 1993–4

3.1 Communication

- Put together Quality Assurance Framework and communicate.
- Awareness of QA procedures.
- Deployment of QA procedures.
- Commitment to the procedures.

4.1 Reward and Recognition

- Informal systems – recognition
- Formal systems – financial reward – criteria etc.

6.1 Data Analysis

- Lack of objective data.
- No analysis of value added factor.

7.3 Customer Satisfaction

- No logging or analysis of complaints.
- No customer satisfaction measurement.

Composition of Quality Groups

Communication	*Reward and Recognition*
Director of Staffing*	Headteacher*
Head of History	Chair of Governors
Head of Year 7	Director of Staffing
2i/c History	Governor – Teacher Rep.
Careers Coordinator	Governor – LEA Rep.
	Governor – coopted

Data Analysis	*Customer Satisfaction*
Director of Assessment and Planning*	Head of Year 7*
Senior Admin. Officer	Head of Years 12 and 13*
Headteacher	Administrative Assistant
2i/c Maths	Science Teacher
2i/c History	3 sixth form students
Careers Coordinator	
IT Coordinator	
KS3 Science Coordinator	

Goals and Objectives of the Groups

Communication

- Staff to have a clear understanding and acceptance of the IBM Model and associated processes.
- There would be a more responsive approach to planning.
- The School Development Plan would be informed by the self-assessment process undertaken by all staff.

Recognition and Reward

- A systematic approach to recognition and reward established and communicated to all staff.
- There would be documentation of the system and a means of making quality measurements, e.g. sets of criteria.

Data Analysis

- Centralize National Curriculum records.
- Use an OMR to improve the efficiency and accuracy of attendance recording.

Customer Satisfaction

- A system for the logging and analysis of complaints.
- An agreed procedure for processing and dealing with complaints.
- Research ways of obtaining customer feedback and running some pilot schemes.

Work of the Groups

1 Customer Satisfaction

Logging of complaints received – by telephone
                                    Heads of Year
                                    Heads of Department
(Research at Marks and Spencer)

Customer feedback – questionnaires to students and parents in Years 7 and 13.
(Research at Leisure Services, Carlisle City Council.)

Involvement of sixth form students in the group and work with the Year 7 Pupil Council Representatives.

2 Communication

Familiarization with the process and ways of 'training' colleagues.
(Research at Allied Signals)

Arranging a programme of familiarization seminars.
Staff involved – Teaching staff
                Administrative Staff
                Governors/Quality Council
                PTA Committee
                Site Manager
Informal networking.

Risks

Examples:

Communication Group

- Perceived as a 'bolt-on' activity.
- Scepticism – irrelevant to teaching.
- 'Flavour of the month'.

Rewards and Recognition Group

- Financial constraints.
- Legislation – New Pay Spine.
- Scepticism – divisiveness.
- Staff would not accept subjective, intangible criteria.

3 Reward and Recognition

Development of criteria against which judgements can be made.

- Teaching and learning
- Management/Leadership
- 'Extra Dimension'

Accountabilities for Heads of Year
                        Heads of Department

4 Data Analysis

Departmental Development Plans on standard pro-forma which is now stored centrally on SIMS>

OMR Attendance procedures being piloted.

Assessment information being centralized.

Statistics on daily cover and subsequent effects.

COMPLAINTS LOG

| | 1. Lost property 2. Illness 3.Homework 4. Academic 5. Staff 6. Travel |
| | 7. Bullying 8. Assault 9. Damage/theft 10. Out of school 11. Other |

DATE	FROM	STUDENTS	TYPE OF COMPLAINT	ACTION	Level of S
			1. 2. 3. 4. 5. 6. 7. 8. 9. 10. 11. Description . . .	Date . . . . 1. No Action 2. Phone back 3. Letter 4. Interview 5. In school support 6. External agencies 7. Recorded on file	1 Low 2 3 4 5 High
			1. 2. 3. 4. 5. 6. 7. 8. 9. 10. 11. Description . . .	Date . . . . 1. No Action 2. Phone back 3. Letter 4. Interview 5. In school support 6. External agencies 7. Recorded on file	1 Low 2 3 4 5 High
			1. 2. 3. 4. 5. 6. 7. 8. 9. 10. 11. Description . . .	Date . . . . 1. No Action 2. Phone back 3. Letter 4. Interview 5. In school support 6. External agencies 7. Recorded on file	1 Low 2 3 4 5 High
			1. 2. 3. 4. 5. 6. 7. 8. 9. 10. 11. Description . . .	Date . . . . 1. No Action 2. Phone back 3. Letter 4. Interview 5. In school support 6. External agencies 7. Recorded on file	1 Low 2 3 4 5 High
			1. 2. 3. 4. 5. 6. 7. 8. 9. 10. 11. Description . . .	Date . . . . 1. No Action 2. Phone back 3. Letter 4. Interview 5. In school support 6. External agencies 7. Recorded on file	1 Low 2 3 4 5 High
			1. 2. 3. 4. 5. 6. 7. 8. 9. 10. 11. Description . . .	Date . . . . 1. No Action 2. Phone back 3. Letter 4. Interview 5. In school support 6. External agencies 7. Recorded on file	1 Low 2 3 4 5 High
			1. 2. 3. 4. 5. 6. 7. 8. 9. 10. 11. Description . . .	Date . . . . 1. No Action 2. Phone back 3. Letter 4. Interview 5. In school support 6. External agencies 7. Recorded on file	1 Low 2 3 4 5 High

Figure 14.4 *Complaints log.*

WILLIAM HOWARD SCHOOL YEAR SEVEN QUESTIONNAIRE FOR STUDENTS

Please fill in the questionnaire below by ticking the approriate box for each question. Consider the answers carefully ... it is important that we obtain accurate results. Please answer the questions yourself without discussing them with anyone. It is your opinion we are interested in. (replies will remain completely anonymous).

The aim of this exercise is simply to identify areas of strength and weakness in the education we are providing for our Year Seven students. This information will help us to make the most of our strengths and improve upon any areas of weakness as we plan for the future.

Thank you for your help.   Students = 172

Derek R. Kay   Head of Year Seven

ARE YOU SATISFIED THAT YOU...

	VERY SATISFIED	SATISFIED	DIS-SATISFIED	VERY DIS-SATISFIED
1. have been sufficiently pushed in lessons to achieve your best				
2. have been offered a variety of lunchtime and after school clubs (Please offer suggestions below.)				
3. are enjoying Year Seven.				
4. were well prepared for entering school through the programme of school visits, induction day, and parent interviews.				
5. have been given enough homework to extend your work in class				
6. have been able to find someone in school to speak to if you have had a question or a problem.				
7. have been helped enough in lessons if you have had a problem.				

PLEASE USE THE SPACE BELOW TO ADD ANY FURTHER COMMENTS ABOUT THE EDUCATION BEING PROVIDED IN YEAR SEVEN

Figure 14.5 *William Howard School Year 7 questionnaire for students.*
Source: R. Alston, William Howard School

WILLIAM HOWARD SCHOOL YEAR SEVEN QUESTIONNAIRE FOR PARENTS

I would be grateful if you could spare a few minutes to fill in the following questionnaire by ticking the appropriate box at the end of each question (replies will remain completely anonymous).

The aim of this exercise is simply to identify areas of strength and weakness in the education we are providing for our Year Seven students. This information will help us to make the most of our strengths and improve upon any areas of weakness as we plan for the future.

Please return the questionnaire in the postage paid envelope provided. Thank you for your help.

Derek R. Kay   Head of Year Seven

	VERY SATISFIED	SATISFIED	DIS-SATISFIED	VERY DIS-SATISFIED

ARE YOU SATISFIED THAT YOUR SON/DAUGHTER

1. has been sufficiently challenged and or helped depending on their needs.				
2. has been offered a variety of educational opportunities outside the classroom. (Please offer suggestions below.)				
3. is enjoying Year Seven.				
4. was given sufficient preparation for entering school through the programme of school visits, induction day, and parent interviews.				
5. has been given enough homework at a level you feel is appropriate.				

ARE YOU SATISFIED

1. with the parents evening arrangements.				
2. with the amount of information you have received regarding the way things are done in school (e.g. homework policy, school visits, etc.)				
3. with the response you have had from school if you have contacted us on any matter.				

PLEASE USE THE SPACE BELOW TO ADD ANY FURTHER COMMENTS ABOUT THE EDUCATION BEING PROVIDED IN YEAR SEVEN

Figure 14.6 *William Howard School Year 7 questionnaire for parents.*
Source: R. Alston, William Howard School

Interesting results have also been produced by other groups. The Data Analysis Group has produced detailed statistics on staff absence, cover and supply provision. This provides useful information on the cumulative effects on each class of staff absences. Alston, prior to this new initiative, has taken steps to flatten the organizational structure of the school, and he sees the prime benefit of the development of the Quality Project Groups as being the development of team-work and the breaking down of functional department boundaries. This leads to a more open communications system and bottom-up rather than top-down driven efforts to improve the school. He recognizes that the experiment is still in its very early stages, and that considerable scepticism exists amongst staff, but he believes that if they persevere, he will eventually obtain 'buy in' from most of his colleagues. As he himself says, 'If the thing works, if it continues to capture people's imagination, then I can see a time when our planning process will come through this quality programme, rather than the other way round' (quoted in *Times Educational Supplement*, May 1993).

We have described the pioneering work of Roger Alston in some detail, but we have not been able to locate the many other schools and colleges which are also experimenting with the Deming paradigm. No doubt their story will emerge one day soon. We can, however, bring to you in his own words the experiences of John Marsh, an independent consultant working with Avon TEC in the south west of England. He has worked closely with Todd Bergman, who is now quality coordinator in Mt Edgecumbe High School, Sitka. This is appropriate since it was the pioneering work of this school which prompted this book, and whose story was described in Chapter 2. Together Todd Bergman and John Marsh developed a three-stage model for the implementation of the quality paradigm in education. This has three levels: TQM applied to the management of the school and its resources; the teaching of the paradigm to students; and the application of the paradigm in the classroom. It may be interesting to note that in Bradford Grammar School, we began at level 2, teaching TQM to Business Studies students. This led naturally to the search for classroom applications, and some of the emphasis on a higher level of 'customer satisfaction' is now infiltrating in a quite natural way into the general management of the school.

The conclusion which we reach is that it is possible for any teacher at any level who may be excited by the ideas in this book to begin to use the paradigm in order to improve his own delivery of good education, starting from wherever in the organization he happens to be at the time.

John Marsh has given us permission to print in his own words his account of his efforts to introduce the Deming paradigm to schools in the south west of England.

A REPORT FROM THE FRONT LINE

John Marsh, Independent Consultant

Background

This update is based on the author's experience of developing and implementing Total Quality in Education. His industrial experience of Total Quality commenced in 1985 and his most recent position was as Total Quality Manager for a Training and Enterprise Council. In this role he was concerned with improving quality of life by achieving systemic improvement.

Methods

One of the major reasons for total quality performing poorly in industry is lack of senior management commitment. This is not a root cause. One reason that managers have lacked real commitment is that total quality has not been promoted as integral to the whole organization through its strategy. As a consequence the methods being developed for education must include strategic planning. Other key elements include leadership, people management and process management. This model is in line with the European Quality Award.

Early implementation was based around this model. However, it is lacking. It took the opportunity of working with Todd Bergman, the Quality and Technology co-ordinator of Mt Edgecumbe High School, Sitka, Alaska, to develop a different way of looking at Quality in Education. Todd and the author developed a three-level framework.

The first and lowest level is applying total quality to the management of schools. The model based on the European Quality Award works well here because, in terms of management, schools and businesses do have similarities. However, their fundamental purposes are very different. Managers of schools find this level interesting but it doesn't tend to excite students and teachers. It is an essential starting point because schools need to improve their management processes in order to get more from less.

The next level up in the model is the teaching of total quality to students. The philosophy, principles, methods and tools are taught to students. This level is more rewarding because, very often, students do not present the same barriers to learning as adults, entrenched in traditional ways of doing things.

The highest level is Total Quality in Learning. This is where the two previous levels come together in the classroom and result in the reinvention of education. Here the results are dramatic and quantum improvements can be made. This level cannot be rushed. It has taken Mt Edgecumbe School eight years of implementation to reach. The previous levels cannot be short-cut.

Progress in the UK

The author is currently working closely with four comprehensive schools in the south west. He has worked with several further education colleges and two universities as well as kindergarten through junior high schools in the USA. Whilst many UK education establishments are making bold claims it is still very early days.

Generally the universities appear to be keener to teach students rather than practise the ideas themselves. This kind of hypocrisy is untenable. FE colleges have Quality clearly on the agenda because of incorporation. Some have taken a very hard systems approach often following BS 5750. Others have taken a very soft approach, only addressing cultural issues. Several are getting a sensible balance, although the author, a member of the International Standards Committee on Quality, believes BS 5750 to be wholly unsuitable to most schools at this point in their quality journeys.

Somervale Comprehensive School, Midsomer Norton, started investigating the quality theme several years ago. Avon TEC agreed to support them to pilot total quality 18 months ago. The process started with a strategic workshop. This involved students, staff, employers, parents and governors. This team developed a full statement of purpose, identified critical success factors and key processes for improvement. As a result a quality forum was established along with two improvement teams.

Unfortunately, owing to the summer holidays and a major accident, there was a delay in communicating with other members of staff. With hindsight, more time should have been spent communicating with all the other stakeholders not directly involved. However, the first improvement team, on internal communications, achieved a very favourable result which, whilst hardly earth shattering, reflected management commitment, saved money and achieved what many thought to be impossible. The second team looked at improving the school's planning process. All improvement teams involve students, staff, parents, governors, etc.

The school is currently designing a Business Centre and it has run a workshop for local employers on the theme of quality. It is currently preparing for Investors in People, the national standard for human resource development. Next stages include training staff and students in the philosophy and tools and testing out these concepts within the classroom. Whilst many teachers have been rightly sceptical, many people outside the school have been keen to help and be involved. Much of the work to date, whilst modest, has helped with immediate pressures, such as OFSTED inspections. This school has a very clear sense of vision and values and a process to review them continually.

Westwood St Thomas Comprehensive School approached a similar process in a different way. The head had been getting training for herself and her senior team over a period of 12 months. They have been testing the philosophy and tools on specifics like pastoral issues. Recently they felt confident and competent enough to involve the rest of the community. On the first day of term they had over 100 students, parents, governors, community members, staff, employers, etc. in the school. In small teams the senior management team facilitated the whole process of identifying wants and needs and key improvement opportunities. By involving so many, the school has a momentum to proceed through the levels of total quality in education.

Key findings

The most important finding is that total quality *is* applicable to education, if not essential. Schools are in a unique position to influence the whole community and to start to break the vicious circle of decline which affects us all. The author sees quality improvement in education as the single most important application because it affects all the systems which operate in the community.

However, there are many things to be learnt about the differences between industrial applications and those in schools. Some of these are apparent now:

Firstly schools, whilst being complex organizations, are not businesses. They do not exist for profit and this must be reflected in any total quality approach. The students are the 'primary customers' and *not* the products. If every child is different then the goal of education must be to provide an environment which meets every child's wants and needs. Quality is not about reducing variety but about increasing it.

There is no prescription for total quality in industry, so there is not likely to be one in education. Every school must adapt the philosophy, principles and tools to create its own way of meeting the wants and needs of its customers. However, the principles and values are important and these are not uniformly agreed in the total quality field. The author, whilst having been exposed to many quality philosophies, finds the teachings of Dr Deming and Stephen Covey most applicable to schools because of their people-centred approach, supported with systems thinking.

However, this philosophy may upset many currently in positions of power. Dr Deming's teachings make a nonsense of grading, league tables, performance-related pay, etc. He deduces this from a technical point of view, not a political one. This raises another key constraint and that is one of control. Companies have far greater control and influence over their key processes than schools. Research and development is an essential process for a manufacturing company. However, schools have lost much of their influence, if not all, over a key process, curriculum design. The author is yet to discover how much flexibility is really possible within the National Curriculum but is concerned that most successful American practitioners have redesigned curriculum for the next century based on the theme of life-long learning.

Total quality in education is not a quick fix. It will take years of systemic improvement in schools to deal with the real root causes. There is no alternative other than continual decline. It is also not free and will require some investment, mainly in training. Creative ways will need to be explored to achieve this. So far several leading industrial practitioners have been keen to help.

To date the management emphasis of total quality in schools has been uninspiring to many teachers. Progression to total quality in learning will correct this because the focus is on the students. In line with this the language of the subject is very off-putting and great care should be taken to adapt it to the language of the organization.

Finally, quality starts and finishes with leadership. It is true that everyone contributes to quality but without principle-centred leadership it is impossible. Are our leaders in education ready for the challenge?

Marsh draws our attention to several points of a cautionary nature, which in concluding this book we would like to endorse.

- Schools are not businesses.
- Teachers mistrust and fear the language of business.
- We must therefore translate the thinking of Deming into a language which reflects the professional aspirations and values of teachers.
- The TQM paradigm runs counter to much of the management style and methods which are being imposed on schools by governments anxious for results and efficiency. These include grading, league tables of results, testing, appraisal of teachers, performance-related pay.
- There is no substitute for leadership. Leadership in the right direction will occur only if teachers and managers recognize the need for fundamental change in a new direction, and are convinced that Deming was right.

The experience of another independent consultant in this field may reinforce the last point. Terri Wilson has considerable experience in her previous employment as a quality manger, and is now offering advice on the introduction of quality management techniques to a variety of firms and organizations. She was recently invited to do a presentation at a comprehensive school in the south of England which sought to improve its performance and public image. She found that her ideas were enthusiastically received by the managers and administrators. They are still seeking to implement a quality improvement programme in the administration department. However, the presentation of the paradigm to the teaching staff and headteacher fell on stony ground. The teachers are taking a very negative attitude to the total quality idea, and this is making it very difficult for the administrators to progress with their experiments. This failure would seem to stem from the apparent incompatibility of the language in which TQM is inevitably presented with the deeply held values many teachers hold about education and its relationship to business. This problem can be overcome with patience and persistence, but a greater problem is that headteachers also hold these values, and find it difficult to provide the right sort of leadership, even if they are superficially convinced of the value of the TQM paradigm. Terri Wilson comments on her experience,'I am afraid that the headteacher appears not to have grasped the concept. He just shouts a lot, and *tells* everyone to work in a quality way.'

If our book helps teachers to understand that TQM is not just a new management fad that may help firms to make more profit, or even exploit their workers more successfully (as some would suggest), we will have succeeded. Out of his scholarly understanding of statistics, Deming, perhaps surprisingly, constructed a philosophy for life which in its positive affirmation of the power of the human spirit should be the guiding light for educators. The total quality idea is potentially a revolutionary tool for the reformation of education. Why not take Deming's advice: 'Now just go do it.'

Postscript

A system of schools is not merely pupils, teachers, governors and parents. It should be instead, a component in a system of education in which pupils – take joy in learning, free from fear of grades and gold stars, and in which teachers take joy in their work, free from fear of [appraisal] and ranking.

W.E. Deming

Edgecumbe Quality Team
1330 Seward Ave
Sitka, Alaska 99835

1993

Dear Educator,

Thank you for your recent inquiry. Quality is many things to many people. In the minds of us at Mt Edgecumbe High School, quality is a dynamic cultural transformation that is here to stay. Quality is a revolution that is sweeping the globe and will forever change the nature of international competition, cooperation and human achievement. The aim of quality productivity and efficiency in the industrial arena paved the way for substantial management developments in business, government and education. In some countries the cultural transformation to quality has been integrated into social entities; through community councils and citizens charters for quality in every aspect of human interaction. Quality is a new dynamic for predominately authoritarian societies and organizations; quality challenges many of our cultural foundations. Quality involves the creative talents of every individual within and connected to an organization. Quality is a new dynamic for perceiving, processing and interacting that seeks to continually improve the world around us. Cultural transformation of an organization can occur using a quality process model allowing receivers (customers), their wants and needs, a vision, mission and purpose, critical success factors, processes, inputs, outputs, tools and techniques and reengineering within the system to all become sustainable for not only the vitality of the organization, but also its competitiveness and ingenuity! The receivers, both internal and external, will experience satisfaction and delight based on the transformation. The quality culture at Mt Edgecumbe High School is rooted in the philosophies of Covey, Senge, Barker, Deming and many others. Essential elements of quality culture at Mt Edgecumbe include quality philosophy and sciences, systems thinking, a focus on processes, teamwork, continuous training and an obsession with improvement. Education needs to develop, implement and sustain a comprehensive quality culture. Transformation to a quality culture will enable us to optimize educational content, delivery and outcomes adaptive to changing personal and societal needs.

Todd Bergman
Quality Coordinator
Mt Edgecumbe High School

Bibliography

Atkinson, Philip E. (1990) *Creating Culture Change*. Bedford: IFS Publications.

Banks, J. (1992) *The Benchmarking Cycle*.

Beare, H. *et al.* (1989) *Creating an Excellent School*. London: Routledge.

Blanchard, K. (1984) *The One Minute Manager*. London: Fontana.

British Deming Association (various authors) (1992) Pamphlet series. Proceedings of National Forum. Salisbury: BDA.

Collard, Ron (1989) *Total Quality: Success through People*. London: Institute of Peronnel Management.

Davies, B. and Ellison, L. (1991) *Marketing the Secondary School*. Harlow: Longman.

Delbridge *et al.* (1992) 'Pushing back the frontiers of management control and work intensification under JIT/TQM regimes'. *New Technology, Work and Employment*, vol. 7.

Deming, W. Edwards (1982) *Out of the Crisis*. Cambridge, Mass.: MIT Press.

Downes, P. (1988) *Local Financial Management of Schools*. Oxford: Blackwell.

Gaunt, Helen J. (1992) *Marketing Your School*. Bradford: Horton Press.

Hannam, R.G. *Kaizen for Europe* (1993) Bedford: IFS Ltd

Likert, R. (1967) *Human Organization*. New York: McGraw-Hill.

Murato, K. and Harrison, A. (1991) *How to Make Japanese Mangaement Methods Work in the West*. Aldershot: Gower.

Oakland, John S. (1989) *Total Quality Management*. Melksham: Redwood Press.

Oakland, John S. and Followell, Roy (1990) *Statistical Process Control*. Oxford: Heinemann.

Scherkenbach, William W. (1991) *Deming's Road to Continual Improvement*. Tennessee: SPC Press.

Taylor, F. W. (1911) *The Principles of Scientific Management*.

Tressell, R. (1905) *The Ragged Trousered Philanthropists*. Reprinted London: Paladin, 1991.

Walton, Mary (1989) *The Deming Management Method*. London: Mercury.

West-Burnham, John (1991) *Quality Management for Schools*. Harlow: Longman.

Wickens, P. (1987) *The Road to Nissan*. London: Macmillan.

Appendix 1

The Red Bead Experiment

In Chapter 5 we explained briefly the manner in which the experiment might be conducted. In this appendix we have set out Professor Henry Neave's slightly amended version of the experiment as carried out by ourselves in school with sixth form pupils. We have done so in the form of OHP slides for the convenience of our readers. We include the method of calculation of results in order to draw up a chart of variance. A fuller explanation may be found in Neave's British Deming Association pamphlet. We have also summarized some of the interpretations which may arise from the experiment.

OHP 1: Staff Required

Staff	Need to
1 Recorder	Write, Perform Calculations
1 Chief Inspector	Compare Figures: Shout
2 Junior Inspectors	Count to twenty: Write Clearly
6 Willing Workers	Obey Orders
1 Foreman	Be Aggressive: Be in control

The above are to be chosen from volunteers from the class or course members, except the Foreman, who is played by the Tutor.

OHP 2: Instructions

The workers should be 'trained' before the experiment commences.

The work standard is 50 units of production per week.

Each worker in turn uses the 'paddle' to take fifty beads from the tray.

The Junior Inspectors must count and record the number of red beads in the batch.

The Chief Inspectors visually checks the count, and if a discrepancy arises must decide which count to take.

The Recorder then writes on the Record Sheet the number of red beads for that worker in that week.

It is important to make sure that the process is carried out each time strictly according to the regulations, which require the following points to be observed:

The tray is first filled by tipping the beads from the box, right hand to left, holding the box 5 cm exactly from the tray. Each worker after completing his task must pour the beads back from tray to box, and from paddle to box before handing over to the next worker.

Each worker carries out the task to complete the week's work.

After two weeks the workers are warned that the percentage of red beads (defective product) is too high and that the following week is to be 'appraisal week'. At the end of the third week the three weakest workers with the highest score of defective products are sacked, and the remaining four work double shifts to maintain production.

The foreman will of course seek reasons for the poor performance of some of his workers. He may seek the advice of the members of the group who are observers.

OHP 3: Scorecard. The Experiment on Red Beads

Name	Week 1	Week 2	Week 3	Week 4		
Weekly total						
Total so far						
	÷6	÷12	÷18	÷24		
Average so far						

Junior Inspector:

Chief Inspector:

Recorder:

OHP 4: Expectations

Since 20 per cent of the beads in the box are red and 80 per cent white, we would expect that each worker would be likely to produce 10 red beads each time.

This will not usually happen. The numbers will probably vary between 7 and 13. To predict that it would be 10 is statistically inaccurate since the sampling method is mechanical, not random. Each bead would have to be numbered, and the 50 beads be selected by a random selection of numbers for this to be so.

We would find that, over time, the number of red beads would settle down to an average, but *not* on the percentage figure we expected because *there are other variables involved*. It may be that the red beads are smaller, or larger, or of a different shape, or of a different tackiness to the white ones *or* it may be that the paddle holes are not identical in size.

But $\bar{x}$ (average) will settle at some value and the process is said then to be in *statistical control*.

There will be some degree of variance around this average ($\bar{x}$). We might expect it to be in the range 8–12. In fact the range will be wider than this.

This can be shown by using the standard calculation for the measurement of *variance* (or variation) around $\bar{x}$.

OHP 5: Calculation of Variance

Six workers work four days, draw (say) 220 red beads.

1. Divide number of red beads by number of 'drawings' i.e. 6 workers x 4 days

   $\dfrac{220}{24}$ = 9.2 daily average

   $\bar{x}$ = 9.2

2. Calculate average proportion of red beads produced per day by *ratio* of red beads to total beads produced

   $\bar{p} = \dfrac{220}{6\text{x}4\text{x}50}$ = 0.18

3. Calculate UCL and LCL (control limits) by using the formula:

   UCL = $\bar{x}$ + 3 $\sqrt{\bar{x}(1-\bar{p})}$

   LCL

   e.g. (9.2 ± 3 $\sqrt{9.2 \text{ x}0.82}$)

4. Draw chart.

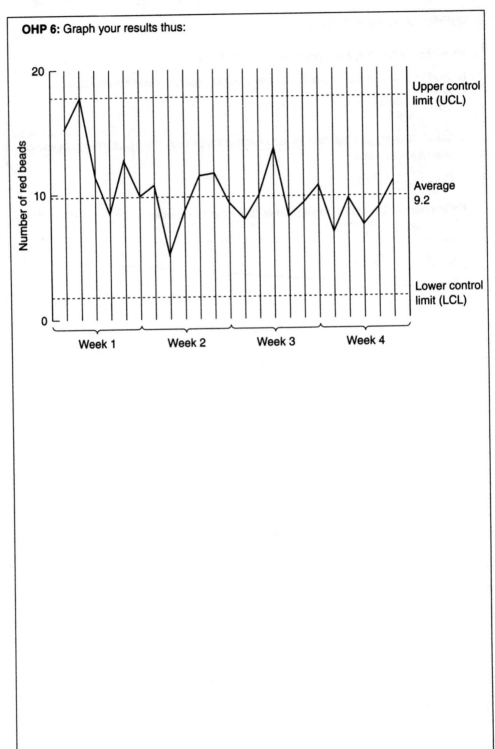

OHP 6: Graph your results thus:

OHP 7: Graph results

What can we observe from the results?

- All of the individual results are within the UCL and LCL lines.

- Therefore we can say that it is a *statistically stable system*. It is therefore predictable.

- It is impossible to explain the variations in the results of individual workers' efforts by reference to 'special causes', e.g. laziness, trying harder, desire to please/displease the boss, etc.

We may therefore conclude:

Barring a change in the system that governs the production line, the number of wrong beads drawn will fluctuate between UCL and LCL, but not exceed them.
This is a rational prediction, which will always hold.

OHP 8: What are the morals of the parable?

- Variation is part of any process.
- Planning requires prediction of performance.
- Workers work within a system which is beyond their control.
- The system determines performance, not skill.
- Only management can change the system.
- Some workers will always be above average, some below.
- The UCL and LCL may be reduced only by improving the system, not blaming the workers.
- We should seek continuous improvement of the system.
- We cannot inspect bad quality out, we must build good quality in.
- With identical tools, tasks and talents, production quality will vary.
- Managers blame workers for bad results which are beyond their control.
- Attempts to identify 'special causes' of variance where the system is in statistical control, and to remedy them is likely to make things worse not better.

Now consider what this experiment has to tell you about your school and the performance of your pupils. Only you as the teacher can remove *some* of the common causes of variance.

Appendix 2

Total Quality Management for Schools

A Total Quality Management training programme for schools
and colleges presented in the form of OHPs

Total Quality Management for Schools

A Total Quality Management Training Programme for schools and colleges described in the book of TQM.

| **Establishing** | Day 1 |
| **TQM** IN OUR SCHOOL | Total Quality Management |

Introduction

This is Day 1 of a two-day course. It is intended to increase understanding of the concept of TQM. This will involve developing activities which are designed to help us to identify both strengths and weaknesses in our school/college.

TQM is not a top-down management initiative which will be a burden to you. It is an attempt to change our culture in a positive way, which involves all of us at every level in the organization.

Throughout the training programme, you are encouraged to think about every aspect of our school life in a critical and challenging way. We hope by adopting an open mind, to develop a culture which will encourage us all to seek opportunities for improvement in all our working practices.

| *Establishing* | Day 1: **OHP 1** |
| *TQM* IN OUR SCHOOL | Total Quality Management |

The objectives of the first day are as follows

- To gain an understanding of the origins and key principles of TQM.

- Identify areas in our school where implementation is possible and desirable.

- Establish the customer/supplier relationships, internal and external.

- Identify what customer requirements are.

- Identify our personal roles in a TQM regime.

It is vital to our future that we implement a TQM programme. To do so requires constant and sustained effort from everybody in the organization, including especially myself as headteacher. This is where the journey begins.

Establishing	Day 1
TQM IN OUR SCHOOL	Total Quality Management

Day 1: Programme

09.00–09.30		Introduction
09.30–10.30	1	Why we are introducing TQM
10.30–10.45		Coffee break
10.45–12.15	2	Defining TQM
12.15–13.00		Lunch break
13.00–14.10	3	External customers
14.10–14.40	4	External suppliers
14.40–14.55		Tea break
14.55–16.10	5	Internal customers and suppliers
16.10–16.20	6	Summary
16.20–16.30	7	Action assignment

Establishing	Day 1
TQM IN OUR SCHOOL	Total Quality Management

Introduction

The purpose of the next two days is to provoke thought and debate about what we do. It is intended that the atmosphere be relatively informal, to promote openness of mind. A great deal of ground will be covered, and we must remember that this is only the beginning of an endless journey of Continuous Improvement.

In each section you will be involved in a series of group activities. In order that we get the best out of each session, we have set out some basic ground rules. These rules are not intended only to apply today, but to become permanent features of the way we work.

- Be open and honest.

- Do not make any assumptions without checking them out. Others may have the same concerns and confusions.

- Do not lose sight of the objective by becoming bogged down in detail.

- Make the meeting more effective by only having one person speak at a time. Asides should be shared, or stifled.

- Be punctual. Waiting for people to turn up spoils a meeting and wastes everybody's time.

- Stick to the agenda.

- Concentrate on getting the best out of every session.

| *Establishing* **TQM** IN OUR SCHOOL | Day 1: **OHP 2** |
| | Total Quality Management |

Introduction:

Ground rules for group sessions

- Be open and honest
- Don't assume, check it out
- Wood not trees
- One speaker at a time
- Be punctual
- Stick to the agenda
- Don't blame and scapegoat
- Make the most of every meeting

Establishing *TQM* IN OUR SCHOOL	Day 1 Total Quality Management

Why are we doing TQM?

Our determined commitment to introduce Total Quality Management is driven by the need to ensure that our school survives and prospers in an increasingly competitive environment. It will benefit the school, its employees and its pupils. The key factors driving us down this road are:

Key factors

- We need to get better at everything we do. We are all aware that there are many areas in which we can do better, for the benefit of our pupils.

- We want to survive. The government has made it clear that no school has a divine right to exist. We must seek to be the best in our market.

- Increasing competition. This makes it imperative that we benchmark our approach, style and product against world-class schools.

- End crisis management.

- We can only be successful if we all work together.

- Job satisfaction is only possible if everybody's ideas and contributions are valued and recognized and implemented.

- The process of continuous improvement must be ongoing in everything we do.

Establishing **TQM** IN OUR SCHOOL	Day 1: **OHP 3**
	Total Quality Management

Key messages

- We need to get better at everything
- We want to survive
- We want to stop firefighting
- People matter
- Job satisfaction is vital
- Continual improvement in everything we do

| **Establishing** | Day 1 |
| **TQM** IN OUR SCHOOL | Total Quality Management |

Why are we doing TQM?

TQM is a vehicle for change. It requires a clear statement of purpose, and must be a managed process. It needs a planned process of implementation, and a means of evaluation and feedback.

There are three stages through which these requirements may be fulfilled:

● Quality audit

● Management commitment

● Establishment and implementation of a plan for quality

Step 1: *Initial Quality Audit*

This is a process by which we collect information on how the school currently operates, covering both formal and informal systems. This process involves the establishment of:

● Employee perceptions

● Customer perceptions

● Supplier perceptions

● Costs of quality

The analysis of this information will enable us to identify the areas where improvement will have the greatest impact on our performance. This is the first stage in seeking improvement across all our activities, in all functional departments of the school. It is a process which will be repeated over and over again.

Establishing *TQM* IN OUR SCHOOL	Day 1: **OHP 4** Total Quality Management

The TQM process

Three elements:

- Quality audit
- Management commitment
- Plan for quality

Establishing *TQM* IN OUR SCHOOL	Day 1: **OHP 5** Total Quality Management

The quality audit

Seeks to identify:

- Employee perceptions
- Customer perceptions
- Supplier perceptions
- Costs of quality

Establishing *TQM* IN OUR SCHOOL	Day 1
	Total Quality Management

Step 2: *Management commitment*

It is vital as a first step to establish with senior management an understanding of and commitment to TQM. Your headteacher has arrived at this commitment as a result of attending a conference. The purpose of this course is to communicate that understanding and commitment to all members of the school, including eventually the pupils. Our school's 'mission' must be to be the best at whatever we have decided to do. We must aim to be a world-class school. This may seem to you to be an impossible dream. It is in fact possible, but will be a long and hard journey to which we must all be committed. We must change the culture; improve the process; and satisfy – indeed, delight – our customers. In this way we will ensure our survival.

Step 3: *Implementation of TQM*

We can only achieve our objectives if we are *all* totally involved, and if the contribution of each member of the school is recognized, valued and celebrated. We can only be involved if we know what it is we are to be involved in. This is why this training course is so vital. Remember it is only a first step. Read all you can about TQM, and think about ways in which what you read might be applied in school.

When this course is over, we shall be setting up Quality Improvement Teams, initially within departments of the school, and then across departmental boundaries. Since everyone who works in the school will have been trained, all will be able to contribute positively, and must be allowed to do so.

The work of these QITs should lead to the preparation initially of Departmental Action Plans. During this course we will begin the process of putting these together.

| Establishing | Day 1: **OHP 6** |
| *TQM* IN OUR SCHOOL | Total Quality Management |

Management commitment

The commitment of top management to the TQM process must be *total* and *evident*. The committment must be to:

- Change the culture
- Improve the process
- Satisfy our customers
- Ensure our survival

Establishing **TQM** IN OUR SCHOOL	Day 1: **OHP 7** **Total Quality Management**

Implementing the TQM process

- Involve everyone

- Train everyone

- Lead from the top

- Set up QITs

- Develop departmental Action Plans

| Establishing | Day 1 |
| *TQM* IN OUR SCHOOL | Total Quality Management |

Defining Total Quality Management

QUALITY is satisfying agreed customer requirements.

TOTAL QUALITY is continually satisfying customer requirements, at minimum cost to the company or school. Furthermore, our ultimate aim must be to go further and 'delight' customers, i.e. do more than they expect in having their requirements satisfied.

TOTAL QUALITY MANAGEMENT is achieving these objectives through the total commitment and personal involvement of *all* members of the school organization.

It has eight guiding principles:

- It is management led.

- It requires good customer–supplier relationships.

- It requires the recognition of customer–supplier relationships which are both internal and external to the school.

- It requires the prevention rather than detection of faults and failures at all points in the system. You cannot inspect quality into an activity, it must be built in to start with.

- Quality is everybody's responsibility.

- In everything we do we must seek to get it right first time so far as humanly possible. Zero defects is our goal, but (since we are human) it is probably unattainable. TQM is a journey, not a destination.

- It requires measurement of the 'costs of quality', i.e. prevention, appraisal and failure. Prevention costs will rise as we eliminate the costs incurred in checking whether we got it right, and then putting it right. Failure is the cost of not doing it right.

- It requires a non-stop search for improvement.

| Establishing | Day 1: **OHP 8** |
| **TQM** IN OUR SCHOOL | Total Quality Management |

Principles of TQM

- Management led
- Customer–supplier interface
- Both internal and external
- Prevention not detection
- Everyone is involved
- Costs of quality
- Continual improvement

| *Establishing* | Day 1 |
| *TQM* IN OUR SCHOOL | Total Quality Management |

Costs of quality

It is easy to see that in a factory there will be costs arising from the occurrence of scrap waste and re-work, and that it might be better to build in quality rather than spotting failure by inspection after production. It may not be so evident that the approach might be useful in a school. It is, both in the operation of the school system and in the classroom interrelationships between teacher and pupil.

There are three categories of costs of quality:

PREVENTION Those activities required to make sure that what we do (teacher or pupil) is done right first time.
1 Clear instructions.
2 Care in preparation.
3 Well-maintained systems.

APPRAISAL Activities used to identify errors.
1 Marking.
2 Checking.
3 Measuring and recording performance.

FAILURE The cost of all failures and errors, and of putting them right.
1 Waste, of time or materials.
2 Scrap; work which is binned.
3 Re-work, which has to be presented again.

Establishing	Day 1
TQM IN OUR SCHOOL	Total Quality Management

Management style

Management culture in the Western world, unlike Japan, tends to stress the importance of activity which might be called 'crisis management', or 'firefighting'. This stress on dealing with immediate crisis situations as they happen, at the expense of seeking ways of providing long-term solutions to the underlying problems which cause the crises, is also inherent in schools. In other words, we emphasize activities involving checking whether things have been done right, and correcting mistakes. Prevention activities tend to be neglected.

It is vital to improve our prevention skills.

| *Establishing* | Day 1: **OHP 9** |
| *TQM* IN OUR SCHOOL | Total Quality Management |

XYZ School: Statement of Mission

We aim to create an educational environment within which each pupil will feel free to achieve excellence in his chosen field through a process of continuous improvement in cooperation with teachers parents and all other members of the school.

We shall seek to achieve this through excellence in the following areas:

- A balanced curriculum.

- Technological and methodological leadership.

- Cross-functional team-work.

- Open and constructive communication.

- A safe and stimulating learning environment.

Our strategic objectives shall be:

- To be responsive to customers, both internal and external.

- Create and foster a committed workforce through training.

- Develop students who will be well qualified, independent and enthusiastic entrants to society and workforce.

- Encourage good and caring attitudes to citizenship.

- We shall achieve these objectives by the implementation of TQM.

Establishing	Day 1: Syndicate session
TQM IN OUR SCHOOL	Total Quality Management

Customers and their requirements　　　　　　　　　Syndicate session 30 minutes
　　　　　　　　　　　　　　　　　　　　　　　　　Group discussion 20 minutes

External customers

1　Who are our external customers?

2　What are their requirements?

3　How can we improve what we do to meet their requirements?

| *Establishing* | Day 1 |
| **TQM** IN OUR SCHOOL | Total Quality Management |

3 External customers and their requirements

Our school serves a number of external 'customers' whose needs differ, and who will all measure the performance of the school in different ways and on different criteria. It is obviously important to be more specific in:

- identifying our 'customers'.

- identifying their requirements.

- measuring our performance in satisfying those requirements.

- reconciling any clashes between those requirements.

Determination not merely to satisfy 'customer requirements', but to delight the customer by offering more than he felt he could expect, is central to TQM.

Clearly we must identify those requirements first, if we are to satisfy them. We must then seek to innovate in order to offer even more to our 'customers'.

Some of these requirements are easy to measure, whilst others, which may be the ones which are most important to our 'customers', are less easily measured, and may be neglected.

The external customers of a school are:

- the pupils, whose education we provide.

- the parents who directly or indirectly pay for this education.

- our feeder schools, who must choose the school which they recommend to their own pupils.

- institutions of higher and further education, to which we supply students.

- employers.

- society.

Establishing *TQM* IN OUR SCHOOL	Day 1: **OHP 10**
	Total Quality Management

External customers and their requirements

Customer	Requirements
Pupils	Stimulating curriculum
	Well delivered
	Producing success
	Offering relevance
	Social, sporting and
	cultural opportunities
	Careers guidance
Parents	All the above, plus:
	Open communication
	Opportunity for participation
Feeder schools	All the above, plus:
	Advantage over competing schools
	Feedback and cooperation
HE/FE institutions	All the above, plus:
	Suitably qualified students
	Capable, self-motivated
	students
Employers	All the above, plus:
	Team-work skills
	Communication skills
	Leadership skills
	Punctuality/self-discipline
	Work ethic
Society	All the above, plus:
	Citizenship knowledge
	Honesty
	Social concern

| *Establishing* | Day 1 |
| **TQM** IN OUR SCHOOL | Total Quality Management |

Measurement of customer requirements

Some of the requirements which we have just noted are easily if crudely measurable, whilst others are more about perceptions of reality. Attempts to measure success in the delivery of a curriculum which reflect the comparative position of the school in relation to both its competitors and national standards are:

Standard Attainment Tests

GCSE results

A level results (and GNVQ)

These are now required to be published by law, as well as being closely scrutinized by independent school inspectors. They have, in the case of A levels, been published in comparative form by the media in recent years.

Readers of this material will already have noted the problems of interpretation. Since the system is geared to the normal curve, 25 per cent plus are doomed in effect to 'fail'. Moreover, the results achieved depend on the starting point – the standard achieved on entry to that school. Hence attempts which are being made to measure 'added value'.

The attitudes and values of the school, which are fundamental to satisfying the requirements of a more intangible nature, are even more difficult to measure. Government sees truancy and absenteeism rates as critical guides, and they must now be measured and published.

Extra-curricular success may be measured crudely by the published sporting successes of the school, the number and quality of concerts and plays staged, etc.

Overall success may be measured by outcome, i.e. university places, jobs, unemployment rates. These presumably will to some extent reflect the more intangible still personal abilities and qualities which we have noted.

The overall image of the school will depend on all the above, but also on the perception which the outsider has of visual presentation, of both pupils, staff and premises.

Remember the customer has a *right* to all this information, and it should be clearly and willingly (not grudgingly) given. The customer also has the right to be invited to offer his opinion; in fact, we need to encourage him to do so, or how else can we improve?

| Establishing | Day 1: Syndicate session |
| *TQM* IN OUR SCHOOL | Total Quality Management |

4 External suppliers

Syndicate session 30 minutes
Group discussion 20 minutes

1 Who are our external suppliers?

2 What do we require from them?

3 How can we help them to meet our requirements better?

Establishing	Day 1
TQM IN OUR SCHOOL	Total Quality Management

4 External suppliers

As it has emerged from the Syndicate session, we can see that broadly we have three group of suppliers:

1. Feeder schools which supply us with pupils.

2. Groups of parents (by class, income, geographical location) which may supply us with pupils.

3. Suppliers of books, materials, stationery, etc., and also of information.

If we are to have a productive relationship with our suppliers, we must see them not as adversaries, but as partners in a joint enterprise. This means that we must communicate clearly to them what our requirements are, and assist them in any way we can to meet these requirements. This comment applies equally to a local feeder school and to, say, a supplier of laboratory materials.

The extent of our dependence on commercial suppliers is easily demonstrated. In a medium-sized secondary school, the total budget will be approximately £1 million. Of this, £300, 000 will be spent on bought in supplies, whilst £700,000 will be spent on salaries. There is plenty of room to reduce waste in a sum of one third of a million pounds.

Unlike a business, we cannot buy in our raw materials. We need the pupils from feeder schools, and the fee or budget income which they attract. Their perception of what we are doing is absolutely critical in a world where pupils and parents choose schools, rather than being allocated to them. We must build trust with all our suppliers.

Establishing **TQM** IN OUR SCHOOL	Day 1: Assignment
	Total Quality Management

Internal customer / supplier chain

Assignment

Syndicate session 30 minutes
Group discussion 20 minutes

TASK

You are working in a small group with members of your own academic or functional department. Consider who are your suppliers, and who are your immediate internal customers.

Customer   *What do they want?*

Suppliers   *What do they supply to you?*

Establishing *TQM* IN OUR SCHOOL	Day 1
	Total Quality Management

Internal customer–supplier relationships

It is relatively easy to recognize the importance of satisfying external customers. It is much harder to recognize that every department in an organization has customer and supplier relationships with other departments.

This connection is best visualized as a network of internal relationships which link the external supplier via the organization to its external customers. It is just as easy, perhaps more so, for that internal relationship to break down. If it does, then the requirements of the external customer will not be satisfied.

This internal customer–supplier chain is made up of long-standing systems and procedures. These often become over-complex and bureaucratic. Delay, waste, departmental imperialism and boundary defence are the result. If things go wrong, blame is apportioned, rather than solutions sought.

If we are to improve the internal chain in order to satisfy external customers better, then the various departments, administrative and academic must talk to each other. This is not something which is normally provided for in a school. Cross-functional teams must sit down and ask the right questions.

- Is what we give you useful? (rooms, equipment, reprographic services, etc.)

- Is it in the right format? (report forms, brochure, application form)

- Is the quantity right? (photocopying, books ordered, etc.)

- Does it arrive when required? (photocopying, book order, materials)

- Any problems with it?

- How can it be improved?

If we find the right answers to these questions, we can ensure that our delivery of the service will meet the requirements of the customer all the way down the chain from external supplier to external customers.

Establishing	Day 1
TQM IN OUR SCHOOL	Total Quality Management

6 Summary: Day 1

The objective of the first day of the course has been to set out the basic principles of TQM, and together to begin to see how these principles might be applied to our school.
It is vital to our future as a school to understand these principles and to develop a plan for implementing them. If we are to succeed, every member of the school community, including pupils and parents, must be involved and committed.

The key elements of TQM are:

Recognize the need for change

Recognize that TQM is the key to our survival through continuous improvement of the service we offer to ALL our customers.

Understand the meaning of TQM

Recognize that TQM is not threatening. It is about harnessing all our talents and commitment on behalf of our pupils, in order to enable them to maximize their talents.

Areas for improvement

By understanding the nature of the customer–supplier chain, begin to identify areas of our organization where improvement is possible and needed.

Team-work for improvement

Recognize that we can achieve improvement continuously only by working as teams with colleagues in other departments, both academic and functional.

Delight all our customers

Recognize that we need to do more than just meet the expectations of our customers, which may be unnecessarily low. We need literally to delight our customers by doing more than they expected.

TQM simply formalizes into a system for continuous improvement of all the values and practices which good teachers intuitively believe in and apply.

Establishing **TQM** IN OUR SCHOOL	Day 2
	Total Quality Management

Introduction

During this second day of the course, we will seek to develop the simple skills which are required by all colleagues if we are to effectively apply TQM to our school.

We will specifically look at the following areas.

- Identifying areas for improvement

- Team-work skills

- The problem-solving process and techniques

- Barriers to TQM

- Making TQM permanent

Objectives

- Establish commitment and involvement at all levels in the school.

- Establish a simple problem-solving process.

- Identify and seek to overcome barriers to TQM.

- Establish what we have to do to make it stick.

Establishing **TQM** IN OUR SCHOOL	Day 2 Total Quality Management

Programme

09.15–09.35	Identifying where to improve
09.35–10.30	Team-work
10.30–10.45	Coffee
10.45–12.30	Problem-solving techniques
12.30–13.15	Lunch
13.15–14.15	Barriers to TQM
14.25–14.30	Tea
14.30–16.15	Making TQM stick
16.15–16.30	Summary

Establishing **TQM** IN OUR SCHOOL	Day 2
	Total Quality Management

Identifying where to improve

Yesterday we set out what we are trying to do. Our aim is to pursue a journey of *continuous improvement* in everything we do as a school community.

The method which we must use is to seek to identify problems in our organization, and opportunities which are presented to us, in order to develop solutions and strategies for improvement. These may be small-scale and limited at first, but will lead on to more radical and large-scale changes in the way we do things. We must learn to love change, not fear it.

If this process is to work, we must be prepared to have an open mind, and look at everything we do with fresh eyes.

Sources of problems for consideration

There are a number of sources from which 'problems' may surface that may then be the subject of an attempt to seek an improved solution to the 'problem'.

● Heads of departments' meetings.

● Complaints from parents or members of the community.

● Customer surveys.

● Parents' evenings.

● Governors' meetings.

● Senior management meetings.

● Staff meetings.

Using problems to generate improvement

Two methods are essential:

● Allocate a presented problem to a suitable *team* who are involved in the appropriate area. This team should where necessary be cross-functional.

● Encourage them to start by 'brainstorming' the problem and possible solutions.

Making TQM *Happen* IN OUR SCHOOL	Day 2
	Total Quality Management

Team-work

Syndicate session 20 minutes
Group discussion 10 minutes

1   What helps to make a successful team?

_____

_____

_____

_____

_____

_____

_____

2   What will stop us making team-work effective?

_____

_____

_____

_____

_____

_____

_____

Syndicate: 20 minutes
Group discussion: 10 minutes

Establishing **TQM** IN OUR SCHOOL	Day 2
	Total Quality Management

2 Team-work

Much of our work to establish and use TQM methods will be undertaken in teams.

Teams will function better than individuals in the following activities:

- generating ideas
- drawing on varied experience and knowledge
- providing self-confidence and motivation in those who have to implement the solutions suggested.

To function well:

- teams must work together, adopting a positive approach to the problem and to each other's contribution. Negative attitudes and defensive argument will damage the teams' efforts.
- the team must be well led, by an experienced individual who is respected by the team members. This will not necessarily be the most senior person in the team. Leadership skills can be learned.

Barriers to team-work to be watched out for include:

- Competitive behaviour – trying to outshine others, insisting on one's own point of view, despite the evidence against, shutting out less confident members.
- Attitudes – fixed ideas, contempt for other members' view, lack of commitment.
- Emotion – personality clashes, old enmities, departmental rivalries, refusing to take an objective stance.
- Unclear terms of reference – confused roles and responsibilities, badly defined objectives, uncertain management commitment.

Positive attitudes required in team leaders:

- Be open and relaxed.
- Be creative and think laterally.
- Watch for the defuse possible areas of conflict.
- Recognize and celebrate the contribution of others, however small.
- Seek compromise.
- Encourage everyone to contribute.
- Have fun.

| *Establishing* | Day 2 |
| *TQM* IN OUR SCHOOL | Total Quality Management |

3 Brainstorming

This a method for identifying problems and possible solutions developed by Edward De Bono, which seeks to use our often latent creative skills. It involves what he calls 'lateral thinking'. This implies that we should stop using our normal linear approach to thinking through problems and generating ideas. Instead we should seek connections which are not at first apparent, and which may even seem to be crazy, without dismissing them out of hand without further thought.

First we will try out a simple example in our groups.

Activity

Syndicate session 10 minutes
Group discussion 10 minutes

Form small groups.

Consider the following problem:

You are asked to find an alternative to a door handle for controlling access/egress from this room.

You have three minutes in which member will silently write down the alternatives which occur to him.

Pool the ideas in a list. Three minutes.

Draw up a short list of three best ideas. Four minutes.

Whole-group feedback session. Ten minutes.

| *Establishing* | Day 2 |
| *TQM* IN OUR SCHOOL | Total Quality Management |

What have we discovered from this experiment? The following simple rules for conducting a brainstorming session should have emerged. I wonder whether they did?

- Record all ideas as quickly as possible.

- Do not evaluate ideas as you generate them.

- Do not criticize.

- Break with convention and think laterally.

- Freewheel and have fun.

Remember that the best ideas may seem silly or ridiculous as well as totally impractical at first – think of the bike which won the Gold Medal for Pursuit in the recent Olympics.

Brainstorming will always be the starting point of the search for solutions.

Establishing **TQM** IN OUR SCHOOL	Day 2
	Total Quality Management

Methods for solving problems

Our first impression of what the problem is, when a system breaks down, may not necessarily be the right diagnosis. We need a rigorous method for identifying problems.

Key steps in problem diagnosis

1 Describe current situation clearly in detail.

2 Define the required situation.

3 Identify causes (as against symptoms).

4 Generate possible solutions by brainstorming.

5 Select a shortlist, and narrow down to preferred solution.

6 Test solution in pilot scheme.

7 Review and, if OK, proceed to implement whole solution, full scale.

8 Feedback – check and monitor results, go back to stage 1 if necessary.

Establishing *TQM* IN OUR SCHOOL	Day 2: **OHP** Total Quality Management

A model of the problem-solving process

1 Describe current situation clearly in detail.

2 Define the required situation.

3 Identify causes (as against symptoms).

4 Generate possible solutions by brainstorming.

5 Select a shortlist, and narrow down to preferred solution.

6 Test solution in pilot scheme.

7 Review and, if OK, proceed to implement whole solution, full scale.

8 Feedback – check and monitor results, go back to stage 1 if necessary.

Establishing **TQM** IN OUR SCHOOL	Day 2: **OHP** Total Quality Management

Problem solving

Stage 1: Describe the current situation

- Describe the state of affairs as it is at present
- Define the key elements
- Define the desired objective

Stage 2: Identify root cause

- Identify symptoms (e.g. declining results, increasing truancy rate, worse behaviour, falling applications)
- Brainstorm root causes (e.g. staff changes, changes in catchment area, changes in feeder schools)
- Brainstorm solutions (only speculatively at this stage – get ideas running)
- Cause and effect analysis (Ishikawa or fishbone diagram)

Stage 3: Generate solution

- Brainstorm possible solutions
- Evaluate and short list in rank order
- Select solution

Stage 4: Test and implement

- Is it viable and practical?
- Pilot scheme/action plan
- Full implementation

Stage 5: Check and monitor results

- Did it work?
- If not, go back to start and try again

Establishing
TQM IN OUR SCHOOL

Day 2: **OHP**

Total Quality Management

The fishbone diagram

(use example from Chapter 8
on Costs of quality)

Establishing *TQM* IN OUR SCHOOL	Day 2 Total Quality Management

Activity

Syndicate session 20 minutes
Group discussion 10 minutes

Think of a problem which has caused your school difficulty.

Draw a cause-and-effect diagram to identify the root cause.

Establishing TQM IN OUR SCHOOL	Day 2
	Total Quality Management

5 Barriers to TQM

TQM is a management system which if applied in a school, or in a classroom, is very different from your usual approach. Its reversal of old-established attitudes may well be very disconcerting for both teachers and pupils. It is so radical that it will not work overnight, but will take years to implement fully. Considerable organizational, institutional and psychological barriers to its successful implementation exist. Constant vigilance is necessary to ensure that the programme does not flag. Remember we are talking about 'continuous improvement', *not* instant success.

- FEAR exists at all levels when status or job are threatened. It destroys commitment, and causes the concealment of information.

- CYNICISM stems from experience of earlier failed experiments.

- UNWILLINGNESS OF MANAGEMENT TO BEAR THE COST – of moving from appraisal to prevention.

These barriers can be overcome, but only by:

- TOP MANAGEMENT COMMITMENT (in deed as well as word)

- OPEN COMMUNICATION

- REASSURANCE AND RECOGNITION

- INVOLVEMENT AND EMPOWERMENT

- TRAINING AND MORE TRAINING

Establishing	Day 2
TQM IN OUR SCHOOL	**Total Quality Management**

Activity

Syndicate session 30 minutes

Group discussion 15 minutes

Barriers to TQM

Identify the five most serious barriers to the implementation of TQM in your school. Then agree action points to overcome them.

Barrier   *Actions*

Establishing *TQM* IN OUR SCHOOL	**Day 2** **Total Quality Management**

6 Making TQM permanent

We cannot afford to allow progress to falter, and all gains made must be consolidated and made permanent. Constant vigilance will be needed.

Above all, we are talking about a complete change in people's attitudes and values, and in the way in which people are managed. TQM is above all else about the *empowerment* of individuals. This means the creation of self-confidence and a sense of self-worth which will free them to work creatively in a team environment, based on mutual trust. This incidentally is true of not only all grades of staff, but also the pupils, parents, and suppliers.

Once we have established a TQM programme in the school it must belong to everyone, not just the quality champions.

The changes in attitude can be summarized thus:

From this   *To this*

FOR EMPLOYEES

Negative	⟶	Positive
Lazy	⟶	Industrious
Disorganized	⟶	Systematic
Don't care	⟶	Conscientious
This is a management problem	⟶	This is our problem

FOR MANAGERS

Won't admit mistakes	⟶	Accept responsibility for their actions
No respect for employees	⟶	Actively empower people to use knowledge and experience
Never listens	⟶	Encourage suggestions
Always blames somebody	⟶	Try to establish and deal with cause of problem

EMPOWER YOUR PEOPLE

Establishing *TQM* IN OUR SCHOOL	Day 2: **OHP** Total Quality Management

7 Summary

The TQM message can be summarized thus:

- We need to improve what we do
- We need to improve the quality of the service we offer
- We want to survive
- We want to stop firefighting and start managing
- We want to empower people and involve them
- We must offer job satisfaction
- We must listen to our customers; internal and external
- We must seek continuous improvement – for ever
- We must delight our customers
- We must communicate constantly to everyone
- We must train everyone and then train them some more

The TQM principles are:

- Management led
- Customers are king
- Prevention not detection of faults
- Everyone is involved
- Aim to get it right first time if possible
- Cut the costs of quality
- Seek continual improvement

Index